THE SCHOOL THAT
REFUSED TO DIE

SUNY Series, Educational Leadership
Daniel L. Duke, Editor

THE SCHOOL THAT REFUSED TO DIE

Continuity and Change at Thomas Jefferson High School

Daniel L. Duke

STATE UNIVERSITY
OF NEW YORK
PRESS

Published by
State University of New York Press, Albany

© 1995   State University of New York

Production by Susan Geraghty
Marketing by Fran Keneston

Printed in the United States of America

For information, address State University of New York Press,
State University Plaza, Albany, N.Y., 12246

Library Of Congress Cataloging-in-publication Data

Duke, Daniel Linden.
    The school that refused to die : continuity and change at Thomas Jefferson High School / Daniel Linden Duke.
        p.   cm.—(SUNY series, educational leadership)
    Includes bibliographical references and index.
    ISBN 0-7914-2331-X. — ISBN 0-7914-2332-8 (pbk.)
    1. Thomas Jefferson High School (Richmond, Va.)—History.
2. Education, Urban—Virginia—Richmond—Case studies. I. Title.
II. Series: SUNY series in educational leadership.
LD7501.R47D85 1995
373.755'451—dc20   94-10030
                                                                      CIP

10 9 8 7 6 5 4 3 2 1

To all those working and studying in the high schools of the United States who believe that excellence and integration are still possible.

CONTENTS

PREFACE

If public education in the United States published an endangered species list, urban high schools committed to academic excellence would be close to the top. It seems that ensuring student safety, regular attendance, and a modicum of order absorb much of the precious time of urban educators. Helping students achieve even basic levels of competence, under such circumstances, becomes a daunting task. When, therefore, a city school district threatens to close a comprehensive high school which, more than any other within its boundaries, symbolizes high academic achievement, the gesture is analogous to pointing a loaded gun at a spotted owl. And when this school also is one of the few high schools with the potential to sustain any semblance of racial integration in a predominantly black school system, the threatened closure strikes at the very heart of the ideals which have shaped the recent history of this country.

This book chronicles the life of Thomas Jefferson High School in Richmond, Virginia. From its opening in 1930, Tee-Jay, as it came to be known, developed a culture of academic excellence that eventually led observers to consider it one of the finest high schools in the South, if not the entire nation. The task of developing such an organizational culture was surpassed only by the struggle to preserve it. Almost three decades of assorted challenges, including desegregation, white flight, changes in leadership, budget cuts, and backroom politics, took their toll. Still, on numerous occasions the faculty, administration, students, parents, and alumni rallied to protect their school. In some cases, this meant initiating change, at other times resisting change.

The history of Tee-Jay, in the final analysis, is a record both of stability and change. Understanding the nature, causes, and meaning of organizational stability and change is one of the central concerns of the organizational historian. While the present study focuses on a single school, and not a typical one at that, it may help people understand more about the forces that threaten the future of comprehensive high schools in general. With all the current interest in "restructuring" high schools, such knowledge cannot come too soon. The tendency for educational reformers to ignore the lessons of the past is pronounced.

The history of a school is best told, I believe, as a story. To permit the story of Tee-Jay to unfold as smoothly as possible, I have tried to reserve comments related to theory and research for the opening and closing portions of the book. The Introduction presents the central research questions and an overview of the book. The concluding chapters cover interpretations of the historical record and their implications. In the Appendix can be found an essay on the methodology of organizational history.

While a narrative format permits readers to understand better how a school like Tee-Jay developed into a successful high school, it does not allow the interweaving of personal insights and references from the literature that often make for compelling reading. Some stories, of course, grab and hold readers' attention from the outset by sustaining a sense of high drama or irony. The history of Tee-Jay's first three decades could not have been written in this manner without betraying its largely tranquil nature. If there is a captivating quality to the school's early development, it must be sought in the refreshing absence of turmoil—turmoil that too often today is taken for granted in urban high schools. Readers who are uninterested in the details concerning how a new high school evolves into an exemplary local institution may wish to go directly to part 2, where Tee-Jay is faced with a series of challenges similar to those being confronted by high schools around the country.

Every effort has been made to write the history of Tee-Jay in as balanced and fair a manner as possible. Great care has been taken, for example, to corroborate descriptive information whenever possible. Over a hundred in-depth interviews were conducted. Retired teachers contributed dozens of letters about their experiences at Tee-Jay. Thousands of primary documents were studied. Nonetheless, it is necessary to acknowledge at the outset that I am a graduate of Tee-Jay (Class of 1965). Furthermore, I would be less than honest if I did not admit to a strong commitment to the ideals of pluralism and school integration.

Having offered these cautionary notes, I also must affirm my belief, as a historian, in the value of honesty. In the long run, no benefit derives from concealing facts or manipulating data to support a particular point of view. Besides, I would betray the very ideals for which Tee-Jay—the school, many of its teachers, and its namesake—stood if I did anything less than present as accurate an account as possible of the school's history.

Before concluding the Preface, I want to thank some of the people who enabled me to undertake this project. The reflections of Tee-Jay principals William Brock, Morgan Edwards, Gordon Hill and Dr. Edward Pruden were critical to gaining perspective on the many challenges faced by the school in its later years. Retired teachers, including Mary Maddox, Ida Wanderer, Virginia Ellett, Dr. Calvin Green, Roland Galvin, Renate Thayer, and Kathleen Hancock shared a rich array of details and stories about key events in school history and some of the less obvious aspects of school culture. Russell Flammia, Larry Volk, Jim Holdren, Dr. Cassandra Fletcher, and Dr. Barbara Ulschmidt provided valuable insights from the vantage point of contemporary members of the faculty and administration. Colleen Boyd, Tee-Jay's librarian, assisted greatly in locating old annuals and school newspapers. Shirley Callihan, the former clerk of the school board and a student of the school system's history, located old board minutes and provided additional data of historical value. My mother, Gale Linden Duke, faithfully combed Richmond newspapers for over four years for any information of relevance to Tee-Jay. Joshua Martin Duke, my son, and Abe Feuerstein, my graduate assistant, assisted me in tracking down reference material in the library. My mentor, Mauritz Johnson, read the entire manuscript with great care, his comments reminding me that I am never too old to be tutored. Paula Price typed and typed and typed, all the while offering encouragement and constructive suggestions. Finally, thanks are due to Priscilla Ross, for her encouragement of this project, and James Pelz, for a splendid job of editing.

Because of the special help provided by these people, along with hundreds of active and retired teachers, students, parents, central office personnel, and alumni, this book in many ways should be regarded as a collective enterprise. In the matter of interpretation of facts, however, the judgments expressed herein are entirely my own.

BRIEF CHRONOLOGY OF
IMPORTANT EVENTS IN
TEE-JAY'S HISTORY

September 1930   Thomas Jefferson High School opens.
                  Ernest Shawen is appointed principal.

February 1931   First issue of the *Jeffersonian* is published.

February 1931   Tee-Jay is officially dedicated.

June 1932   First graduation ceremony is held.

Fall 1934   Ability grouping introduced in Senior
                  English.

Fall 1935   Student Participation Association is orga-
                  nized.

Fall 1937   Ability grouping initiated in history, science,
                  and remaining English courses.

July 1938   Richmond Vocational School opens.

September 1938   Maggie Walker Vocational High School
                  opens.

September 1942   Shawen retires and Coalter C. Hancock
                  becomes principal. Cadet Corps is started.

September 1943   Units needed to graduate are reduced from
                  18 to 16.

September 1944   Compulsory school age is raised from 15 to
                  16.

September 1948   Richmond Public Schools shifts from an
                  eleven to a twelve-year system. High school
                  involves grades 9L to 12H. Revised course
                  of study is implemented.

February 1957   Honor Council is created.

September 1957   Advanced Placement courses in European
                      history, chemistry, and mathematics are
                      inaugurated.

September 1958   William Brock becomes principal; the prac-
                      tice of mid-year promotion is discontinued.

September 1959   High school is extended from four to five
                      years.

September 1960   George Wythe High School and the new
                      John Marshall High School open. Two
                      black students attend Chandler Junior High
                      School, marking the beginning of school
                      desegregation in Richmond.

September 1962   First black student attends Tee-Jay.

June 1965   First black student graduates from Tee-Jay.

September 1965   First black teacher is hired at Tee-Jay.

August 17, 1970   Judge Mehrige orders Richmond Public
                      Schools to implement busing.

August 31, 1970   Court-ordered busing begins in Richmond.
                      Tee-Jay's student body becomes 45 percent
                      black and the faculty 50 percent black.

June 1976   William Brock retires as principal and is
                      replaced by Morgan Edwards III.

November 1977   Superintendent Dr. Richard Hunter makes
                      first public statement by a Richmond school
                      official concerning the possibility that Tee-
                      Jay might have to be closed.

November 1978   School board votes to accept Plan G, which
                      calls for the creation of three high school
                      "complexes."

September 1979   Jefferson-Huguenot-Wythe complex begins
                      operation.

April 1985   Judge Mehrige approves neighborhood
                      school plan submitted by Richmond Public
                      Schools, paving the way to an end to busing.

July 1986   Judge Mehrige officially relinquishes court
                      control of Richmond Public Schools.

September 1986	Complex system ends; Tee-Jay reopens as a separate comprehensive school.
September 1988	Lois Harrison-Jones leaves Richmond Public Schools; Dr. James W. Tyler assumes interim superintendency.
December 1988	School board votes 6 to 1 to close a second Richmond High School (Maggie Walker High School had been closed earlier).
March 1989	Tee-Jay students march from the high school to city hall to attend a hearing on the fate of their school.
April 1989	School board decides not to close any comprehensive high school.
July 1989	Dr. Albert Jones becomes superintendent and begins to press for magnet programs.
September 1990	Tee-Jay's magnet program begins; Gordon Hill is appointed principal.
June 1991	School Board votes to replace Superintendent Dr. Albert Jones. Lucille Brown is appointed Acting Superintendent.
September 1991	Governor's School for Government and International Studies opens at Tee-Jay.
February 1992	Superintendent Brown endorses both neighborhood schools and open enrollment.
March 1992	Superintendent Brown announces that Tee-Jay will be allowed to draw students only from Hill and Binford Middle Schools.
June 1992	Gordon Hill is removed as Tee-Jay principal and replaced by Dr. Edward Pruden, Jr.
April 1993	Virginia Department of Education urges Richmond Public Schools to decide on a permanent home for the Governor's School.
December 1993	Richmond School Board votes 6 to 1 to maintain "dual occupancy" at Tee-Jay if the Governor's School refuses to be relocated.

INTRODUCTION

The sight was a truant officer's worst nightmare. Two hundred students marching along Broad Street during school hours.

But these students were not a riotous band of young truants intent on mischief. Far from it. The group of predominantly black students had left Thomas Jefferson High School ("Tee-Jay") shortly after lunch on Wednesday, March 22, 1989, in order to reach City Hall in time to secure seats for the evening meeting of the Richmond Board of Education. The agenda that night contained an item of great concern—a hearing regarding the future of a number of Richmond schools. Two high schools were among those targeted for possible closure—John F. Kennedy High School, located in the largely black East End of the city, and Tee-Jay, in the largely white West End. The Tee-Jay students planned the march in order to dramatize opposition to closing their school. They left before the end of school to make certain they arrived early enough to prevent students from other schools on the "hit" list from filling the small chamber where board meetings were held.

Had the march been conducted several decades earlier, the journey would have penetrated the commercial heart of a thriving downtown district. Years of suburban expansion, however, had rendered the 3.6-mile strip of Broad Street a tableau of lost enterprise and urban decline. The closer the students got to City Hall, the more obvious the signs—the huge empty hulk of Sears Roebuck, boarded up stores, vacant lots of abandoned car dealerships, pawn shops, adult bookstores, and clusters of people milling around, headed nowhere in particular.

Had the students decided to turn left rather than right when they first reached Broad Street, they would have headed west and encountered a more promising landscape. For it was to the west, and to some extent southward, that commerce and well-to-do Richmond residents had migrated. West Broad Street housed thriving shopping centers, hotels, restaurants, and business parks.

For Richmonders, the Promised Land refused to stand still. As if secured to some nervous tectonic plate, it moved inexorably toward the setting sun—and the county. Henrico County, in fact, was listed as one of the fifty wealthiest counties in the United States in 1989.[1]

Tee-Jay once stood on the very frontier of the West End. For all intents and purposes, it had been created as a suburban school on the outskirts of an urban school district. By 1989, however, the high school seemed closer, in many ways, to downtown than to the suburbs. Despite the beautiful Monument Avenue homes that bordered the school, Tee-Jay clearly had become an urban school. Only 126 of its more than 600 students came from west of the Boulevard, the traditional starting place of West Richmond.[2] Fewer than 100 white students were enrolled on the eve of the march.[3]

How had it come to pass that a group made up mostly of black students was marching on City Hall to fight for the life of a school that twenty-five years before had been the very symbol of white elitism in Richmond? What strange set of circumstances had caused the Acting Superintendent of Richmond Public Schools—a system where almost nine out of every ten students were black—to propose closing one of the few secondary schools with any potential to attract white students? During a time when the public was demanding higher standards for all students, how could district officials contemplate shutting down a high school that, more than any other public school in Richmond, embodied a tradition of academic excellence?

To answer these and related questions, it is necessary to understand the history of the city of Richmond, the Richmond Public Schools, and especially Thomas Jefferson High School. Little can be learned from studying an organization at one point in time or in isolation from its context. Schools, like people, experience birth, youth, maturation, and death. They face challenges, occasionally life-threatening ones. Sometimes the challenges originate from within; at other times they result from external forces. How schools respond to these challenges reflects and helps determine their character and culture. To understand a school's present circumstances, it is essential to trace its development, to learn how it became the school it is. The best predictor of how a school will fare in a crisis usually is how it has fared in previous crises.

Schools, of course, change. They also remain the same. Patterns of continuity and change constitute the storyline of school history. Trying to explain why and how a school changes under certain conditions and not others reveals important clues concerning the nature of the school and the sociopolitical context in which it operates. The history of a school is more than the chronicle of a public organization and the people who have worked in and were served by it. It is a window on the community and a reflection of the times through which it has passed.

KEY ISSUES

To preserve the integrity of Tee-Jay's historical narrative, a general discussion of the broad issues on which the school's experience can shed light has been reserved for the concluding section of the book. This arrangement means that readers are exposed to considerable detail before they encounter an assessment of the school's wider significance. It may help readers, therefore, to be alerted in advance to some of the key issues that will be addressed at the end of the narrative. In my judgment, the history of Tee-Jay illuminates three contemporary social concerns—school desegregation, school improvement, and school survival.

Many Americans in the nineties openly question the impact of efforts to desegregate public schools. Initial gains seem to have evaporated in many cities as well-to-do families have moved to suburban communities or opted for private schools. A front-page article in the December 14, 1993, issue of the *Washington Post* summarized a recent study of Department of Education data that indicated seven out of ten black and Hispanic students attend "racially isolated" classrooms. The article went on to observe that

> the trend away from integration is . . . being fed by the abandonment of mandatory school desegregation orders in many areas and the belief among local school officials that integration is no longer viewed, or enforced, as an important national goal.[4]

The United States, for all practical purposes, has "turned its back upon the moral implications, if not yet the legal ramifications, of the *Brown* decision," concludes Jonathan Kozol in his disturbing analysis of urban and suburban schools.[5] Gary Orfield and Carole Ashkinaze, in their comprehensive investigation of black opportunity in Atlanta, are compelled to conclude that, despite favorable economic conditions and strong local leadership by blacks, the dream of equal opportunity is disappearing for young blacks.[6]

How can Tee-Jay's experience help readers understand the changing circumstances of school desegregation? Tee-Jay enrolled its first black student in the fall of 1962, eight years after *Brown v. Board of Education of Topeka*. Consistent with the philosophy of Richmond's Board of Education, only small numbers of blacks attended Tee-Jay until court-ordered busing in 1970 compelled the school district to comply with the intent of the *Brown* decision. Ensuing efforts at Tee-Jay to accommodate large numbers of black students and teachers, to forestall white flight, and to maintain academic quality reflect challenges recognizable to anyone involved in urban education over the past thirty years. Readers will discover, however, that these familiar challenges did not always result in familiar responses. A sense of context is vital to understanding why Richmond Public Schools, in the wake of busing, experimented with public alternative schools for gifted students, complexes consisting of several high schools, and magnet programs. A sense of context is also needed to explain why a school system that once tried and abandoned neighborhood schools and freedom of choice would embrace anew these strategies two decades later. A sense of context is necessary as well to comprehend the turn of events that led a school system presumably committed to the goal of school integration to try repeatedly to close one of the few Richmond schools with any possibility of retaining more than token numbers of white students.

The history of Tee-Jay reveals a context characterized by competing special interest groups, politics masquerading as educational decision-making, and district leadership more apt at times to symbolize confusion than clarity. Perhaps the word that best describes this context, though, is *complexity*. No decision regarding schooling in Richmond has been simple. No decision has been free of serious costs. And no decision has gone uncontested. At times, readers may wonder how learning could have taken place at all, so preoccupied were educators with other matters. Yet the school system continued to address the needs of Richmond's young people, and Tee-Jay managed to preserve some semblance of its commitment to excellence.

Excellence is a term frequently heard in contemporary conversations about public schools. Typically, the word is used to describe what schools should strive for rather than what they have achieved. The history of Tee-Jay is instructive in that, for a time, before and after desegregation, the education offered within its walls could legitimately be called excellent. How Tee-Jay's culture of academic excellence was established, and how it eventually was placed at risk, may offer important insights for readers concerned about contemporary school improvement efforts. For example, recent initiatives aimed at raising the quality of teaching and learning have demanded quick action. The history of Tee-Jay suggests, however, that the formation of a strong academic culture may take years.

Excellence often is associated with a clear sense of organizational mission. Most observers acknowledge that no single organization can be successful if it tries to be all things to all people. Readers should consider the mission that guided the Tee-Jay faculty and how it compares with contemporary interpretations of the purpose of the high school. Has Tee-Jay's commitment to prepare well-rounded students lost relevance in a society that seems to value education primarily for its contribution to economic competition? What factors enabled Tee-Jay to sustain high academic expectations without diminishing the importance of school citizenship, extracurricular participation, and exemplary personal conduct?

The third key issue illuminated by Tee-Jay's history concerns organizational survival. Once considered secure, urban high schools increasingly face the threat of closure. Readers should note the various arguments for closing Tee-Jay and how they shifted over time and across special interest groups. The expressed reasons for keeping the school open are equally revealing. Taken together, this information illustrates the extent of politicization of educational decision-making in urban communities. Consensus is rare, and opportunism holds coherence hostage.

That Tee-Jay has remained open, despite three serious attempts to shut it down, casts light on the contemporary politics of school survival. As readers will discover, Tee-Jay's recent history demonstrates the value of changing while remaining the same. Continuity is necessary to retain the support of traditional constituents, while change is crucial to win over many newcomers. How Tee-Jay achieved this marriage of opposites is one of the most interesting sidelights of its story and, perhaps, a source of lessons for other high schools threatened with extinction.

The story of Tee-Jay begins with the rise of the Richmond Public Schools. Chapter 1 offers background information on the city of Richmond, its commitment to education, and the creation of its public school system. In addition, the chapter describes the circumstances leading to the opening of Tee-Jay in 1930 and its early days of operation. The school's determined efforts to foster an academic culture are discussed in chapter 2, which covers the years from 1931 to 1946. The period following World War II was a favorable one for Richmond and Tee-Jay. The local economic picture brightened, and the city's West End expanded. Chapter 3 details the process by which Tee-Jay grew into an outstanding center of learning. From 1946 until the beginning of desegregation, the school's academic culture continued to develop, eventually achieving a solid reputation for excellence.

The next section of the book covers the period from 1962 through the present, a time of numerous challenges—both internal and external—to Tee-Jay's culture of academic excellence. The struggles to preserve this culture and the impact of these efforts on Tee-Jay as an organization serve as the themes of chapters 4, 5, and 6.

Chapter 4 describes the early years of desegregation from 1962 through 1977. Small numbers of black students attended Tee-Jay until 1970, but the school avoided the trauma and tension experienced by many schools elsewhere. Richmond's school system meanwhile was accused of purposefully slowing the progress of desegregation efforts. A lengthy court battle ensued, resulting eventually in a court-ordered desegregation plan and busing. Court-ordered busing in 1970 provided the next challenge for Tee-Jay. The student body and faculty became increasingly black. Racial incidents and discipline problems were experienced in substantial numbers for the first time. A large group of veteran white teachers retired or were reassigned during these years. In 1976 Tee-Jay was assigned its first black principal, and Richmond's first black superintendent was selected. An alternative public high school for academically gifted students, Richmond Community High School, opened in 1977, thereby creating yet another challenge. Tee-Jay's academic culture depended on the availability of a core group of bright students. Now these students could opt to attend Community High School.

In an experiment ostensibly aimed at forestalling school closings, Richmond's high schools were combined into three "complexes" in 1979. Tee-Jay was grouped with two high schools located in the southern part of the city, across the James River. Chapter 5 recounts the period of the complex system, from 1979 until 1986, and how Tee-Jay confronted the prospect of losing its identity as a result of school consolidation. The chapter then examines the aftermath of complexes, when the Richmond school system was forced to explore other ways to cope with declining enrollments and budget problems. Tee-Jay, during this period, faced not only the challenge of preserving its academic culture, but also one of surviving as a school.

The success of the SOS (Save Our School) Campaign in the spring of 1989 brought but temporary relief. The early nineties witnessed the creation of a citywide set of magnet schools and an open enrollment plan, the School Board's recommitment to neighborhood schools, the opening of a Governor's School at Tee-Jay, and the drafting of a plan for phasing out Tee-Jay as Governor's School enrollments grew. Chapter 6 discusses these developments and the strains that resulted when the high school once again battled to survive.

The last section of the book considers the lessons to be learned from the Tee-Jay experience. Chapter 7 focuses on what the history of Tee-Jay means in terms of the goal of school integration. An effort is made to understand why a school with the capacity to attract and serve the needs of a diverse student body would be faced periodically with closure by school officials and local politicians presumably committed to desegregation.

The meaning of the Tee-Jay experience for those in search of academic excellence for urban comprehensive high schools is the focus of chapter 8. Cities around the United States have struggled to create what some Richmonders seemed willing to abandon—a high school with a track record of academic excellence *and* the ability to retain a relatively diverse student body. The chapter seeks to understand how Tee-Jay was able to sustain its academic culture for so long in the face of so many challenges.

The final chapter concerns what the history of Tee-Jay can teach about organizational survival. To survive, organizations presumably must deal successfully with the twin challenges of internal integration and external adaptation.[7] In other words, they must keep their members moving together in the same direction while ensuring that the direction is acceptable to their clients and local community. For three decades Tee-Jay dealt with an array of challenges, including desegregation, busing, racial tension, white flight, declining enrollment, school consolidation, faculty and administrator turnover, open enrollment, alternative schools, magnet programs, the Governor's School, and repeated threats of closure. The organizational adjustments and changes that were made in order to respond to these challenges are a major part of the Tee-Jay story.

In order to tell the Tee-Jay story, various sources of data were tapped. These included local newspapers, such as the *Richmond Times-Dispatch*, the *Richmond News Leader*, the *Afro-American*, and the *Richmond Free Press*; school publications such as the *Jeffersonian* (newspaper) and *The Monticello* (annual); minutes of the Richmond Public Schools Board of Education; and the Superintendent's *Annual Report*. More than a hundred key informants were identified and interviewed, sometimes on several occasions. They included principals and their assistants, central office administrators, board members, previous and current faculty members, school secretaries, parents, students, and community members. Informative letters were received from twenty-three retired members of the Tee-Jay faculty. Archives and private collections of papers held by the Virginia Historical Society and the Valentine Museum were reviewed. Secondary resources included several masters theses on Tee-Jay and the Richmond Public Schools, Robert Pratt's recent history of desegregation in Richmond, and Virginius Dabney's chronicle of the city of Richmond. A general description of the methodology of organizational history—the approach followed in this study—is contained in the Appendix.

The story that unfolds in the following pages touches on the lives of hundreds of dedicated educators and thousands of committed students. It encompasses the politics of education in a southern city and the changing world of public secondary education in the United States. First and foremost, however, *The School That Refused to Die* is the record of an exceptional public school—a kind of organizational biography. Exceptional organizations often serve as symbols, invested with meanings that extend far beyond bricks and mortar and the lives of their employees. Tee-Jay is such an organization. During its more than six decades, Tee-Jay embodied the dreams and aspirations of Richmond's white community and, later, some of its most influential black citizens. The high school has been both an icon of resistance to integration and a symbol of Richmond's last hope for integration. A paragon of continuity and tradition in its early years, Tee-Jay eventually came to represent flexibility and innovation as it adapted to a changing student body, declining resources, and new educational priorities. Perhaps the one area where the school's symbolic value over the years remained relatively stable was its commitment to academic excellence—a commitment worthy of the school's namesake.

PART 1

Creating an Excellent High School

Although many people trace the origins of a school to its construction, a school—in the sense of an organization with clearly understood ways of conducting business and a culture characterized by shared values and expectations—is far from complete when the final brick is laid and the last coat of paint is applied. In a real sense, of course, a school is never completed, but it is fair to say that a school undergoes a process of initial invention or creation. This process cannot be separated from the temporal and sociopolitical contexts in which it occurs. It begins well before the digging of the foundation, perhaps with a dream and a gleam in the eyes of planners, and it can continue for years as teachers, administrators, students, and community members debate and clarify what they want from the school and what they are prepared to contribute. Finally the awareness emerges that that which has been the goal of creative energy for years actually exists as a distinct entity, complete with reputation, history, and traditions. The dream has been realized.

This section describes the process by which Thomas Jefferson High School—Tee-Jay—was created. It is a story that opens with the development of the city of Richmond and the westward migration of white families seeking a better life. The story continues with the construction of Tee-Jay and the subsequent crafting of an academic culture amidst the challenges of the Depression and World War II. The section concludes with Tee-Jay's post-war "glory days," the time fondly recalled by many of those who worked in and attended the school as the defining period in the school's history.

CHAPTER 1

Richmond, Its School System, and the Origins of Thomas Jefferson High School

Gazing at the imposing edifice of Thomas Jefferson High School on opening day, September 11, 1930, an observer might have understood why education sometimes is considered to be the secular religion of the United States. A block long, three stories high, crowned with a central pyramidal tower, and highlighted by a massive set of stone steps flanked on each side by bas relief pylons, the gleaming finished concrete building resembled an art deco temple. Eyes could not help being drawn up the external stairway and heavenward to the tower, flanked on either side by busts of Thomas Jefferson and containing a large clock. Even the clock seemed appropriate—the educational equivalent of the cross that capped many houses of worship. Instead of scripture, the left pylon contained the following Jeffersonian inscription: "To enable every man to judge for himself what will secure or endanger his freedom."[1] What better patron saint to invoke than Thomas Jefferson, the father of the University of Virginia and the individual who, more than half a century before Horace Mann's initiatives in Massachusetts, called for a comprehensive system of public schools?

What kind of community would have commissioned and paid for such an impressive facility? What kind of community would have celebrated the opening of such an expensive school less than a year after Black Friday and the collapse of the U.S. stock market? What kind of community would have supported the placement of its second high school—a school ostensibly created to relieve severe overcrowding—at a bucolic site far removed from the areas of greatest population density?

The Tee-Jay story cannot be appreciated fully without some awareness of the city of Richmond and its school system. Only by knowing the background of this proud southern city is it possible to understand the evolution of the high school that for over half a century symbolized Richmond's commitment to public education. The chapter opens with a brief overview of Richmond's early history. The next part begins with efforts after the Civil War to create a system of public education in Richmond and continues through the late 1920s, when construction of Tee-Jay was authorized. The conclusion covers Tee-Jay's first days, a time when pride in the new school helped offset, however briefly, the distressing onset of the Great Depression.

RICHMOND—A SENSE OF PLACE

The history of Richmond, Virginia, reflects a certain ambivalence, symbolized by its location at the fall line of the Piedmont plateau. The oldest part of the city lies east of the first series of rapids on the James River, the place beyond which commercial boat traffic in the early years was impossible. The newer part of the city lies west of the rapids, which once marked the gateway to the frontier and the end of the genteel colonial plantations scattered along the lower James. The river also bisects the city along its north-south axis. The seats of government, banking, and culture are located north of the James, while much of the city's industrial and commercial activity occupies the flatlands south of the river.

Richmond's ambivalence extends beyond geography to its very identity—or identities. A patrician realm of Anglophiles and magnificent estates, Richmond also is home to working-class residents with little use for foreign culture or aristocratic tastes. A city closely identified with the South's struggle to preserve slavery, Richmond boasts an old and powerful community of black middle-class residents. Richmond's black population mirrors the complexity of the city as a whole. The city's young black professionals in many ways have more in common with white Yuppies than with fourth- and fifth-generation black gentry. A city of enormous wealth, Richmond sometimes appears a bit shoddy and down-at-the-heels, like a proud but impoverished spinster. Some claim that the reason Richmond has so much money is that Richmonders do not like to spend it. Southern cities such as Charlotte and Atlanta have eclipsed Richmond in influence and growth. While recent urban development schemes such as Project I testify to Richmond's commitment to the future, novelist Tom Robbins is guilty of only modest overstatement when he writes in *Even Cowgirls Get the Blues* that Richmond is "not a city at all but the world's largest Confederate museum." Cradle of the New South or last bastion of the Old South? The only answer for Richmond is "Yes!"

Richmond was founded in 1733 by William Byrd II and named for Richmond, England. Nine years later it was incorporated by the General Assembly, but the settlement's place in history was insecure until 1780, when it replaced Williamsburg as Virginia's capital. For the next eighty years, Richmond grew as a center of government, commerce, and manufacturing. By the 1850s the city had become, in local historian Virginius Dabney's words, "the industrial center of the South and the region's wealthiest city, based on per capita property valuation."[2] In fact, the claim was made that Richmond was "the wealthiest city of its size in America and perhaps the world."[3] On the eve of the Civil War, approximately 38,000 people lived in the city—a figure that represented a 37 percent increase from 1850. Tobacco was the leading, but by no means the only, source of Richmond's wealth. Flour, coal, iron, and transportation contributed to the city's diverse and prosperous economy.

Richmond's formative years were not without problems, of course. In 1800, a plot by Gabriel Prosser, a slave from a Henrico County plantation, nearly led to the wholesale massacre of Richmond residents and the burning of the city. The abortive insurrection, betrayed by two slaves loyal to their master, dramatized the agonies of slavery and the inescapable insecurity that must characterize any society that relies on keeping humans in bondage. Nat Turner's Southampton County revolt in 1831 again filled white Richmonders with alarm, though the initial location of the uprising was more distant than Gabriel's Insurrection. Fears of slave revolts actually prompted Virginia's General Assembly during its 1831–32 session to debate the merits of repatriating blacks to Africa and abolishing slavery altogether.[4] No substantive action, however, was taken by the legislators.

The Civil War brought Richmond increased fame and eventual destruction. On April 27, 1861, fifteen days after rebel cannons fired on Fort Sumter, the Virginia Secession Convention invited Jefferson Davis to move the capital of the Confederacy from Montgomery, Alabama, to Richmond. Given Virginia's location and importance to the war effort and Richmond's strong economy, Davis accepted the offer. From that point virtually until the Civil War's end, Richmond served as the primary target for Union forces. Several campaigns to take the city were repulsed, but eventually Richmond was compelled to surrender. Before evacuating, Confederate troops torched the city's supply of tobacco, lest it fall into enemy hands. The fire spread to nearby warehouses, and together with other fires deliberately set by looters and escaped prisoners reduced much of the once prosperous downtown area to ashes.

In the aftermath of the war, Richmond, along with other southern cities, attracted large numbers of ex-slaves seeking employment and safety. Approximately 15,000 blacks flocked to Richmond, nearly doubling its black population.[5] Unlike their counterparts elsewhere, however, Richmond's blacks dispersed throughout the central city. In the words of urbanologist Christopher Silver, "Although blacks concentrated most heavily in the Jackson Ward area, virtually the entire city possessed at least some black representation."[6] Jackson Ward, located north of Broad Street, served as the commercial center of Richmond's black community. This neighborhood, in fact, was home to Maggie Walker, who founded one of the country's first black-owned and black-operated banks in 1903. Next to Durham, North Carolina, Richmond constituted the "most progressive Negro business center in the nation."[7]

Despite the growth of Richmond's black community, the overall percentage of blacks in the city actually declined as the twentieth century approached. By 1900 the nonwhite percentage declined to 38 from 44 percent two decades before.[8] Richmond's diversified economy made the city a mecca for those in search of employment. As well-to-do residents of the city moved to outlying areas, the central city filled with working-class whites and blacks. Between 1906 and 1914, annexation efforts resulted in Richmond more than doubling its size and reclaiming many one-time residents who had sought refuge in the suburbs.

The pattern and process of Richmond's growth has been explained in terms of a combination of urban boosterism and the politics of race.[9] Annexation, for example, was used not only to expand the tax base, but also to ensure a preponderance of white voters. Committed to efficiency in government and economic growth, Richmond's progressive elite did not support other planks in the platform of America's urban boosters in the years following Reconstruction. Reforms in race relations and the status of organized labor were all but ignored. It is understandable why a visitor to Richmond in 1919 described the city as embodying the "heart of a modern city" and "the very heart of the Old South."[10]

THE EARLY YEARS OF RICHMOND PUBLIC SCHOOLS

Although a statewide public system of schools had been proposed in Virginia just prior to the Civil War, no action toward this end was taken until after the war. A condition of Virginia's readmission to statehood was the drafting of a new constitution, one providing for, among other things, free public schools supported by taxes. A constitutional convention was convened on December 3, 1867, in Richmond.[11] The president of the convention was New Yorker John C. Underwood, whose name is forever linked to the constitution. Because many of the commonwealth's leading citizens were yet to be reenfranchised, convention delegates included a large number of out-of-staters and ex-slaves. Some delegates pressed for a provision requiring racially integrated public schools, but disagreement among radicals led to its defeat.

The residents of Richmond did not wait for the details of a state system of schools to be worked out by the convention. In 1866, the city fathers appropriated four thousand dollars to continue operation of the Lancasterian School and various ward schools.[12] Dating from 1816, Richmond's Lancasterian School had been created through a city council donation and private pledges. Originally an elementary school with free tuition for white students lacking adequate means, the Lancasterian School was converted to a high school shortly before the Civil War. As a consequence, an elementary school was opened in each ward. Several private schools served Richmond's more affluent residents.

In 1869, after the Underwood Constitution had been adopted but prior to its full implementation, a system of free schools was organized in Richmond. The action followed a petition from a number of citizens, many of whom could no longer afford to educate their children privately. Ten thousand dollars was appropriated by the city council to operate separate schools for white and black students beginning in October. A matching sum of money was awarded by the Peabody Fund and the Freedmen's Bureau.

Andrew Washburn, an educator from Massachusetts, was selected as the superintendent.

October 1869 found 1,008 white students and 1,769 black students enrolled in Richmond's public schools. Initial reluctance to accept "charity" on the part of some of Richmond's white majority diminished in succeeding years, and universal free schooling was fully embraced. Richmond took entire control of the system of free schools in 1870, thereby creating Richmond Public Schools. James H. Binford, a graduate of the University of Virginia, was chosen as the school district's first superintendent. In 1870 the state school system was formed under William Ruffner's leadership, and Richmond Public Schools became a part of it. The only substantive change which resulted from this shift in authority was the replacement of black teachers with white teachers in Richmond's "colored" schools.

The idea of publicly funded high schools was not universally accepted in the 1870s. Not until the landmark Kalamazoo case in 1874, in fact, did a court extend the principle of tax-supported public education to secondary schools.[13] As late as 1880, the Richmond *Standard* questioned the need for free public schooling beyond the elementary level.[14] Despite such feelings, Richmonders in the early 1870s generally supported construction of a high school facility to replace the rented quarters being used at the time. Located at 805 East Marshall Street, Richmond High School opened its doors on October 1, 1873. Built to accommodate 222 students, the school initially failed to attract a full complement and so had to share space with district administrative offices. William F. Fox served as the first high school principal, supervising two teachers and 49 students.

The course of study for the three years of high school, which ended at the eleventh grade, consisted of mathematics, natural science, English, foreign language, and miscellaneous other courses.[15] In the first year of high school, students learned arithmetic and algebra; physical geography, map drawing, and physiology; grammar, composition, etymology, reading and elocution, and orthography; ancient history; and penmanship. In addition, they could elect to study Latin, German, or French. Subjects offered to second-year students included algebra, geometry, and commercial arithmetic; natural philosophy (listed as a natural science) and descriptive astronomy; composition, rhetoric, reading and elocution, and orthography; modern history; bookkeeping;

and foreign language. The final year of high school found students studying geometry and trigonometry; chemistry, geology, and botany; English literature, composition, reading and elocution, and orthography; civil government; mental science; political economy; and foreign language.

News of Richmond High School's first graduating class was carried in the Richmond *Dispatch* on July 1, 1874. Despite the oppressive heat, every seat in the school's third-floor assembly hall was filled three hours prior to the graduation ceremony. In the presence of the mayor, the school board, and leading citizens, Superintendent Binford conferred diplomas. Awards in recognition of individual academic achievement, including a medal to a student who spelled correctly all 1440 words dictated by her teacher, were presented by the Reverend J. E. Edward. In light of current demands for more rigorous student assessment and accountability, it is worth noting that in the early years of the Richmond Public Schools the examinations upon which high school promotions and graduation were based were personally developed and graded by the superintendent. Copies of the examinations were printed, bound, and made available to the public.

Between 1870 and 1900 Richmond's population burgeoned from 50,000 to 85,000.[16] As the city grew, the ability of Richmond High School to serve the educational needs of white adolescents diminished. By 1908 the school strained to accommodate a faculty of 33 and student body of 950. Realizing that a larger facility was required, the school board authorized the construction of John Marshall High School. The half-million dollar, three-story granite building opened in the fall of 1909 on a site adjacent to the one-time home of its namesake.[17] Located in the very center of Richmond on a full city block, John Marshall contained fifty-five rooms for general instruction, four laboratories, and a library.[18] Little more than a decade after opening, John Marshall found itself so crowded that it could no longer accept first-year students. By this time, the length of high school had increased from three to four years. Freshmen were required to remain in their junior high schools until they were prepared to commence the second year of high school. Despite this stopgap measure, the high school still was forced to hold some classes in corridors and initiate double shifts. Seniors and juniors attended school from 8:20 a.m. until noon with no recess, while sophomores arrived at 12:30 p.m. and stayed until 4:10 p.m. With nearly 100 faculty and over 2600 students, John Marshall clearly was outgrowing quarters once thought to be spacious. George Wythe Junior High School was built in 1923 across the street from John Marshall, but by the time the facility opened, it had to be utilized as an annex by the overcrowded high school.

Richmond's population continued to grow during the twenties, but increasing numbers of white residents opted to settle in the city's newer and less commercial West End. While the westward exodus sometimes has been attributed to overcrowding in the downtown area by blacks migrating from other areas, the more likely cause seems to have been commercial expansion.[19] Richmond's black population actually grew relatively slowly between 1910 and 1940. In fact, while Richmond's black community actually dropped by 2 percent between 1920 and 1930 (from 54,041 to 53,055), the white population climbed from 117,626 to 129,874.[20] As the white population grew and located further from the central city, the need for a second high school became more apparent. Each year from 1919 through 1928, in fact, Richmond's director of high and junior high schools included in his section of the superintendent's annual report a recommendation for a second high school.

By the late twenties, when the nation unknowingly stood on the brink of economic disaster, Richmond found itself in the midst of a renaissance. The uncertain days of Reconstruction had given way to vigorous programs of economic expansion and development. In 1914 Richmond beat out Baltimore for the site of the Fifth Federal Reserve Bank. During the years following World War I, Richmond boasted the world's largest cigarette factory, cigar factory, woodworking plant, mica mills, baking powder factory, and plant for reproducing antique furniture.[21] Annexation in 1914 added 12.21 square miles and thousands of residents. The cultural life of the city thrived with the growing popularity of local writers such as Ellen Glasgow, James Branch Cabell, and Douglas Southall Freeman. Interestingly, however, Richmond, for all its wealth and culture, was the last city of its size in the country to establish a free public library, waiting until 1924 to do so.[22]

Not all of Richmond's citizens shared equally in the city's prosperity. Virginius Dabney cites a 1927 study of blacks in Richmond that indicated widespread discrimination.[23] Perhaps nowhere were inequities more obvious or harmful than education. Restricted to a separate system of schools under the supervision of

Richmond's superintendent, black students attended inferior schools staffed by poorly trained and poorly paid teachers. Illiteracy among blacks was reported to be fourteen times that of whites.[24] In the area of labor, blacks earned far less (on average) than whites, worked longer hours, and lacked access to more desirable jobs. Blacks frequently lived in substandard housing located on unpaved streets. Circumstances for Richmond's black residents did not begin to improve until after World War II, and even then progress was measured in inches, not feet.

On November 15, 1928, less than a year before the collapse of the New York Stock Exchange, the Richmond City Council approved an $850,000 bond issue to finance construction of a "western" high school. If council members argued over whether or not to construct the school or where to locate it, there is no record of such debate. At the time, John Marshall was operating on a double shift and straining to accommodate over 3,000 students in its main building and annex. Approximately 900 of these students lived in the area known as the West End.[25]

While it is impossible to reconstruct the negotiations and political bargaining that may have preceded the decision to locate a new high school in Richmond's far West End, the school district's architect, Charles M. Robinson, had stressed the need for a West End high school as early as 1925.[26] In a survey of building needs, Robinson noted Richmond's shifting demographics:

> A new high school in either the north, south, or east cannot well serve any other location, while by means of the Boulevard a West End High School will not only serve all portions of the "fan Belt" but can also reach the North Side or the South Side by bus along the Boulevard. Here it is practical to build a much larger building than in the center of the city as the traffic can be better handled and future traffic routing can be arranged to provide for the school needs. City planning is comparatively new, but can be made by the means of such as that of making no provisions for bypassing traffic around schools.

Was Robinson's reasoning really designed to serve the interests of well-to-do Richmond residents whose vision of the city's future followed the setting sun? The possibility of collusion between the school district's architect and city power brokers is conceivable, but unlikely. At the time a new high school was planned, Richmond's largest center of residential affluence was in

Northside, not the West End.[27] Christopher Silver, a student of Richmond's urban growth, concluded, furthermore, that Richmond lacked a true comprehensive planning process—either overt or covert—during the twenties and early thirties.[28] What public planning did occur focused primarily on engineering issues such as street improvements and sewer lines. Silver notes that planning "only abetted the insatiable urge of the private sector to develop as rapidly as possible the suburbs surrounding Richmond."[29] By doing nothing to moderate the expansion of suburban areas, Richmond officials, of course, were actually sowing the seeds of eventual deterioration of the city's central core.

Robinson clearly was aware of Richmond's suburban expansion, and his 1925 survey and recommendation of a West End high school reflected this awareness. In the following passage, he anticipated future annexation of part of Henrico County and the westward movement of city residents. Whether Robinson's prescience derived from insider information or keen predictive skills is unknown, but whatever the source, his awareness led to the recommendation that a new high school be placed well beyond the existing center of western settlement.

> Due to the approach of time when Westhampton [a Henrico County high school] will be annexed with a consequent shift of the population center of the West, this building should be placed well beyond the present center of the West End population. You already have a lot on Grove Avenue of sufficient size and admirably located. It possesses the advantage of by-passing the main thorofares lying north and south of it, yet being centrally located between them.
>
> At first glance, it might appear that this location is too far out. The theoretical proportion of the school population which should be in the high school is approximately 25 percent of the total school population. As better education is being demanded throughout the commercial world, pupils are staying in school longer. The extremely rapid growth of this higher grade proves that a fairly close approximation of this theoretical figure is no idle dream, but an approaching reality which must be faced by all city administrators. In figures, this would mean, at present, over 6,000 white high school pupils, on whom less than 1/4 can be housed in your present building. The next building must, therefore, be so arranged that at no distant future, it will handle the pupils from Lombardy Street to Richmond College, and

unless it is to be limited to a local area in its use, should be near the center of its district.

The Richmond City Council and School Board would take four years to act on Robinson's recommendation. While agreeing that the new high school should be located well beyond the center of western settlement, officials eventually opted for a site on West Grace Street rather than the Grove Avenue property mentioned by Robinson. On May 31, 1929, a committee of the school board recommended that the new school be named for the nation's third President, native son Thomas Jefferson.[30] Completed a year later, the high school cost $811,695, somewhat less than the projected cost of $850,000, but a substantial sum for the times nonetheless.

A profile of Richmond Public Schools on the eve of Tee-Jay's completion reveals a complex and growing educational enterprise. Besides segregated programs for K–5 students (19,571), junior high students (8,406), and high school students (4,597), the district operated its own normal school (187) to prepare elementary teachers (numbers in parentheses represent total numbers of white and black students).[31] The K–5 enrollment had risen by 240 students from the previous year, while the junior high and senior high enrollments had jumped by 54 and 217 students respectively. The district also ran an open air program (437), special programs for "subnormal" students (360), delinquent classes (112), a class for deaf students (8), and a night-school program (3,730). Students were distributed among thirty-eight elementary, four junior high, and two high schools. The per pupil cost of operating all-white John Marshall High School was $89.17, compared to $54.80 for all-black Armstrong High School.[32] No junior high schools existed for black students. The cost of operating the white junior highs was $87.48 per pupil. Elementary schools for white students cost $68.07 per pupil, compared to $41.29 per pupil for black schools.

A SCHOOL IS BORN

On a late summer day in 1930, when the League of Nations convened its eleventh annual session in Geneva and agricultural reports indicated that the U.S. corn crop would be the smallest in two decades, Richmond Public Schools began its sixty-first year of operation. Nearly 30,000 students traded queues at the Virginia

State Fair and John Barrymore's "Moby Dick" for registration and cafeteria lines at forty-five city schools. The newest of those schools was Thomas Jefferson High School.

The *Richmond Times Dispatch* reported that 715 students enrolled at Tee-Jay on September 11, while John Marshall welcomed 2,715 students.[33] The combined total of 3,430 represented an increase of 481 from the previous year, when John Marshall was forced to accommodate 2,949 students—294 over capacity. The newspaper article noted that, citywide, nearly a thousand students in the fall of 1929 had waited to register until the second and third days of school. Hence, it was anticipated that the two white high schools would enroll additional students.[34] Of Richmond's 29,156 total students, 20,408 were white. Black enrollment reached 8,848, an increase of 407 over 1929 and more than double the percentage increase for white schools. Still, only 87.9 percent of the black school-age population was enrolled for the 1930-31 school year, compared to 92 percent of the white school-age group. The official school-leaving age at the time in Virginia was fifteen.

On Monday, September 8, 1930, the principal of Tee-Jay, Ernest Shawen, met for the first time with his faculty and briefed them on the impending school opening. In the audience were thirty-two teachers, a librarian, and an assistant principal.

The man who presided over Tee-Jay's first faculty meeting was fifty-six years old and a veteran school administrator. Shawen grew up on a farm in rural Loudoun County and attended the one-room school at Wheatland.[35] Credit for his academic development and eventual matriculation at William and Mary was given to William B. Carr, principal of the three-room school in Waterford to which Shawen transferred after Wheatland. A retired professor of ancient languages at Randolph Macon College, Carr had the ability to illustrate his lessons with fascinating stories. Shawen was one of three boys coached by Carr "at odd times and after school in Latin, algebra and geometry" to prepare them for college.

Shawen's professional path to the Tee-Jay principalship began at the one-room school in Clark's Gap, Virginia, where he served as teacher and janitor. Since he had studied only two years at William and Mary in order to earn his licentiate of instruction, Shawen desired eventually to return for a bachelor's degree. In 1897 he reentered William and Mary, eventually graduating with an outstanding academic record and election to the nation's first Phi Beta Kappa chapter.

After completing college, Shawen taught high school for four years before becoming an elementary principal in Norfolk, Virginia. For three summers he also headed Seaside Normal, a coaching school for teachers intending to take the state examination for a teaching certificate. Shawen served as an elementary principal in Norfolk for eight years prior to accepting a comparable position in Richmond in 1911. Thus began thirty-one years of administrative service to the youth of Virginia's capital city.

Shawen's early years in Richmond were spent under the direction of Superintendent Dr. Julian Alvin Carroll Chandler, who later became president of William and Mary College. Shawen regarded Chandler as the best supervisor he ever had. Principals who desired promotion at the time were expected to earn a master's degree in educational supervision. Shawen, along with many of his peers, wound up heading north to Teachers' College, Columbia University, to complete their graduate studies. Reflecting on the experience, Shawen concluded, "While I may not have gained much from Columbia, except atmosphere, I learned a great deal in exploring the great city. . . ."

During Chandler's tenure, monthly meetings were held with all Richmond principals. Reports were heard and future plans discussed. Shawen recalled one meeting where the superintendent asked whether there were any problems to discuss. When no problems were offered, he responded that "the principal who had no problems was not making progress." Chandler initiated many improvements in Richmond's school system, including a building campaign, curriculum changes, a more selective process for hiring teachers, the replacement of white principals of black schools with black principals, and a plan for the distribution of free textbooks.

Chandler was succeeded in 1919 by Albert H. Hill, who Shawen remembered as "another progressive educator," though a man "of less ability" than his predecessor. Hill promoted Shawen from principal of Binford Junior High to principal of Tee-Jay. The superintendent originally felt that the new high school should be devoted primarily to college preparatory studies, given the aspirations of West End residents and the existence at John Marshall of a wide range of vocational offerings.[36] Shop facilities therefore were not provided in the architectural plans for Tee-Jay. By the time the school opened, however, economic uncertainty convinced district officials that Tee-Jay should offer a relatively comprehensive course of study, accommodating the needs of both college-bound students and those concluding their formal education upon graduation.

The initial course offerings at Tee-Jay included all the same courses available at John Marshall except for German, vocational trades, home economics, and military. In addition, Tee-Jay students were offered the first high school physical education classes in the Richmond area. All students were required to take two periods of physical education a week during the first semester. In the second semester, the requirement was dropped for upperclassmen. The new school's curriculum will be described in the next chapter.

A Richmond high school education in 1930 officially ended at the conclusion of the eleventh grade. High school consisted of four years, though most students completed their first year of high school in a junior high school building. Junior high school, available only to white students, housed grades six and seven, plus levels IL and IH of high school. Many students remained in high school past graduation in order to earn additional credits.[37] Students were allowed to conclude their studies either in February or June, but commencement was held only once a year, in June.

Tee-Jay opened without a senior class, so it was not until February, 1932, that the first students completed their studies. Diplomas reflected six possible areas of concentration: Latin, modern language, history, science, commerce, and electives. Diplomas for "special students" and students majoring in vocational education and home economics were only available from John Marshall.

The school day in 1930–31 consisted of six fifty-minute periods and a twenty-five-minute period for assemblies and other student activities. A wide range of extracurricular activities were offered to Tee-Jay students from the very outset. Athletics, publications, service clubs, social clubs, and academic groups competed with classwork for students' attention. An editorial in the first issue of the *Jeffersonian*, which appeared on February 13, 1931, at the beginning of the second semester, captured the enthusiasm and optimism of the school's first months of operation:[38]

> January 31 closed the first half session of Thomas Jefferson. It has, perhaps, been as successful a semester as there has ever been in a new school. A record was established in September, when classes were organized and schedules straightened in two days.

A Sophomore and a Junior class were organized later on and both have enjoyed many social activities. Very successful athletic teams were formed, considering the shortage of time and material. A show was given, the proceeds of which amounted to almost two hundred dollars.

In the first of what would become a rich array of rituals of recognition, "honors certificates" were awarded to seventeen students at the end of the first semester. Each student had to have earned a grade-point average of 90 percent or better in every course, accumulated no more than one demerit, and possess no tardies or unexcused absences. Room 224 was lauded in the school newspaper as the homeroom providing the largest number of honorees—four. So began the encouragement of academic competition which was to become a hallmark of Tee-Jay. Homerooms even competed for the best average daily attendance each month, with winning rooms receiving monthly recognition in the *Jeffersonian*.

Second semester found the student body enlarged by two hundred students. Growth, too, would become a hallmark of the new high school. Among the newcomers were eighty-six Binford Junior High students, seventeen from Northside Junior High, thirty from Lee, and fifteen from private schools and out of town.[39] Six new teachers were hired to accommodate the increased enrollment. A double lunch period was inaugurated to relieve crowding in the cafeteria, but excessive noise and disorder during lunch persisted throughout the second semester.

On February 20, 1931, the high school was officially dedicated in a ceremony held in the auditorium. Dr. Roshier Miller, chairman of the school board, presided and delivered the opening address. A representative of the Daughters of the American Revolution presented Ernest Shawen with an American flag and a Bible. Later in the year Tee-Jay again opened its doors to the general public, this time for its first Visitors' Day. Patrons were invited to spend May 26 at the school, observing classes and inspecting the building and exhibits of student work. These events marked the beginning of a longstanding close relationship between Tee-Jay and its community.

As the 1930–31 school year came to a close, all who had been involved in launching Tee-Jay—faculty, administrators, students, and patrons—could take justifiable pride in a job well done. Not only had the establishment of routines and the scheduling of classes been handled with remarkable efficiency, but there were even some demonstrable academic successes about which to boast. Tee-Jay acquired its first silver trophy when a contingent of math scholars defeated counterparts from John Marshall in a trigonometry competition.[40] In addition, a Tee-Jay student took second place in the Randolph-Macon College Latin Tournament, missing first place by a single point.[41]

The general success of Tee-Jay's first year was hardly a matter of luck. While fledgling organizations often feel their way through the early months of operation, an ethos of determination and intentionality characterized Tee-Jay's infancy. Teachers and administrators alike *expected* success. So did students. When these high expectations occasionally encountered disappointment, as occurred in late winter when a series of locker thefts were reported, an editorial in the *Jeffersonian* reminded students:

> We have a new school without a reputation as yet. Make it good.[42]

CHAPTER 2

Building an Academic Culture

In one sense a high school is finished when mortar has set and paint has dried and the school board has accepted the building from the general contractor and declared it satisfactory. Tee-Jay officially was accepted by the Richmond School Board on July 30, 1930. If the culture of a school is the focus of attention, however, the work of creation only begins when the physical structure is ready for occupancy. The culture of a school embodies the norms, values, and beliefs shared by the individuals who work and study in it, or as Edgar Schein puts it:

> a pattern of basic assumptions—invented, discovered, or developed by a given group as it learns to cope with its problems of external adaptation and internal integration—that has worked well enough to be considered valid and, therefore, to be taught to new members as the correct way to perceive, think, and feel in relation to those problems.[1]

The process of forging a school culture is complex and time-consuming. As Schein indicates, it occurs at the same time as the organization must deal with both its external environment and its internal operations. Not all schools succeed in creating a strong organizational culture. Those that do not may be characterized by ambiguity, lack of clear direction, and internal friction.

Tee-Jay developed its culture during the nation's most serious economic downturn and the world's most devastating war. The task was all the more daunting because Tee-Jay's faculty and administration were committed to building an *academic* culture during an era when public opinion regarding intellectual development was ambivalent.

Writing of the context in which the modern high school was formed, Robert Hampel has noted that fewer than one in four adults aged twenty-five or older were high school graduates in 1940.[2] He contested the recollection that yesteryear's high school was typically a seedbed of scholarly endeavor (see figure 2.1):

The joy of a stimulatng lecture, the give-and-take of sprightly discussion, the intrinsic satisfaction of learning: these were not the foundation on which high schools in 1940 built their authority to run each day with bell-ringing precision. It is wrong to memorialize yesterday's high schools as citadels of order fortified by strong minds. Order, yes, but its acceptance was not contingent on academic excellence; often the strength of young minds was a secondary consideration.[3]

FIGURE 2.1
School Days Give a New Thrill!
Richmond Times-Dispatch September 11, 1930

How was Tee-Jay able to resist those who perceived intellectual pursuits as frivolous and create a school culture committed to academic growth? Before addressing this key question, it is first necessary to describe how Tee-Jay coped with growth of a different kind—the steady increase in enrollment. This chapter covers the period from the opening of the high school through the fall of 1946. Until September of 1940, enrollment increased substantially each year. The first part of the chapter discusses the challenges presented by a decade of steady growth and how they were met by Tee-Jay faculty, administration, and students.

Subsequent parts focus on key elements in the process of building an academic culture at Tee-Jay, beginning with curriculum and programs and continuing with the formation of a faculty. The penultimate part describes the variety of ways in which student competition was encouraged and celebrated. The chapter concludes by making the case that Tee-Jay, by the end of World War II, had consolidated its academic culture and was poised to pursue greater goals.

The fall of 1946 serves as a useful watershed for two reasons. First, the dislocating effects of the Depression and World War II finally abated, marking the first time in Tee-Jay's brief history when the full energies and resources of its staff and student body could be concentrated for a sustained period on the pursuit of educational excellence. Second, 1946 represented the end of an era for Tee-Jay's crosstown rival. James C. Harwood, the only principal John Marshall High School had ever known, retired, thereby creating an opportunity for Tee-Jay to escape the long shadow of the older school.

DOING MORE WITH LESS

Ernest Shawen, writing his annual report in the late spring of 1938, noted with alarm that his school was overcrowded.[4] Less than a decade old, the high school built to accommodate 1800 students "comfortably" was bursting at the seams with 2,011. Almost two hundred more were expected to enroll in the fall of 1938. Tee-Jay continued to grow, in fact, until the 1939–40 school year when its enrollment peaked at 2,367.

Enrollment growth affected all of Richmond's high schools throughout the 1930s (see table 2.1). In fact, Jesse H. Binford,

TABLE 2.1
Richmond High School Enrollments
(Regular Day Program)

Year	TJ	JM	Armstrong	Walker	Westhampton High (1–1–42)
1931–32	1,435	3,104	1,809		
1932–33	1,650	3,195	1,988		
1933–34	1,949	3,271	2,146		
1934–35	2,047	3,390	2,282		
1935–36	2,047	3,615	2,356		
1936–37	2,146	3,514	2,334		
1937–38	2,226	3,623	2,352		
1938–39	2,279	3,664	1,448	1,067	
1939–40	2,367	3,696	1,721	1,037	
1940–41	2,350	3,517	1,667	1,253	
1941–42	2,292	3,130	1,574	1,387	368
1942–43	2,222	2,893	1,471	1,322	382
1943–44	1,862	1,940	1,170	808	
1944–45	1,730	1,806	1,252	965	

Enrollment figures were taken from the Annual Reports of the Richmond Public Schools.These numbers represent the total number of students enrolled during the year, not the census on a given day or an average enrollment for the year.

who succeeded Albert Hill as superintendent, warned in 1935 that Richmond would need another white high school unless enrollments stabilized within two years.[5] John Marshall grew every year but one between 1931 and 1940, hitting a high enrollment of 3,696 students. Armstrong High School became so overcrowded that a second black high school, Maggie Walker Vocational High School, was opened in 1938 on land donated by Virginia Union University. Richmond Vocational School also began in 1938, providing a citywide center for white students interested in practical trades. In January 1, 1942, annexation resulted in Westhampton High School leaving the Henrico County school system and joining Richmond Public Schools. After two years, most of Westhampton's students were transferred to Tee-Jay, partially stemming a precipitous wartime decline in enrollment, and the school was converted to an elementary–junior high facility.

The steady growth in Tee-Jay's enrollment throughout the 1930s can be attributed to several factors. As noted in Chapter 1, Richmond itself had been growing, the result of a diversified economy. As the Depression deepened, however, jobs became harder to find, especially for teenagers. With the option of employment diminishing, more students elected to remain in high school.[6] A substantial number of students still left school before graduating, however.[7] Had they not done so, overcrowding would have been even more serious.

As its reputation grew, Tee-Jay began to attract a number of transfers from John Marshall and tuition-paying students from areas around Richmond. The March 4, 1938, issue of the *Jeffersonian* carried an article, for example, about Virginia Stanley, a senior who traveled 135 miles each day from Gordonsville to attend Tee-Jay. Stanley said she endured the four hours of daily train travel because Tee-Jay offered a "better education" with "newer and more complete" course offerings.[8] Many of Tee-Jay's transfers came from private schools, the Depression having forced their parents to choose free schooling. By the fall of 1937 Tee-Jay's regular enrollment was so large that Shawen announced the high school no longer would accept postgraduate students.[9] He further justified the decision on the grounds that older students constituted a "disturbing element."

While postgrads no longer attended Tee-Jay, the school continued to serve large numbers of students who failed to complete graduation requirements on time (see table 2.2). For example, of 746 students who entered Tee-Jay's sophomore (2L) class in 1933, only 309 or 41.4 percent graduated in 1936. It is interesting to note that, as late as 1950, almost three out of every ten students at Tee-Jay needed an extra semester to graduate. Why John Marshall's percentages generally were lower is unclear; although one reason may have been the higher percentage of Tee-Jay students in college preparatory programs after 1940 (see table 2.6).

Coping with rapidly growing enrollments can be challenging under the best of circumstances. While Richmond weathered the Depression better than many cities, the 1930s hardly qualify as the best of circumstances. School revenues shrank by almost $200,000 between 1930 and 1933.[10] Confronted by austerity, the

TABLE 2.2
Percentage Of Students Graduating On Time

	TJ			JM		
	% Who Graduate in Normal Time	% Who Graduate a 1/2 Session Late	% Who Graduate 2 Years Late	% Who Graduate in Normal Time	% Who Graduate a 1/2 Session Late	% Who Graduate 2 Years Late
1938–39	47.1	20.8	6.8	36.6	30.8	5.6
1939–40	39.2	27.1	3.7	40.5	31.9	2.6
1940–41	37.9	31.2	3.9	39.6	30.8	4.2
1941–42	38.5	33.2	1.6	45.0	27.9	2.0
1942–43	49.5	30.6	1.4	55.7	26.2	1.5
1943–44	N.A	N.A	N.A.	N.A.	N.A.	N.A.
1944–45	70.9	21.5	0.3	75.2	19.6	0.5
1945–46	N.A	N.A	N.A.	N.A.	N.A.	N.A.
1946–47	N.A	N.A	N.A.	N.A.	N.A.	N.A.
1947–48	65.0	23.8	1.2	74.0	17.6	0.4
1948–49	67.4	23.1	1.2	72.9	17.7	N.A.
1949–50	54.4	29.8	0.9	75.1	16.7	N.A.

N.A. = Not Available
Figures were taken from Annual Reports of the Richmond Public Schools.

school board abolished evening schools, summer schools, the Richmond Normal School for white elementary teachers, and the Armstrong Normal School for black elementary teachers. The school board also curtailed expenditures for supplies and maintenance, added to teachers' workload, and reduced salaries by one-tenth.[11] Had it not been for a series of budget surpluses accumulated by Albert Hill prior to the Depression, cuts would have been even greater. In 1934 consideration was even given to preventing married women from teaching.[12] Proponents reasoned that employment was scarce and households in which both husband and wife held jobs were a luxury society could not afford. While the counties surrounding Richmond adopted restrictive personnel policies, Superintendent Binford opposed the move, much to the relief of the city's 229 married women teachers.

By 1935 the economic picture in Richmond had begun to brighten. Serious consideration was given to building a second black high school and establishing a special center for vocational training for whites. The impact of the Depression lingered, however. As will be seen in the next part, years of economic insecurity and budget restrictions compelled educators at Tee-Jay and elsewhere to approach program development with a healthy measure of pragmatism.

SHAPING TEE-JAY'S COURSE OF STUDY

On February 20 and 21, 1894, thirty-six years before Tee-Jay opened, Richmond hosted a national meeting of individuals concerned about the future of secondary education in the United States. The ostensible purpose of the gathering was to discuss, for the first time in public, the recent report of the Committee of Ten, a blue-ribbon panel appointed by the National Education Association and headed by Harvard president Charles W. Eliot.[13] While the report hardly constituted a radical departure from past practice, it stressed the importance of solid academic courses of study, whether or not students intended to go to college. Recommended courses of study were presented under four headings: Classical, Latin-Scientific, Modern Languages, and English. A distinguishing feature of each program was its particular configuration of foreign languages. Historian Edward Krug believed that the message of the report ran along the following lines:

> There should be no difference made in the teaching of any subject on the ground of whether or not a pupil was going to college. The modern academic subjects should be rescued from their scrappy inferiority. . . . One could get good mental training and should be admitted to college even though he had never studied either Latin or Greek. The elective principle was clearly endorsed. . . .[14]

Whether Richmond school officials were directly influenced by the recommendations of the Committee of Ten is unknown, but throughout the early decades of the twentieth century they insisted on the value of rigorous academic preparation for all students, not just the college-bound. The Depression, however, brought reconsideration of the high school curriculum. The 1935–36 Annual Report of the Richmond superintendent indicated that economic realities compelled him to place greater emphasis on vocational subjects:

> The function of the high school has and is radically changing. It is no longer a selective agency for the college. Due to compulsory attendance laws and changed economic conditions, it has had thrust upon it some very definite social demands, whether they [sic] like it or not. Because of these changes, the classical work of the school must be supplemented or replaced by courses in the fields of the Fine and Industrial Arts.[15]

The 1935–36 report continued with references to the ways in which the high school curriculum was being adjusted to accommodate practical concerns:

> Work in the Social Studies is becoming more practical and concerned with the present; in the field of science some very definite things have been done to show its relation and use in everyday life; the growing popularity of music, art, home economics, and industrial arts points toward better preparation either vocationally or avocationally; and teachers in other fields are trying very definitely to show how their subject works in the world of industry and business today.[16]

The Tee-Jay faculty recognized the importance of curriculum balance. Furthermore, they saw no contradiction between rigorous academic preparation and the need for coursework to be of practical value. Academic preparation, to them, implied serious study, diligence, high levels of performance, competition, and a broad base of knowledge. Today such beliefs may be associated primarily with a college preparatory mission. In the 1930s, however, when only one in five Tee-Jay graduates attended college after four years of high school, academic study was not associated exclusively with preparation for college.[17]

Throughout the 1930s, efforts were made to expand the Tee-Jay course of study and increase the number of practical offerings. By 1935, students could select courses from the following areas of study:

English	Typewriting	Science
Public Speaking	Art	Bookkeeping
Business Correspondence	Mechanical Drawing	Shorthand
Mathematics	Music	Band
Latin	Physical Education	History
French	Home Economics	Spanish
German	Orchestra	Voice

By the end of the decade, the only courses available at John Marshall that could not be taken at Tee-Jay were in vocational education and military. A Cadet Corps finally was established at Tee-Jay in September 1942, amidst the pressures of wartime mobilization. Aviation training, preparatory to service in the U.S. Air Corps, served as the focus of instruction for Tee-Jay's cadets. A full program of vocational-technical offerings, however, never was initiated at Tee-Jay, despite annual recommendations by the central administration. In March of 1940, the Tee-Jay faculty added their voice to the district's when a study group authored a report stressing the need for an addition to the school to house shop facilities for electrical trades, woodworking, metal, printing, automobile essentials, commercial arts and crafts, mechanical drawing, and home economics.[18]

One explanation of why these recommendations were not acted upon immediately was the advent of World War II. Capital improvements for Richmond Public Schools were curtailed during the war. By the time the war ended, attention had shifted to the construction of new elementary schools to accommodate Richmond's baby boomers. As these youngsters matured in the 1950s, the school system focused on building new high schools rather than expanding existing facilities. The closest Tee-Jay ever would come to obtaining a full vocational educational program was a request in the 1939–40 district budget for $300,000 to build an industrial and practical arts wing across the street from the school.[19] A year before, the Thomas Jefferson Men's Association, a boosters club, helped the school acquire a half-block of land on the south side of Grace Street for the addition.

No records exist to indicate whether other reasons besides bad timing played a part in preventing Tee-Jay from developing a vocational education program. Since recommendations for such a program began as early as 1932, World War II alone cannot explain the lack of action on the part of the school board. Inadequate finances during the Depression might be offered as an explanation, except that the district found the funds to construct a new, vocationally oriented black high school and to establish Richmond Vocational School in 1938. An argument could be made that the latter facility, located in a remodeled school at Broad and Twenty-second Streets, obviated the need for vocational education at Tee-Jay. When the forementioned faculty study group issued its 1940 report, however, the justification for a new vocational wing was based on the school's large number of work-seeking dropouts (see table 2.5) and the hundreds of enrolled students waiting for openings in available vocational courses.[20]

One further comment on vocational education is needed. The plans for Tee-Jay were drafted prior to Black Friday, when the economic picture was bright. Why, then, was no provision made for vocational classrooms in the original plans? Is it possible that influential Richmonders never envisioned that the new western high school would be a truly comprehensive facility?[21] They may have felt that John Marshall's vocational education programs were capable of accommodating the need, or perhaps they desired Tee-Jay to be more of an elite institution then its crosstown rival. If they changed their minds later, in the face of the Depression, overcrowding at Tee-Jay meant that any attempt to add vocational education necessitated costly alterations to the existing facility or an expensive new addition.

Whether by design, coincidence, or poor planning, the failure of Tee-Jay to develop a full vocational education program contributed substantially to the particular nature of the school's academic culture. After World War II, as interest in college grew and the word "academic" became virtually synonymous with a college preparatory curriculum, Tee-Jay would have no established vocational education program to compete for resources, accommodate during curriculum planning, or counter its growing image as an elite school.

While Tee-Jay's curriculum was never expanded to include a full range of vocational courses, the school did not ignore external pressures for subject-matter relevance. In 1939, for example, one year after its sister high school, Tee-Jay initiated a Cooperative Work-Study Program, otherwise known as "Distributive Trades." Juniors and seniors in the program attended school for a half-day and received on-the-job training for the other half day. Courses in consumer problems and salesmanship were added in 1941. Table 2.3 shows the numbers of students involved in vocational programs at Tee-Jay and Richmond's other three high schools at the beginning of World War II.

Following December 7, 1941, the impetus for curriculum improvement shifted somewhat from labor-market concerns to the needs of a nation engaged in global conflict. As indicated earlier, a Cadet Corps under the leadership of Captain Bernard Dabney, Jr., was formed in September of 1942. Approximately four hun-

TABLE 2.3
Vocational Enrollments In Richmond High Schools:1941–42

Tee-Jay	John Marshall	Armstrong	Maggie Walker
Distributive trades (22)	Distributive trades (26)	Woodworking (89)	Barbering (109)
Diversified occupations (27)	Diversified occupations (20)	Automobiles (70)	Diversified occupations (35)
Mechanical drawing (280)	Mechanical drawing (670)		Building maintenance (83)
	Automobiles (149)		Cosmetology (31)
	Electricity (203)		Masonry (77)
	Metalworking (245)		Public foods (83)
			Shoe repairing (33)

Seventy-third Annual Report of the Superintendent of the Public Schools of the City of Richmond, Virginia:1941-1942, pp. 56–57.

dred boys became involved in the first year. The Annual Report for 1942–43 indicated that certain courses, particularly in mathematics and science, also had been revised to help prepare students for military service. Greater emphasis was placed on physical education, with junior and senior boys receiving one period of P.E. every day. In the fall of 1943, classes in family relations were introduced on a once-a-week basis through the Home Economics Department. Offered only to female students and taught by the wife of a local minister, the classes focused on relationships between boys and girls in high school, the value of friends, the problems of dating, marriage, and how to choose a "life partner."[22]

As of February 1, 1943, graduation requirements for high school students were lowered from eighteen to sixteen credits.[23] This move meant that fewer students needed to remain in high school longer than four years, thereby increasing the pool of high school graduates available for military service and employment in wartime industries. The Richmond High School Teachers Association petitioned Superintendent Jesse Binford the following year to reinstate the eighteen-credit graduation requirement, but he rejected the request, pointing out that the "present requirements benefit pupils who 'will do well to get 16 credits,' but do not hamper college-preparatory students who wish to get extra units."[24]

While pressures for curricular practicality were consistently strong during Tee-Jay's first decade and a half, it would be wrong to assume that no countervailing pressures affected school programs. Foreshadowing similar queries in the late 1950s and early 1980s, Richmond's influential assistant superintendent, Forbes H. Norris, asked the following questions in 1942:

> What place do standards have in a modern school? Should all standards be individual, or are there degrees of attainment that all should reach? What should be the relationship between standards and student effort?
>
> Are we thinking too much of the slowest, least promising of our school population, and not enough of the pupil who has average or above average ability?[25]

Norris's questions were intended to introduce a report on new policies adopted by Richmond Public Schools in 1941. The policies encompassed a new course of study for all city schools, a uniform system for reporting pupil progress, and an "approximation of grade standards for pupil promotion."[26] The Tee-Jay faculty, however, had begun to focus on academic standards almost as soon as the school opened. On February 9, 1932, for example, the English Department met to establish minimum standards for grammar and a "correct form for all English papers."[27] The meeting engendered considerable debate, particularly regarding the width of margins and whether students should be able to write on both sides of a sheet of paper. Concern over the waste of paper during a period of economic retrenchment prevailed.

Ability grouping was initiated in the 1930s as a mechanism for ensuring that all students, regardless of aspirations or ability, met basic standards. Years later, questions would be raised about the effectiveness of this innovation, but at the time, considerable support existed for it.[28]

A two-level English course began at Tee-Jay in September of 1934. The "X" level was designed for students interested in college, and the "Y" level catered to students taking "life preparatory classes."[29] By 1937, English, history, and science courses at Tee-Jay were being taught on two levels.

A further indication of concern for less able students involved a new course in remedial reading. Pioneered by Lucy Henderson in 1935, the course provided drills in specific reading skills and ample time for free reading. Of seventy-five remedial reading students tested during the 1937–38 school year, the average gain in reading ability was over one-and-a-half years.[30] Only fifteen students made no gain. The Annual Report for 1937–38 boasted that the attitudes of students in remedial and Y courses were more positive and their rates of promotion were higher than before the introduction of these courses.[31]

By the end of World War II, Tee-Jay offered students a wide range of courses in traditional academic areas and electives. Only German had been dropped, the victim of wartime feelings of resentment. A particularly strong set of offerings were available in art, band, orchestra, vocal music, and drama. Students had numerous opportunities to display their artistic talents at exhibitions and concerts, in plays and operettas, and on a weekly radio program. The needs of lower ability students were addressed in Y-level classes and remedial reading. Non-college-bound students could choose from a variety of business and commercial courses, some with opportunities for work-study. Only the absence of offerings in vocational trades prevented Tee-Jay from being a truly comprehensive high school.

FORMING A FACULTY

Creating a course of study requires awareness of subject matter and sensitivity to the needs of young people. Transforming dozens of educators into a faculty is a more complex process. Working in the same school under the same leader does not guarantee that a collection of teachers will coalesce into a compatible team of professionals pursuing common goals. Without such teams, strong school cultures are unlikely to emerge.

Veterans of Tee-Jay's formative period indicated that a true sense of faculty unity did not develop immediately. In fact, teachers initially tended to cluster, depending on whether they had been assigned to the school or personally selected by Shawen.[32] Whether the eventual formation of a unified faculty occurred despite, or as a result of, the early challenges faced by the school is unclear. There is simply no way of knowing what would have happened had the school developed during a period of prosperity and peace. What is apparent in the recollections of retired teachers is that Tee-Jay's teachers thrived on adversity, be it overcrowding, severely limited financial resources, or wartime shifts in priorities. When the school's roof burned on November 21, 1932, and classes had to be canceled, teachers came to school anyway so that offerings for Thanksgiving baskets for the needy still could be collected. When depleted revenues forced Tee-Jay to absorb 145 new students in 1937 without adding new teachers, the faculty closed ranks and got the job done.

A culture entails, above all else, a sense of shared values and beliefs. What the Tee-Jay faculty ultimately came to share included a deep enjoyment of teaching and of each other, a commitment to continuing professional development, high expectations for students, and a willingness to exercise leadership. Each of these aspects of Tee-Jay's culture will be addressed in this section.

Between 1930 and 1937 the number of teachers at Tee-Jay more than doubled from thirty-two to seventy-two. With newcomers joining the ranks virtually every semester until February 1937, little opportunity existed for an "old Guard" to form. Barely a year after the school opened, teachers agreed on three distinct purposes for faculty meetings—business, professional development, and social activities.[33] The Mathematics Department hosted card parties to raise money during the Depression to purchase badly needed curriculum materials. Playing together seemed a natural outgrowth of working together. Teachers attended parties at each other's homes and christened each other with nicknames. G. Ray Bennett, an English teacher and Yale graduate, headed a squad of nine faculty bowlers who competed against teachers from other Richmond schools. Faculty men practiced basketball together under the tutelage of "Spud" Bloxsom, Tee-Jay's coach, in order to compete against a team of students. Faculty members even joined students on stage, taking roles in dramatic productions and benefit performances.

Tee-Jay's teachers enjoyed and took pride in teaching. Departments frequently met to coordinate activities. For example, in the spring of 1932, when all Richmond teachers were struggling to adjust to a 10 percent reduction in salary, science teachers, under the leadership of Roland "Chunky" Galvin, conferred with both the Mathematics and the History Departments to identify common curriculum concerns. Out of such gatherings came shared knowledge of what teachers of different subjects covered in their courses and their instructional objectives. An article in the October 22, 1937, *Jeffersonian* noted that faculty and students sometimes were found by custodians working at school as late as 10:00 p.m. Teachers at Tee-Jay seemed to appreciate the fact they were engaged in the process of building a new school.

Credit for bringing together such a dedicated group of educators must go, in large part, to Tee-Jay's principal. Ernest Shawen, in his memoirs, claimed that he looked for four primary qualifications in teachers: (1) a liking for children, (2) a willingness to work, (3) thorough knowledge of subject matter, and (4) a sense of humor.[34] Just how he assessed these attributes was not specified, but Shawen expressed admiration for Superintendent Albert Hill's policy of according Richmond principals considerable discretion in teacher selection.[35] Tee-Jay's first principal valued a college education, but he also believed that teachers were born, not trained.[36] As a result, he occasionally bucked the trend of the times and hired teachers without degrees. Two such individuals were Marjorie Davis, an art teacher who knew "how to make her group feel that art was an important part of life," and Susette Tyler, the head of the Commercial Department, who made certain her students were "in constant demand by business organizations."[37]

One mark of capable and committed educators is a desire for continuing professional development. Tee-Jay teachers manifested such a desire in various ways. Many teachers found the time and resources to take sabbaticals and earn master's degrees. They played active roles in professional organizations, and several even undertook professional writing. Roland Galvin authored a chemistry lab manual. Ruth Wilson, head of the Mathematics Department, published an article in 1937 in *The Mathematics Teacher*. The piece described her annual exhibition of calculating machines and student work covering every branch of mathematics, including charts on how math was used in industry.[38] Innovative teaching ideas such as this were a hallmark of the Tee-Jay faculty and a further indication of ongoing professional growth. Tee-Jay teachers were the first in Richmond to use "portable talking movie machines" for instructional purposes.[39] History teachers ventured beyond their textbooks and provided opportunities for students to select and discuss topics of current interest.[40] Science teachers at Tee-Jay were the first high school teachers in Richmond to utilize field trips, taking their students to chemical plants and local colleges. New approaches to teaching often were introduced in faculty meetings devoted to professional matters.

While teaching methods varied across departments, most Tee-Jay teachers agreed that all students benefitted from high expectations. High expectations were conveyed in various ways. For instance, teachers planned assemblies to introduce students to exemplary thinkers such as Dr. Negus, head of the Chemistry Department at the Medical College of Virginia, and Douglas Southall Freeman, editor of the *Richmond News Leader* and a prominent historian. Freeman gave a dramatic Memorial Day address on May 28, 1931. Following the introduction of several Civil War veterans and the singing of "Way Down South" and "Old Black Joe," he spoke of the ideals of the Confederacy:

> The most somber fact of the present day is that we have not taken as our heroes such brave men as Lindbergh. Our demigod is Henry Ford. We need in America to select heroes for something else than their power of acquisition. That is why the Confederate age stands out. Lee, Jackson, and Stuart were the three greatest men the South produced during the war, according to Virginians.[41]

That all three of Freeman's heroes hailed from Virginia suggested that teachers did not have to venture across state lines in search of role models. Virginia boasted an abundance of famous sons and daughters, and Tee-Jay's faculty, most of whom came from the state, rarely overlooked opportunities to remind students of their illustrious heritage.

High expectations also were conveyed through ritual and routine. Tee-Jay's students were encouraged, for instance, to break local precedent and conduct graduation ceremonies in academic robes.[42] While such a choice could have been influenced by economic considerations, asking all students to don robes rather than costly suits and dresses also represented a conscious effort to emulate college graduations. Furthermore, the use of academic robes served to distinguish Tee-Jay's graduation ceremony from John Marshall's. Faculty agreed that students should serve as the principal graduation speakers. The four student speakers at Tee-Jay's first graduation on June 10, 1932, addressed their peers and parents on the changing American high school.[43]

National Honor Society served as the embodiment of high faculty expectations, since selection depended on excellence across various dimensions of school life. In 1937, when faculty felt that the academic standard for admission was not rigorous enough, they insisted that the cut-off grade-point average be raised from eighty-five to eighty-seven. The induction ceremony for National Honor Society was an elaborate and solemn ritual in which unknowing students were silently "tapped" as they sat amongst their peers, while carefully sequestered parents watched with pride.

The routine of homework afforded teachers another opportunity to reinforce high expectations. Students, however, pointed out that all expectations had their limits. An editorial in the March 31, 1932, *Jeffersonian* echoed a sentiment heard frequently over the years at Tee-Jay:

> The faculty has either forgotten its high school trials or methods of procedure have "stiffened" since the good old days. Imagine the plight and vexation of a student who carries five subjects and who is greeted with an hour assignment in each class. . . . The principal says three hours of outside work should be sufficient; the teachers say, "My class requires an hour's home work."

The frequency of student editorials decrying heavy workloads indicated that the Tee-Jay faculty, while unresponsive to the complaint, was receptive to students who spoke their mind. As long as students conducted themselves responsibly, they were treated as adults. Athletes were not held to a separate standard. Head football coach Shelburne Carmack believed, for instance, that the ideal athlete

> is the boy who is a real gentleman at all times. He attends to his studies diligently, does not give his athletic work as an excuse for nonpreparedness in the classroom, and does not try to impress others with his importance.[44]

High expectations were not limited to academic activities. Tee-Jay became the first high school in the area to introduce student government, doing so in the fall of 1932.[45] In the fall of 1935, "Student Participation" replaced student government, the faculty having determined that it was misleading to suggest that students actually "governed" Tee-Jay. Student opinion and advice were highly valued, however, and a variety of formal opportunities to share views were provided under the rubric of Student Participation. Each year student officers were installed in an impressive ceremony held in the auditorium. The event served to reinforce the faculty's high expectations for students, particularly student leaders. As an editorial in the school paper indicated:

> Such a ceremony does more, perhaps, than anything else toward making the school as a whole feel that it must live up to an ideal. Each student is given a feeling of personal responsibility for upholding the standards set by those with the highest degree of leadership and ability to be found in the school.[46]

One component of Student Participation was a Club Council, made up of representatives of various student organizations. It was created soon after Tee-Jay opened to coordinate nonathletic extracurricular activities. A unique "point system" was begun in 1941 to increase student participation in service activities. Each student activity carried a specific point value, based on the estimated amount of time and responsibility involved. A limit of fifteen points per semester was placed on each student, thereby preventing students from overcommitting themselves and coincidentally providing opportunities for a greater number of students to participate. A premium was placed on the quality, rather than the quantity, of student involvement. Service awards, based on point accumulations and faculty judgments of the quality of participation, were presented annually to seniors.

In 1934 students gained a voice in the disciplinary process. A committee of students and teachers, headed by Harriet Snow, determined that students who consistently obeyed school rules and met academic expectations should be entitled to attend "honor" study halls.[47] Roughly one-quarter of Tee-Jay's students qualified during the program's first semester of operation. These students also were allowed to function as cafeteria monitors and tour guides for school visitors.

High expectations also were transmitted through collegiate awareness building. News of the college successes of Tee-Jay alumni was covered regularly in the school newspaper. Reports typically dealt with academic honors, elections to class office, and selections by prestigious fraternities and sororities. Coverage of the successes of Tee-Jay graduates who did not attend college was virtually nonexistent until the advent of World War II. Graduates were encouraged to return from college to share their experiences with upperclassmen, thereby providing academic role models. Occasionally Tee-Jay students were taken on field trips to local colleges to hear lectures and meet professors.

A by-product of faculty emphasis on high expectations was an increase in what students expected of each other. An editorial in the September 30, 1932, issue of the *Jeffersonian* is illustrative. Addressed to incoming students, the piece concluded:

> The upperclassmen also expect something of these newcomers. The school is new and a great deal remains to be done to build up its ideals and institutions. The new students are invited to take part in student enterprises and asked to do their bit for the support of student organs. By doing this a school will be made of which all will long be proud.

Tee-Jay's teachers could not be accused of making substantial demands on students while going easy on themselves. Not only did they expect quality teaching of themselves and their colleagues, but they assumed that faculty members would play active leadership roles in the school. Sixty years before "teacher empowerment" became the battle cry of beleaguered educators across the United States, Tee-Jay's teachers participated extensively in school decision making. Once again, Ernest Shawen, along with Superintendents Albert Hill and Jesse Binford, deserve some of the credit. They believed in shared decision making and teacher leadership. Of course, with only one assistant principal for a school that grew to well over 2,000 students, school officials had little choice but to rely on teacher leadership. Teachers served on various school and district task forces and curriculum committees. They also shaped the extensive extracurricular program through their roles as sponsors of student clubs, activities, and classes.

The most visible manifestation of teacher leadership, however, was the department chair. Unlike many high schools where department chairs were "compromise candidates" or the teachers with the greatest seniority, Tee-Jay chairs typically were chosen because of their expertise and leadership ability. For example, Virginia Sydnor, first chair of the History Department, completed graduate work at Yale and Paris, earned a master's degree from Columbia, and taught at Greenville Women's College in South Carolina. Department chairs like Sydnor, Roland Galvin (Science

Department), and Ruth Wilson (Mathematics Department) did more than order textbooks and convene meetings. They functioned as instructional leaders—to use a recent term—supervising colleagues, helping new teachers, initiating curriculum reviews, and planning new courses. Retired teachers recalled the high esteem in which department chairs were held by their peers and the vital role they played in shaping Tee-Jay's academic culture.

Because teachers were involved in practically every aspect of life at Tee-Jay, they quickly developed a strong loyalty to the school. Those who transferred from other schools, including venerable John Marshall, soon switched their allegiance. Each victory over John Marshall, whether in a Latin tournament or on the playing field, was hailed as evidence that Tee-Jay was no longer a fledgling operation. Teachers in the early years insisted on referring to Tee-Jay as "Thomas Jefferson," lest it be confused with Jefferson (High School) in Roanoke.[48] By the late 1930s, the faculty began to exude a quiet confidence that Tee-Jay was well on the way to becoming a first-rate high school.

CELEBRATING COMPETITION

If one belief distinguished the Tee-Jay faculty from many of its counterparts today, it concerned the value of competition. Competition constituted a central element of school culture. Regarded as a healthy mechanism for reinforcing high expectations, recognizing exceptional performance, and boosting school spirit, competition could be found at all levels and in virtually every aspect of school life. Not only did students compete with each other in class, but classes and homerooms competed against one another. Competition was not limited to academic activities, either. Recognition was given to the homeroom with the best attendance for the month, the most *Jeffersonian* subscriptions, and the greatest number of donations during charity drives. Homerooms participated in a bowling league as well. Students also competed as individuals to get into band, orchestra, plays, and social clubs. In 1933, when Shawen became concerned that competition to join social clubs was unconstructive, however, he abolished them. Interscholastic competition was highly valued, not just in athletics, but in music, art, forensics, publications, and academic subjects. Tee-Jay students were exhorted to try hard for the sake of their school, homeroom, class, and club, as well as themselves. In Tee-Jay's culture, achievement was not justified solely in terms of individual advancement.

The importance of the homeroom in the organization and culture of Tee-Jay cannot be overstated. Homerooms served a key integrative function, as students from various junior highs were purposely mixed by homeroom to break down neighborhood identities and promote new loyalties. That this process succeeded is evidenced by the fact that some homerooms continued to hold reunions years after graduating.[49] The Tee-Jay faculty was responsible for deciding that it was best for students if the members of each homeroom remained together with the same homeroom advisor throughout their years at Tee-Jay. In this way, advisors got to know their students and were able to provide advice and support.

The bonds forged through daily contact in the homeroom were strengthened as a result of competition among homerooms.[50] Sometimes competition was arranged between particular homerooms, as occurred in the fall of 1931 when rooms 315 and 316 vied for the lowest number of absences and tardies during the month.[51] Victorious room 315, with twenty-two absences and four tardies (as opposed to twenty-five absences and ten tardies for room 316), was rewarded with entertainment by students from the losing homeroom.

On other occasions, all homerooms were engaged in competition. Such was the case with the monthly honor roll report in the *Jeffersonian*. Each month the school newspaper reported the homeroom with the highest percentage of students on the honor roll and the names of the students. A place on the honor roll required a grade-point average of ninety or better and an attendance record with no absences or tardies. When the percentage of Tee-Jay students on the honor roll dropped to 2 percent in January of 1932, an editorial appeared in the *Jeffersonian* decrying students who caved in to negative peer pressure regarding grades:

> The statistics concerning honor rolls . . . demand some comment. Ninety-eight per cent of the Thomas Jefferson students are not missing the honor roll because of a lack of intelligence. There must be some other reason! This statement is backed by the recent request of a boy that his name be left off of the honor roll because his "pals" razzed him for getting high grades.

What a shame such jealous busybodies can't be confined in
an air-tight cell or be made to visit a nice abattoir for nuisances.
Since what date has dumbness become a virtue, knowledge a dis-
grace?[52]

Competition was encouraged within class as well as between
homerooms. Results frequently were reported in the *Jeffersonian*.
For example, the March 27, 1931, issue carried news that the boys
had defeated the girls in Miss Wilson's third period Geometry II
class in an "original exercise" contest.

Of all the opportunities to compete available to Tee-Jay students, those involving crosstown rival John Marshall probably
were perceived to be the most important—by teachers and students alike. Tee-Jay, after all, was the newcomer—the school with
something to prove. John Marshall enjoyed its position as the
established academic and athletic power. No matter what the
focus of competition, it was not until John Marshall had been
defeated that Tee-Jay could feel truly successful. In many sports,
the game between Tee-Jay and John Marshall officially ended the
season. A losing season could be redeemed with a victory against
the Justices. The honor of defeating John Marshall for the first
time in a major sport went to the Tee-Jay girls' basketball team,
which defeated the Lady Justices 34 to 20 on February 5, 1932. A
short time later, school board chairman Dr. Roshier Miller was
quoted as saying that he and his fellow board members considered
Tee-Jay to occupy the same "level" as John Marshall "in every
way."[53] While a difficult-to-prove generalization, the comment
indicated that comparisons between the two schools were not limited to Tee-Jay faculty and students.

It is common today to read and hear about the dangers of
competition among students.[54] Part of the "philosophy" supporting the contemporary movement for middle schools, in fact,
involves an explicit rejection of such competition. Among the students attending Tee-Jay in the 1930s and early 1940s there doubtless were some who were harmed by the institutionalization of
competition. Many students seemed to rise to the occasion, however. Competition so pervaded the school that most students
could find some competitive opportunity to match their abilities
or aspirations.

Tee-Jay students compiled a solid record of achievement during the school's formative years. Typically, at least three out of

every four students obtained grades high enough to pass their courses (see table 2.4). It should be remembered that this period predated the days of "grade inflation" when students in many schools were virtually assured of receiving passing grades if they simply showed up for class. The data on John Marshall's promotion rates reveal that Tee-Jay's figures were not out of line for white students in Richmond.

Students who consistently failed their courses frequently dropped out of school, but these individuals did not represent the typical dropout of the prewar period. For example, in the 1937–38 school year, Shawen reported that 162 students left Tee-Jay. Sounding a cautious note of accountability, he added that, of this number, "only forty-two—two for conduct trouble, and forty for failure, indifference, inability or discouragement—could possibly be considered the fault of the school."[55] The category accounting for the largest number of dropouts was "went to work," a pattern that continued through the early 1940s (see table 2.5). Interestingly, greater percentages of John Marshall students left school to secure employment than Tee-Jay students, a fact that suggests Richmond's shifting demographics.

While the days when a majority of Tee-Jay's graduates attended college still lay well in the future, college performance provided an important indicator of the school's success from the earliest days. Of the ninety-four students who first crossed the Tee-Jay stage to receive their diplomas on June 10, 1932, ten were awarded college scholarships. The institutions represented by these awards included the University of Virginia, the University of Richmond, the College of William and Mary, Westhampton College, Hollins College, Shenandoah College, Washington and Lee College, and Randolph Macon College.[56]

In the years prior to World War II, the practice at both Tee-Jay and John Marshall was for the school administration to publish lists of graduates who were "recommended" for college matriculation. These students presumably manifested the academic ability and maturity to succeed in postsecondary study. To make the recommended list, students had to maintain an average of 80 percent in every course. Both high schools tracked their recommended and nonrecommended students to determine how well they performed in college. In 1935, for instance, Shawen was pleased to report that 11 of the 46 "recommended" students who entered the University of Richmond

TABLE 2.4
Percentage of John Marshall and Tee-Jay Students Promoted by Subject Area

	JOHN MARSHALL							THOMAS JEFFERSON						
	ENGLISH	HISTORY	MATH	SCIENCE	PE	FRENCH	BOOKKEEPING	ENGLISH	HISTORY	MATH	SCIENCE	PE	FRENCH	BOOKKEEPING
Feb. 1932	75.4	75.1	69.3	80.4	—	69/3	79.0	75.6	69.2	67.8	71.4	97.4	63.2	63.0
June 1932	80.0	82.5	72.8	74.8	—	70.6	71.3	77.6	72.1	68.2	72.7	93.7	67.1	70.0
Feb. 1933	75.8	72.5	67.4	69.7	—	67.4	70.4	75.9	72.5	63.0	71.9	94.6	60.5	64.0
June 1933	80.5	74.4	71.1	73.9	—	75.3	73.5	72.7	73.4	70.3	71.4	93.3	72.1	67.2
Feb. 1934	81.5	78.6	67.7	72.7	95.3	73.5	71.0	78.0	74.5	70.9	77.7	94.0	77.8	55.5
June 1934	81.4	73.1	72.4	73.5	89.5	80.2	77.9	74.9	71.3	75.7	77.9	95.3	78.7	66.4
Feb. 1935	84.3	83.3	72.4	80.6	98.1	86.5	81.2	78.7	75.5	76.4	75.9	94.8	83.5	68.8
June 1935	85.4	82.6	76.3	91.1	96.2	86.0	80.2	82.4	80.9	78.1	85.3	91.8	78.3	70.0
Feb. 1936	86.4	82.8	74.2	83.8	97.2	78.6	81.8	83.8	84.9	77.1	80.5	94.7	83.5	70.9
June 1936	87.5	83.9	75.5	86.2	97.6	80.4	77.9	81.7	82.9	76.8	82.0	91.8	81.9	72.3

Date														
Feb. 1937	84.2	83.7	74.2	82.4	97.5	85.2	75.9	85.7	86.1	80.6	84.3	91.4	85.2	71.6
June 1937	82.7	84.1	75.7	85.5	95.4	84.0	76.6	85.7	86.1	80.6	84.3	91.4	85.2	71.6
Feb. 1938	83.6	83.5	73.1	81.5	99.4	78.6	81.4	82.3	85.5	77.3	80.4	94.8	82.3	78.6
June 1938	87.1	87.1	76.6	84.9	97.4	81.0	79.3	86.3	87.2	81.2	85.8	94.4	81.9	77.2
Feb. 1939	87.3	85.6	72.6	78.5	99.4	83.1	77.6	83.4	84.2	78.6	83.4	94.2	81.4	77.3
June 1939	84.3	85.7	77.0	86.2	98.4	84.2	74.5	84.8	86.2	78.9	83.8	95.2	82.1	73.6
Feb. 1940	85.3	81.1	75.4	83.9	92.1	82.7	73.6	80.5	87.5	78.1	80.9	95.2	82.1	75.7
June 1940	85.8	82.1	74.3	84.6	95.8	88.9	74.8	81.7	88.5	81.9	93.4	95.1	81.8	73.8
Feb. 1941	83.2	81.7	71.7	81.3	100	81.0	72.9	81.7	88.4	78.4	81.7	96.5	76.6	80.3
June 1941	83.6	82.2	74.3	82.9	92.5	83.8	68.9	82.5	88.2	81.5	86.8	96.9	79.5	80.2
Feb. 1942	82.5	79.5	72.7	82.2	97.8	84.0	73.0	86.4	90.0	81.9	85.0	96.9	78.9	80.2
June 1942	84.3	83.5	71.8	83.6	97.2	87.7	72.1	85.9	89.9	83.4	86.8	97.1	83.6	73.1
Feb. 1943	84.3	82.4	73.1	79.4	100.0	87.5	71.5	86.2	91.0	80.0	85.9	94.6	81.1	74.6
June 1943	83.8	82.8	77.0	81.3	100.0	77.9	65.1	85.9	91.2	84.1	85.7	92.6	82.6	70.5
Feb. 1944	84.1	83.9	73.5	74.0	93.0	76.6	65.7	92.9	85.4	80.3	96.9	94.0	84.5	77.4
June 1944	81.1	83.8	73.8	92.2	99.3	91.9	65.4	82.6	88.6	79.1	85.0	93.1	80.0	81.5
Feb. 1945	85.2	84.4	74.7	80.8	86.7	67.6	92.4	81.2	87.7	75.9	83.6	91.4	66.0	62.9
June 1945	86.6	84.7	77.6	85.6	91.8	87.4	86.3	82.0	88.1	78.9	85.8	95.2	78.8	88.1

Figures were taken from the Annual Reports of the Richmond Superintendent.

TABLE 2.5
Reasons for Dropping Out of School

YEAR	THOMAS JEFFERSON		JOHN MARSHALL	
	No. and % of Students Dropping Out to Go to Work	No. and % of Students Dropping Out Due to Failure in School Work	No. and % of Students Dropping Out to Go to Work	No. and % of Students Dropping Out Due to Failure in School Work
1940–41	43 (1.8%)	11 (0.5%)	168 (4.8%)	23 (0.7%)
1941–42	88 (3.8%)	0 (0%)	207 (6.6%)	30 (1.0%)
1942–43	62 (2.8%)	0 (0%)	220 (7.6%)	11 (0.4%)
1943–44	N.A.	N.A.	N.A.	N.A.
1944–45	21 (1.2%)	1 (0.0%)	86 (4.9%)	10 (0.6%)

N.A. = not available
Dropout data were taken from Annual Reports of the Richmond Superintendent.

from Tee-Jay in the fall of 1934 made the Dean's List.[57] In 1938, Shawen indicated in his end-of-year report that the 146 recommended students from Tee-Jay passed 93 percent of their freshman courses.[58] The 32 nonrecommended students passed "only" 88 percent of their courses. In 1939, Shawen reported that the 163 recommended graduates passed 96.5 percent of their freshman courses, while the figure for the 43 non-recommended students dropped to 80 percent.[59]

Helen Gill, who started teaching chemistry at Tee-Jay in 1942, recalled that the school resembled a junior college more than a high school. She took pride in the letter written to her by a professor at Virginia Military Institute. He indicated that a "C" student from Tee-Jay was preferable to "A" students from many other schools. Roland Galvin, who headed the Science Department until 1946, when he left Tee-Jay to assume the principalship of Westhampton Elementary and Junior High School, boasted that no student who passed physics at Tee-Jay ever failed physics in college (at least through 1945). When the parent of one graduate notified Galvin that his son was struggling with college physics and might flunk, Galvin phoned the student, providing assistance and reminding him of Tee-Jay's perfect track record. The student's grades improved.

Student achievement was not limited to coursework and college performance. As Roland Galvin put it, "Tee-Jay was the first school I was in where *all* the talents of the students were used." The school newspaper and annual routinely won awards in national and regional competition. Tee-Jay's music program, under the leadership of Frank Wendt, was outstanding. Tee-Jay students played in the Richmond Symphony Orchestra and earned superior ratings at the Virginia Music Festival. Tee-Jay's athletes also achieved distinction, especially in basketball, tennis, golf, and field hockey. If the academic culture, high expectations, and competition at Tee-Jay failed to benefit large numbers of students, it is difficult to find supporting evidence. When an evaluation committee, headed by University of Virginia professor W. R. Smithey, assessed Tee-Jay in March of 1941, it awarded "superior" ratings for "Philosophy of Education, School Spirit, Standard Equipment, and Outcome of Its Educational Program."[60]

POISED FOR EXCELLENCE

The war years confronted Tee-Jay with a variety of challenges as well as its first change of leadership. By this time, however, the school possessed both a sufficiently strong culture and a faculty capable enough to handle such contingencies.

In September of 1942, Ernest Shawen was succeeded by Coalter C. Hancock. The October 16, 1942, *Jeffersonian* characterized the new principal as "progressive" and "sympathetic." Hancock previously served for sixteen years as the first principal of Chandler Junior High, one of Tee-Jay's feeder schools. A Richmond native, Hancock graduated from Richmond High School and the University of Virginia and completed a master's degree at Columbia University. For one year at Bellevue Junior High, Hancock had served as Ernest Shawen's assistant principal.

One of Hancock's first official duties was to dedicate an athletic field behind the school to his predecessor. The ceremonies were held during halftime of the Tee-Jay–Hopewell football game on November 25, 1942. Shawen Field became the first school facility in Virginia to be named for a principal.[61] Of Shawen's tenure at Tee-Jay, Hancock earlier had told a *Jeffersonian* reporter:

> He was our first principal, the man who bore the burden of our entire future. There were no traditions then [1930], no ceremonies, no songs, no memories. His was the spirit that launched and guided us in the first hard years.
>
> It wasn't his way to herald his actions with trumpets or to parade himself in front of students. But quietly and unassumingly, things were done—and Tee-Jay, finished materially, was built spiritually.[62]

In his memoirs, Shawen revealed how he wished to be remembered. Relating a charming story of a trip along Richmond's Monument Avenue that he had taken with his five-year-old granddaughter, Shawen recalled the young girl asking why there was no monument among the avenue's many to honor him. "Aren't you a great man?" she inquired. Shawen replied that he was not on an equal footing with the likes of Robert E. Lee, Stonewall Jackson, J. E. B. Stuart, Jefferson Davis, and Matthew Fontaine Maury. He added that he preferred to think of the "monument" to his life's work in terms of "the success of the inspiration toward a better life which I have tried to instill in the minds of the 26,000+ young people who have come under my influence in 46 years."[63]

Shawen's successor inherited a school with an enrollment slightly down from the high figure of 2,367 in 1940. Along with students from Hill, Binford, Chandler, and Bainbridge Junior Highs, Tee-Jay drew nine transfer students from John Marshall and twelve from Westhampton High School, which joined Richmond Public Schools on January 1, 1942, as a result of the annexation of a western portion of Henrico County. The city also annexed part of Chesterfield County at the same time. In September of 1943 Westhampton became Richmond's westernmost elementary and junior high school, as its high school students were transferred to Tee-Jay. Hancock also welcomed to Tee-Jay twenty students from private schools, forty-eight students from elsewhere in Virginia, and forty-one students from outside the state.[64]

With enrollments shrinking a little, Hancock was not required to devote a substantial portion of his energy to the management of growth, as his predecessor had been compelled to do. He immediately went to work to reduce some of the coordination problems that had developed during a decade of rapid expansion. Within his first month, Hancock created a Coordination Committee, made up of representatives from important school groups, to plan the extracurricular program for the year.[65] By adjusting the school schedule, he also enabled the orchestra and the glee club to work together.[66] The Tee-Jay Cadet Corps was launched at this time under the direction of Captain Bernard Dabney.

The exigencies of war prevented Hancock and his faculty from undertaking an extensive program of reform, however. First of all, class and personnel adjustments were necessitated because teachers and students left school to join the armed forces. Eight Tee-Jay teachers were furloughed for military service during Hancock's first year. Competent replacement teachers were hard to find, and regular substitutes with emergency certificates often had to be hired. Forty-nine Tee-Jay students, along with ninety-four from John Marshall, signed up in 1942–43 as well.[67] A bronze plaque in the front hall of Tee-Jay serves as silent tribute to the seventy-three young men from the school who lost their lives in the war.

Second of all, schools became centers for such wartime activities as the distribution of ration books, the sale of war bonds and war stamps, charitable and relief efforts, and the collection of salvageable materials. These activities required considerable coordination and supervision on the part of administrators and faculty. A third impact of the war involved shortages of resources. An editorial headline in the October 30, 1942, *Jeffersonian* dramatized the concern over scarcity: "Saboteurs Slink Through Halls; Look Strangely Like Students." The article went on to ask: "Do you carelessly destroy school property, dishes, silverware, desks, or typewriters that cannot be replaced? Now is the time when everything must be saved to provide for lean days ahead."[68] By 1944, even textbooks were affected as a result of paper and labor shortages. An ominous, and somewhat ironic, note was sounded in the *Jeffersonian* regarding the lack of replacement texts: "With the number of texts dwindling at the present rate, it will soon be necessary to resort to the lecture method of teaching, which at best is unsatisfactory."[69] World War II may have been one of the few times in the history of modern schools when students actually defended textbooks!

If the war did not present enough of a challenge, Tee-Jay also faced a major initiative by the Richmond School Board. In May of 1943 the report of the Survey Commission was published. Appointed by the State Superintendent of Public Instruction at the behest of the Richmond Board of Education, the Survey Commission authored a number of recommendations regarding administrative reorganization and program priorities for Richmond schools.[70] Among the recommendations most relevant to Tee-Jay were the following:

- Development of a course of study for each subject
- Improvement of spelling performance at all levels
- Initiation of more cooperative planning among teachers, including special teachers
- Development of courses in office practice
- Evaluation of the practice of ability grouping in high school
- Development of a plan to interest more students in the study of foreign language
- Improvement of library facilities
- Expansion of guidance services in junior and senior high schools
- Provision for daily physical education for all students
- Requirement that all principals possess at least a master's degree in Education

While Tee-Jay and its sister schools attempted to respond to these recommendations, other changes were taking place. The Virginia General Assembly raised the compulsory school age from fifteen to sixteen in 1944. Two years later Richmond caught up with many school systems in the United States when it moved from an eleven- to a twelve-year program of instruction. The make-up of the school board was switched in the same year from nine members, selected by districts, to five members, appointed by the city council from the city at large. Even the hand on the rudder changed, as H. I. Willett assumed the superintendency on January 1, 1946, and began to steer the district through shifting, though not necessarily treacherous, currents.

By the mid-1940s, Tee-Jay was well prepared for the voyage. The school had confronted the two primary challenges faced by all organizations—external adaptation and internal integration—and fared reasonably well.

Externally, Tee-Jay achieved harmony with its surroundings. An academic reputation sufficiently strong to please the middle- and upper-middle-class residents of the West End and lure students away from local private and parochial schools had been earned. Parents appreciated the orderliness and discipline of the school. In 1938, Tee-Jay became the first Richmond school to boast a boosters club. The purposes of the Tee-Jay Men's Organization were to promote good citizenship, support athletics, assist graduates in finding jobs, help dropouts to continue their studies, and "interpret aims of the school to citizens of the city."[71]

Internally, Tee-Jay possessed an organizational structure and culture that complemented each other. "Teachers," according to Helen Gill, "could count on cooperation from the office." Faculty and administrators served the same end—academic achievement. Factors that might have deflected or undermined this singular commitment, such as a large vocational education program, never materialized. By 1944, it had become clear that vocational education in Richmond would be concentrated at John Marshall, the Virginia Mechanics Institute, and the two black high schools.[72]

TABLE 2.6
Senior High School Enrollment by Area of Concentration

	TEE–JAY		JOHN MARSHALL	
AREA OF CONCENTRATION	1939–40	1944–45	1939–40	1944–45
General	1,733	901	2,066	860
Home Economics	0	0	150	0
College Preparatory	481	782	543	448
Commercial	131	225	921	637
Vocational	22	58	30	305
Total Enrollment	2,367	1,966	3,710	2,250

These data were taken from the Annual Reports of the Superintendent. It is unclear why some of the total enrollment figures in table 2.6 do not agree with the total enrollment figures in table 2.1. It is possible that some students were able to declare more than one area of concentration or that students who switched areas of concentration were listed twice.

A compatible and talented faculty led by knowledgeable administrators and department chairs guided a substantial proportion of Tee-Jay's students to graduation and subsequent success in college, business, and the professions. This record of success, coupled with numerous extracurricular accomplishments, helped Tee-Jay rival the older and larger John Marshall. By 1945 Tee-Jay actually had surpassed John Marshall in the preparation of students for college, while the latter high school served a growing percentage of vocational and commercial students (see table 2.6). With approximately two-fifths of its students preparing for college, Tee-Jay's percentage was double that of John Marshall at the end of the war. After World War II, and particularly after June of 1946 when the only principal John Marshall had ever known retired, Tee-Jay increasingly looked beyond Richmond city limits for schools with which to compare itself. Whatever rivalry remained with John Marshall was limited primarily to the playing field.

Having established a viable academic culture during the school's first decade and a half, the faculty and administration would spend a comparable period of time after World War II refining the culture into one that symbolized academic excellence and the ideal of the well-rounded student. How this process unfolded is the subject of the next chapter.

CHAPTER 3

Glory Days and Well-Rounded Students

Most were white. Six or seven were black. The youngest was pushing fifty, and many were well over eighty years of age. Some climbed the steps of the Engineers Club unassisted, despite the oppressive noonday heat of August in Richmond. Others relied on a cane or a colleague's arm. A few were barely audible, while others spoke in stentorian tones reminiscent of classroom lectures long ago. Each shared at least one thing—he or she had worked at Tee-Jay prior to the fall of 1970, when court-ordered busing transformed the landscape of public schooling in Richmond.

These educators gathered for lunch this day, as in Augusts past, to honor Tee-Jay's "glory days." While this period unofficially extended from 1930 until 1970, many of those in attendance believed that the school's true golden age was confined to the period between the end of World War II and the mid-sixties. At this point, the ferment throughout the country caught up with Tee-Jay. Some white students began to question authority, and the beginnings of desegregation introduced a degree of student diversity for which certain individuals were unprepared.

This chapter seeks to understand what teachers and administrators meant by the term "glory days." What was it like to work in and study at Tee-Jay in the years from 1946 through 1962? In what ways did the school change during this time? Has memory improved upon experience, or did this period deserve its epithet?

FOND RECOLLECTIONS

When teachers and administrators who had worked at Tee-Jay were asked to reflect on the "glory days," their responses revealed four recurring themes. Students were bright and motivated to learn. Discipline problems were relatively small. Parents supported the school, and teachers respected and valued one another.

The remembrances of Renate Thayer, a history teacher, are illustrative:

> As far as problems were concerned, there were none. I believe the faculty was so academically knowledgeable—their "control" of the classroom was their ability to stimulate and present their subject in logical methods to a captive audience. Students came to Tee-Jay with the thought impressed upon them that they were there to learn, to get an education. . . . It seemed to me that faculty and parents were always in agreement as to why you were at Tee-Jay. Tee-Jay was an academic high school which in some ways could compare to the German "gymnasium" (except that Tee-Jay did not offer Greek). I think, too, that the faculty "loved" to teach. We knew what students needed to learn in order to succeed at college or university.

Catlin E. Tyler, Commandant of the Cadet Corps from 1946 until 1956 and a retired Army Colonel, shared like views:

> To me, the outstanding quality of Tee-Jay was the dedication of faculty and students to be the best in every way. It was evident on College Night when nearly every school of higher learning east of the Mississippi was represented in the gym to advise students and parents. . . .
> I would venture to say that the faculty was better than most small colleges have to this day. They inspired all Tee-Jay boys and girls to forge ahead and keep up the work.

Alumni often expressed similar memories. Patricia Young, who attended Tee-Jay in the fifties and returned in 1963 to teach history, recalled the quality of her alma mater's educational experience:

> I was a student at Tee-Jay as a freshman (1955–56) and as a senior (1958–59). The two years in between I was at Collegiate [a private school in Richmond]. I returned to Tee-Jay my senior year because I finally convinced my parents that Tee-Jay had a much better faculty and more challenging courses than Collegiate. At that time Collegiate did not even offer Advanced Placement courses like Tee-Jay did. In fact, my senior history course in European history under Mary Maddox was harder than my course in European history in college!
> As a student, I remember the dedicated and demanding

teachers at Tee-Jay. The entire faculty seemed to look upon their jobs as avocations rather than vocations.

Though he did not come to Tee-Jay until the fall of 1958, few individuals were more closely associated with the "glory days" than William W. Brock, Jr. Replacing Coalter C. Hancock, "Bill" Brock served as principal of Tee-Jay for eighteen years. He was highly regarded by his faculty as indicated by Margaret Campbell's remembrance:

> To me, Mr. Brock was a living symbol of the school itself. He not only exhibited fairness, industry, and high moral character each day, but he also expected these attributes to be present in faculty and in students. Under his leadership the school was highly respected, and it was considered an honor to be a student or a teacher there.

A 1929 graduate of John Marshall, Brock remembers that school's legendary principal, James C. Harwood, as a scholarly leader who wrote Latin poetry and insisted on making all decisions himself. When Brock became principal, first at Albert Hill Junior High School and later at Tee-Jay, he preferred a different approach. Teachers and, on occasion, students actively participated in school decision making. Brock recognized that most academic matters were best handled by teachers, either at the department level or in the faculty senate, but he also displayed little reluctance to intervene in the face of conflict or when difficult nonacademic issues arose. Such initiative hardly was surprising from a man who had attained the rank of major during World War II and who eventually retired from the Army reserves as a brigadier general. During his tenure as principal, Brock helped guide Tee-Jay in its transition from a large, all-white, suburban-style high school to a smaller, desegregated, urban high school. To his credit, the process was accomplished with relatively little rancor and disruption.

After retiring, Brock initiated an annual August luncheon for those who had taught at Tee-Jay prior to the fall of 1970. He has continued to host the well-attended affair, displaying the low-profile gentility and school pride that characterized his leadership style as principal. When asked to reflect on what was significant about Tee-Jay, Brock recalled the school's high educational standards, talented students, involved parents, and competent teachers.

This litany of strengths was repeated in scores of interviews with retired teachers and alumni. In fact, no one who provided information concerning the period from 1946 to 1962 noted anything resembling a serious concern. Such unanimity invites skepticism. Were these fond recollections more reflective of subsequent events than the actual time period in question? Did the fifties and early sixties seem so wonderful because of later tensions and turmoil? Were Tee-Jay's "glory days" more fantasy than reality?

A review of primary documents from the time period—particularly school newspapers, local newspapers, district annual reports, and yearbooks—suggest that the answer is "yes and no." Yes, memory in some cases did improve on reality, obscuring differences of opinion, unpleasant challenges, and unexpected changes, while simultaneously magnifying successes. No, the "glory days" were not a complete fabrication. There was, in fact, much about Tee-Jay from 1946 to 1962 that deserved the pride and recognition of those who were members of the school community during those years.

In order to achieve a balanced account of Tee-Jay's "glory days," a sense of historical context is needed. While the postwar era has been associated with general stability, a cessation of hostilities, American preeminence, and economic prosperity unparalleled in the nation's history, the period also encompassed the Korean conflict and the beginning of the Cold War, the Brown decision and the commencement of the Civil Rights movement, and the emergence of the Soviet Union as a scientific and military power. So concerned were Americans over the last development that a wave of educational reforms were promulgated in the late fifties. Public schools, particularly high schools, were subjected to intense criticism, as if they had been largely responsible for the failure of the United States to place a satellite in orbit before Sputnik.

Tee-Jay was affected directly by efforts to promote educational excellence. Along with high schools across the United States, Tee-Jay teachers took a careful look at their courses of study, particularly in the areas of mathematics, science, and foreign language. A variety of Advanced Placement courses were developed, and the content of other offerings was upgraded. Richmond Public Schools extended the length of a high school education from four to five years, as the eighth grade became part of high school, and eliminated mid-year promotions. These changes were not the first to mark the postwar period, however.

No sooner had World War II ended than school officials in Richmond pressed for an extra year of public education. White schools were reorganized from a 6-2-3 to a 6-3-3 configuration, while black schools went from a 7-4 to a 6-3-3 arrangement of grade levels. In the late fifties, schools were reorganized again into a 6-2-4 arrangement and high school was expanded to included grades 8 through 12, with the eighth grade continuing to be offered in junior-high-school buildings. The decision in 1946 to shift from an eleven- to a twelve-year school program was justified as an effort to help Richmond students succeed in college.[1] A full scale revision of the existing course of study for all Richmond students accompanied the move to a twelve-year plan. Letter grades replaced numerical grades in 1947. Along with these academic changes came overcrowding. Finding adequately trained teachers and space to accommodate Richmond's "baby boomers" became major concerns for school officials. By the mid-fifties Richmonders acknowledged that their existing high schools could not handle the increased numbers of students. In 1960, a brand new John Marshall High School opened in Northside, replacing its outdated downtown namesake. The same year saw the opening of George Wythe High School in South Richmond, an event that meant South Richmonders no longer would have to send their children across the James River to attend high school.

The fifties and early sixties in Richmond witnessed the beginnings of pressure by blacks for improved educational opportunities and desegregation. While Richmond school officials did not adopt the openly defiant anti-integration stance of many Virginians, they also were slow to embrace more than token racial mixing.[2] The story of desegregation in Richmond is a chronicle of political and legal maneuvering and persistence on the part of both blacks and whites. More will be said of these matters at the close of this chapter.

This brief overview of the postwar period suggests that images of stability and continuity implicit in recollections of Tee-Jay's "glory days" are belied somewhat by actual events. In reality, the years from 1946 to 1962 represented a time of considerable ferment—political, demographic, racial, and educational. Still, it would be unfair to discount the "glory days" as sheer nostalgia.

In the years following World War II, the numbers of Tee-Jay students preparing for college grew steadily. Their parents increasingly were convinced that the road to the American Dream led through postsecondary education. By 1955, seven of every ten graduates entered college. Tee-Jay students distinguished themselves and honored their teachers in college, consistently passing well over 90 percent of their freshman courses (see table 3.1). Increasing numbers of Tee-Jay's students gained admission to prestigious colleges and universities. The percentage of students graduating from Tee-Jay "on time" also climbed after the war, rising from approximately 59 percent in 1947 to almost 89 percent in 1963 (see table 3.2). Tee-Jay students won regional and state contests in science, music, and foreign language. They became National Merit scholars and received college credit for Advanced Placement courses as a result of outstanding performance on AP tests. By the end of the fifties, according to Bill Brock, Tee-Jay was considered one of Virginia's two best high schools, along with Washington and Lee in Arlington.

Tee-Jay administrators had no problems recruiting talented teachers, given the school's reputation for bright students and supportive parents. That is, if there were openings. An indication of the school's desirability was its low teacher turnover rate. Half of the teachers on the faculty in 1946 still were teaching at Tee-Jay in 1958, when Bill Brock became principal. Low turnover not only meant continuity of school culture, but the availability of experienced teachers to serve in various leadership capacities. Teachers enjoyed working at Tee-Jay, according to many veterans, because they were never subjected to heavy-handed top-down administration. In part, this situation resulted from the enlightened leadership of principals Hancock and Brock. Credit also must be given to the Tee-Jay faculty for their willingness to assume responsibility when it was delegated.

When Bill Brock left his position as principal of Albert Hill Junior High School (one of Tee-Jay's feeder schools) to become principal of Tee-Jay, he inherited a faculty of eighty-five. Thirty-three teachers possessed master's degrees.[3] Only four teachers had not earned a college degree of any kind, and they all taught "non-academic" subjects. Five teachers were members of Phi Beta Kappa. Brief profiles of two teachers serve to illustrate the quality of the Tee-Jay faculty.

TABLE 3.1
Thomas Jefferson High School Graduates Who Enter College

	1950	1951	1952**	1953#	1955#	1956#	1957#
Number of graduates	480	257	305	414	423	377	488
Number reported entering college	333	146	205	271	294	249	313
Per cent of graduates entering college	69.4%	56.8%	67.2%	65.5%	69.5%	66.3%	64.1%
*Number of freshman classes in which students enrolled	1896	906	1218	1577	1640	1428	1697
*Number of freshman classes successfully passed	1701	788	1146	1472	1568	1349	1578
*Per cent of freshman classes passed	89.7%	87.0%	94.1%	93.3%	95.6%	94.5%	93.0%
Number of colleges in which students enrolled	67	36	39	68	61	55	65

*Based on first semester reports of Freshmen furnished by the colleges.

**The 1952 class was the first to graduate under the 12-year plan

#Based on second semester grades.

Jeffersonian, 10 April 1959, p. 1 (data were not collected for 1954 graduates).

TABLE 3.2
Progress of Tee-Jay High School Students

	% of students who graduated in normal time	% of students who graduated 1/2 year late	% of students who graduated 1 year late
1946–47	58.7	25.8	10.3
1947–48	65.0	23.8	7.9
1948–49	67.4	23.1	6.4
1949–50	54.4	29.8	13.6
1950–51	37.0	42.0	16.4
1951–52	91.0	1.7	3.1
1952–53	82.9	12.5	3.8
1953–54	78.4	17.8	3.8
1954–55	85.4	10.7	3.3
1955–56	84.9	9.6	4.0
1956–57	79.4	16.5	2.7
1957–58	81.6	11.7	5.4
1958–59	84.9	10.8	3.8
1959–60	82.6	13.8	2.8
1960–61	77.8	18.9	2.1
1961–62	83.3	12.1	4.0
1962–63	88.9	4.0	5.9

Statistics are derived from Annual Reports of the Richmond Public Schools.

Virginia Ellett first learned of Tee-Jay when she attended Westhampton College and met young women who had graduated from the school. She was impressed that these students had been prepared so well that they rarely needed to study. When an opportunity came in 1954 to teach chemistry at Tee-Jay, Ellett jumped at the chance. Three years later she was called on to design and teach the new Advanced Placement (college-level) chemistry course. Of the new course she said, "I loved it; it made students think." She coaxed sixteen of her first nineteen AP students to develop projects for the National Science Talent Search Contest.

Ellett's love for chemistry and teaching led her in 1961 to apply for and win a summer fellowship to study nuclear energy in Oak Ridge, Tennessee. She recalled one experiment in which she injected radioactive phosphorus into a rat, killed it, removed its organs, and then, using a Geiger counter she built herself, determined where the phosphorus had settled. Upon returning to Richmond, Ellett was asked to lecture on "atomic structure" and "the biological effects of radiation" to students throughout the Richmond school system. She insisted, however, on continuing to teach her AP chemistry course at Tee-Jay while she undertook these new responsibilities. After earning a master's degree in guidance at the University of Virginia, Ellett became a counselor at Tee-Jay. Despite her new role, she still taught AP chemistry until eventually she was offered a full time position at the new Richmond Mathematics and Science Center.

Mary Maddox came to Tee-Jay in 1939 to teach European history and eventually taught every course in social studies except economics. Having studied history with Virginia Sydnor at John Marshall High School, she was delighted to have a chance to teach in a department chaired by her former mentor. Like many unmarried teachers, Maddox was wedded in numerous ways to her students. She served as a class sponsor, Forum sponsor, and Quill and Scroll advisor. Every morning before school she dutifully read the sports pages and comics in order to facilitate casual conversations with her students. When Sydnor retired after twenty-eight years at Tee-Jay, Maddox succeeded her as History Department chair, a post she would hold until her own retirement in 1971.

Maddox is best remembered by her students and colleagues for her unabashed love of history and travel. When she was not spending her summers studying history at prestigious universities such as Chicago and Berkeley, she was likely to be walking Hadrian's Wall or traipsing through Eastern Europe. In 1954, she won a Fulbright Fellowship to serve as an exchange teacher in England for a year. Six years later Maddox was one of eighty-three U.S. teachers to be awarded a John Hay Fellowship.[4] The award allowed her to study international relations at Berkeley.

Maddox developed and taught the Advanced Placement course in European history and a new course on the "World in the Twentieth Century." She decried parochialism and always felt that Richmond school officials placed too much stress on state and national history and too little on international studies.

Ellett and Maddox were exceptional educators, but they were not atypical of the Tee-Jay faculty. The faculty boasted an abundance of dedicated and gifted individuals whose names continue to be invoked whenever Tee-Jay graduates or teachers gather. Over the years certain teachers came to exemplify key values in the school culture. When teachers wished to convey the importance of dedication to newcomers, for example, they mentioned physical education teacher and coach Spud Bloxsom. Before being halted momentarily by a bad cold in 1959, Bloxsom went twenty-nine-and-a-half years without an absence—from the very day that Tee-Jay opened![5] Nicknames were sometimes employed to convey a value exhibited by a particular teacher. Such was the case with mathematics teacher Katherine Brumble, otherwise known as "Duty."

It would be unlikely that teachers as talented and devoted as those at Tee-Jay would have remained for long periods of time had the school's organizational structure and culture failed to support and honor professionalism. The previous chapter suggested that such a structure and culture were in place almost from the school's inception. While Ernest Shawen must be cited for initially fostering an environment where teachers felt valued and supported, credit for perpetuating and improving the environment should be given to his successors and their faculties. The latter came to *expect* to be involved in school decision making. The formal mechanisms by which faculty views were expressed have already been noted—the ten academic departments and the faculty senate. On an informal basis, senior teachers generally enjoyed ready access to the principal's office.

Coalter Hancock and Bill Brock believed in teacher leadership. Unlike some latter-day principals who strive to function as instructional leaders, they did not initiate lots of programs, press for new instructional methods, or involve themselves deeply in departmental affairs. Out of respect for the capabilities of their faculties, particularly the department chairs, and perhaps because of some discomfiture dealing directly with matters of curriculum and instruction, Tee-Jay's first three principals established a pattern of low-profile management in academic matters. When they exercised leadership, it tended to focus on student affairs, community relations, and the acquisition of resources.

HOW GOOD WAS TEE-JAY?

In recent years, schools have been exhorted to strive for excellence. The word, in fact, has assumed the status of a shibboleth among critics of contemporary education. According to Thomas Toch, advocates of excellence in education share two fundamental beliefs:

> First, virtually all students should receive an education emphasizing "book learning" through high school, regardless of their future plans. Second, standards in academic subjects should be raised significantly.[6]

To what extent would Tee-Jay during its "glory days" have met these conditions of excellence? For students enrolled at Tee-Jay between 1946 and 1962, "book learning" was a clear and common expectation, whether or not they intended to go to college. Teachers did not regard curriculum relevance and rigorous standards as mutually exclusive. As will be shown later, all students—no matter what the focus of their programs—were expected to gain a solid foundation in English, mathematics, history, and science.

Where Tee-Jay would have failed to meet the contemporary conditions of excellence, so too would many high schools of the postwar period. By excluding black students and referring some vocational education students elsewhere, Tee-Jay did not truly accommodate "virtually all" students.

To judge the Tee-Jay of the past by current conceptions of excellence may be an interesting exercise, but for the purposes of an organizational history, such a tactic smacks of what historians call "presentism." Douglas Wilson describes presentism as the application of "contemporary or otherwise inappropriate standards to the past."[7] To avoid presentism, it is necessary to understand what excellence in education meant to those living during the period under examination.

The term "excellence" was not used widely until the success of the Soviet space program shocked American policymakers and academics into questioning the quality of public schooling in the United States. Among the leaders of the jihad against mediocrity were Carnegie Corporation of New York president John Gardner; the Reverend Theodore Hesburgh, president of Notre Dame; and Harvard sociologist David Riesman. In a 1958 report of the Special Studies Project, funded by the Rockefeller Brothers Fund, the trio set as the proper course for American schools the "pursuit of excellence."[8] This journey would require improving deteriorating and outdated school facilities, raising teacher salaries, upgrading the quality of teacher education, and developing a curriculum which would permit "every child" to attend college. Furthermore, the pursuit of excellence demanded early identification of bright children—the top 2 percent—and provision of college-level courses for them while they were still in high school. These students eventually would be the scientists and skilled teachers who would ensure America's preeminent place in the world order.

Reports of the "sorry state" of the nation's schools that surfaced during congressional debates over federal aid to education in 1958 should have caused Tee-Jay's students, parents, and teachers to feel fortunate indeed. Among the litany of obstacles on the nation's road to excellence were the following:

- Of all high school graduates in the top 30 percent of their class, only half ever go on to college. About one in five of the students in the top quarter does not even stay in high school long enough to graduate.

- Two out of three high school students do not take chemistry, three out of four avoid physics, seven out of eight get no trigonometry or solid geometry. Some 100,000 seniors attend high schools that offer no advanced mathematics. . . .

- Last year 14 states did not require even a single course in science or mathematics for a high school diploma.

- Fewer than 15 percent of U.S. high school pupils are taking a foreign language; half the U.S. high schools do not offer a foreign language at all.[9]

While Tee-Jay in 1958 may not have arrived at its final destination, the school certainly found itself well down the road to excellence. A large percentage of the school's graduates attended college, and faculty expected the number to keep growing. Editorials appeared annually in the *Jeffersonian* with statistics regarding how many students entered college the previous year and how well they did in their freshman courses. In the spring of 1959, for example, the newspaper reported that an average of 66 percent of Tee-Jay's graduates over the past eight years attended college.[10] Current students were urged to raise the percentage! All Tee-Jay students, regardless of their postgraduation plans, were required to take multiple courses in mathematics and science. More able students enjoyed what was reported to be the largest selection of advanced courses in Virginia. Foreign language programs were well subscribed, and Tee-Jay students were the first in Richmond to travel abroad in school-sponsored groups to enrich their language skills and knowledge of foreign cultures.[11] During the fifties, Tee-Jay students consistently passed over 90 percent of their classes—an impressive figure for the days before grade inflation.[12]

Concern for high academic achievement among Tee-Jay's parents, teachers, and students was great during the late fifties and early sixties, but it was never the solitary focus of attention that it later became for some schools. Academic achievement was regarded as a crucial component of the ultimate mission—preparing well-rounded citizens. Contemporary reformers, with the exception of Ernest Boyer and a few others, have not regarded this goal as particularly important, preferring instead to stress the acquisition of knowledge and skills that can directly benefit economic productivity.[13] For parents and educators in the fifties and sixties, however, the desire for a balanced school experience was strong.[14] Besides "book- learning" and the valuing of academic coursework, "well-roundedness" also necessitated involvement in school activities, good citizenship, and respect for the school's code of honor. In the view of the Tee-Jay faculty and administration, good schooling was more than preparation for college or employment; it was preparation for life. Helping students make the most of the high school experience became a primary commitment. The second stanza of the school's "Alma Mater" put it well:

We love thy teaching and traditions
The things no books can ever give,
For thou has shown a deeper meaning,
Thou hast taught us how to live;
And we are glad to be thy children,
To toast thy future worth and fame,
So sing we now to Thomas Jefferson,
God's blessing on her name.

The belief that schooling involved more than academic development received further reinforcement in the School Pledge and School Philosophy. Recited at every school assembly, the School Pledge acknowledged the moral dimension of a Tee-Jay education:

> We pledge allegiance to Thomas Jefferson High School and to the ideals for which it stands: honesty, courtesy, self-control, cooperation, and obedience to authority with kindness and justice to all.

When Coalter Hancock passed away in 1978, his obituary suggested the high value placed on character at Tee-Jay:

> The school pledge at Thomas Jefferson emphasized the ideals that Hancock sought to instill in students—honesty, courtesy, self-control, obedience, kindness, and justice. "I'd rather teach you these principles," he was once quoted as telling students," than teach you reading, writing and arithmetic."[15]

The School Philosophy also underscored the central values expressed in the School Pledge. The basic goals for all Tee-Jay students, as listed in the School Philosophy, were

> To acquire the knowledge and appreciations requisite for responsible citizenship
>
> To think logically, comprehensively, and without prejudice
>
> To understand and practice the rules of sound mental and physical health
>
> To adjust themselves to many personalities
>
> To adhere to high moral standards
>
> To enter upon a spiritual and cultural growth which will help them adjust their lives to an ever widening, complex society.

The penultimate section of the School Philosophy stated that the above goals would be accomplished through the school's program of studies, guidance services, and student activities program. The Philosophy concluded with the words of Thomas Jefferson:

> Finally, our hope for all boys and girls who enter our school is embodied in the inscription upon the entrance "To enable every man to judge for himself what will secure or endanger his freedom."

While the sentiments expressed in Tee-Jay's "Alma Mater," Pledge, and Philosophy seem to be missing in many of the recommendations of today's educational critics and reformers, they apparently were meaningful during the "glory days." The deprivation and uncertainty of the Depression and World War II were still fresh in people's memories. They could not help thinking that life was precious. To justify school solely in terms of preparation for college or work for a generation that had witnessed many of its sons graduate from high school only to lose their lives in war made little sense. A generation that observed highly educated people in other countries use their intelligence to subjugate and slaughter could not be expected to divorce education from values. A generation compelled to cope with sustained economic crisis easily recognized that academic prowess did not ensure food was on the table. They knew first hand that no education was complete without learning the importance of cooperation and civic-mindedness.

These observations in no way suggest that academic achievement was devalued during the postwar period. The middle- and upper-middle-class parents of the Tee-Jay community were well aware of the vital role of a college education in the struggle for upward mobility. Tee-Jay would have been roundly criticized had a large percentage of its graduates been unable to gain admission to or excel in the colleges of their choice. The ideal of the well-rounded person simply dictated that "book learning" was necessary, but not sufficient for a balanced and meaningful life. Upcoming sections will examine four aspects of the Tee-Jay experience from 1946 to 1962 that symbolized this idea. These aspects include a rich and rigorous course of study for all students, the organization of student life, opportunities for extracurricular involvement, and the institutionalization of core values.

A RIGOROUS ACADEMIC PROGRAM

For students who attended Tee-Jay during the postwar period, common observations regarding the school's academic offerings were that courses were "challenging" and "demanding." While teachers and administrators seconded this assessment, their comments also included references to the changing nature of the curriculum. Far from a static entity, the curriculum underwent a series of alterations after World War II. These alterations were relatively modest until the mid-fifties. The impetus for change often derived from forces external to the school. For instance, the move from an eleven- to a twelve-year course of study in 1946 and the shift from four to five years of high school in 1959 resulted from action by the school board. The creation of Tee-Jay's trademark Advanced Placement courses can be traced to a joint committee of professors from the University of Virginia and educators from Richmond Public Schools. Most of the changes reflected a common commitment to high quality curriculum content and learning experiences for students.

From 1943 until the expansion of high school from four to five years in 1959, Tee-Jay offered four distinct diplomas—college preparatory, elective, business, and vocational. Each diploma required sixteen units, including four units of English, two-and-a-half units of social studies, one unit of science, and a minimum of one unit of mathematics (see table 3.3). Students were allowed to select electives in each diploma program.

Throughout the late forties and fifties, Tee-Jay faculty tinkered with offerings in all four diploma programs, modifying required courses and occasionally adding new ones. In the fall of 1947, for example, the motoring public of Richmond doubtless was relieved to learn that driver education would be available to Tee-Jay students. A nursery school was introduced by the home economics teachers in the spring of 1949, thereby providing students with opportunities to study child development. In the fall of 1952, the mathematics faculty boasted that, with the addition of General Math 3 and 4, Tee-Jay had become the first high school in Virginia and one of "less than a dozen" schools in the nation to offer a complete program of mathematics courses.[16] Several months later new turf again was broken when a section of mechanical drawing was opened to female students. While Tee-Jay offered the section on a non-coeducational basis, John Marshall allowed boys and girls to study mechanical drawing together.

With the creation of a course in "advanced science" in September 1954, Tee-Jay once more entered new territory, anticipating by several years the post-Sputnik curriculum reform movement. Covering physics and chemistry and stressing mathematical concepts, advanced science was designed to enable Tee-Jay graduates to enter special college classes.[17] To be eligible for the course, students needed to have completed a year each of physics and chemistry and be enrolled in or have taken solid geometry or trigonometry. To allow select students to qualify more easily for the course, biology was shifted to the freshman year.

By the mid-fifties, Tee-Jay students enjoyed access to a reasonably full range of academic courses as well as a variety of business, commercial, homemaking, music, and art offerings (see table 3.4). The only area where offerings were deficient was vocational education.

The mid-fifties marked the point at which Tee-Jay began to be regarded primarily as a college preparatory high school. Well over half of its graduates by this time were entering college each year. A fitting symbol of the growing orientation to postdiploma study was College Day. Every fall from 1950 on, the school's Guidance Department and senior class hosted the event, which brought together during school hours representatives from dozens of colleges to provide advice and assistance to students.[18] As the only high school in the Richmond area to offer such an opportunity, Tee-Jay welcomed students from nearby public and private schools to College Day.

Efforts like College Day were continually made by the Tee-Jay faculty and administration in order to promote and facilitate college attendance. Scholarships for graduating seniors were solicited from civic groups and alumni. News of the collegiate successes of Tee-Jay graduates was regularly carried in the *Jeffersonian*. In 1961, a special fall induction was added to the regular spring National Honor Society ceremony just so that eligible seniors could list their membership on college applications and qualify for National Honor Society scholarships.[19]

Skip Ledbetter, currently a field representative with the Virginia Department of Education, recalled that he had no intention of attending college when he first entered Tee-Jay in 1955. His first love, he freely admitted, was football. Even in the locker room, however, Ledbetter could not escape the pervasive emphasis on preparing for college. So persistently did one of his coaches stress the importance of college that Ledbetter eventually applied for and won a football scholarship to the University of Mississippi. Had he attended another high school, Ledbetter doubted that he would have ever attended college.

By the early sixties, Tee-Jay students identified so closely with the goal of attending college that their unofficial "preppy" dress

TABLE 3.3

Diploma Options for Students at Thomas Jefferson High School During the 1950s

ELECTIVE DIPLOMA REQUIREMENTS		COLLEGE PREPARATORY DIPLOMA REQUIREMENTS	
Units	*Subject*	*Units*	*Subject*
4	English	4	English
2 1/2	Social Studies	2 1/2	Social Studies
1	Mathematics	2	Algebra
1	Science	1	Geometry
7 1/2	Elective Units	1	Laboratory Science
16	plus Physical Education (3 semesters for girls) (8 semesters for boys) or Military (8 semesters)	2	Foreign Language
		3 1/2	Elective Units
		16	plus Physical Education (3 semesters for girls) (8 semesters for boys) or Military (8 semesters)

TABLE 3.3 Continued

BUSINESS DIPLOMA REQUIREMENTS

Units	Subject
4	English
2 1/2	Social Studies
1	Mathematics
1	Science
4	Business subjects in one of the following combinations
	1. 1 units in Shorthand and 2 units in Typewriting
	2. 2 units in Bookkeeping. 1 in Typewriting—1/2 in Filing—1/2 in Office Machines.
	3. 2 units in Bookkeeping and 2 units in Typewriting.
	4. 2 units in Typewriting, 1/2 in Filing--1/2 in Clerical Practice and 1 in Algebra, Practical Mathematics or Shorthand.
3 1/2	Elective Units
16	plus Physical Education (3 semesters for girls) (8 semesters for boys) or Military (8 semesters)

VOCATIONAL DIPLOMA REQUIREMENTS

Units	Subject
4	English
2 1/2	Social Studies
1	Mathematics
1	Science
4	Vocational Units from the subjects listed below:
	1. Distributive Education
	2. Mechanical Drawing
	3. Jewelry
	4. Ceramics
3 1/2	Elective Units
16	plus Physical Education (3 semesters for girls) (8 semesters for boys) or Military (8 semesters)

TABLE 3.4
Curricula of Thomas Jefferson High School

COURSES OFFERED	9th Grade	10th Grade	11th Grade	12th Grade
Units Required	*Freshman Year*	*Sophomore Year*	*Junior year*	*Senior Year*
English 4 Units required	English 1–2 Dramatics 1–2	English 3–4 Dramatics 1–2 Speech 1–2	English 5–6 Dramatics 1–2 Speech 1–2	English 7–8 Dramatics 1–2 Speech 1–2
Social Studies 2 1/2 Units required	Geography Government 9	World History 1 World History 2	U.S. Hist. 1 U.S. Hist. 2	Government 12 Economics
Mathematics 1 Unit required plus a one semester couse in arithmetic for all who are not exempt by test score	General Math 1–2 or Algebra 1–2	General Math 3–4 Practical Math 1–2 Algebra 1–2 Geometry 1–2	Practical math 1–2 Algebra 1–2, 3–4 Geometry 1–2	Senior Arithmetic Advanced Arithmetic Algebra 1–2, 3–4 Geometry 1–2–3 Trigonometry Trigonometry-Algebra 5–6
Science Any 1 Unit required	Science 1–2	Biology 1–2	Biology 3 (boys) Biology 4–5 (girls) Chemistry 1–2, or 3 Physics 1–2, or 3–4	Biology 3 (boys) Biology 4–5 (girls) Chemistry 1–2 or 3 Physics 1–2, or 3–4 Advanced Science

COURSES OFFERED	9th Grade	10th Grade	11th Grade	12th Grade
Units Required	*Freshman Year*	*Sophomore Year*	*Junior year*	*Senior Year*
Foreign Language (No credit for less than two years)	Latin 1–2 French 1–2 Spanish 1–2	Latin 1–2, 3–4 French 1–2, 3–4 Spanish 1–2, 3–4	Latin 1–2, 3–4, 5–6 French 1–2, 3–4, 5–6 Spanish 1–2, 3–4, 5–6	Latin 3–4, 5–6, 7–8 French 3–4, 5–6, 7–8 Spanish 3–4, 5–6, 7–8
Business		Typing 1–2	Typing 1–2, or 3–4 Shorthand 1–2 Bookkeeping 1–2	Typing 1–2, or 3–4 Shorthand 1–2, 3–4 Bookkeeping 1–2, 3–4 Office Practice 1–2 Clerical Practice Filing Office Machines Business Law
Homemaking 1–8	Interior Decoration Foods Clothing	Home Nursing Interior Decoration Foods Clothing	Home Nursing Interior Decoration Foods Clothing	Home Nursing Interior Decoration Child Care Foods Clothing Sr. Homemaking
Art 1–8	Art-Design Basic	Art-Design Basic Jewelry Ceramics Painting	Art as assigned	Art as assigned

TABLE 3.4 Continued

COURSES OFFERED	9th Grade	10th Grade	11th Grade	12th Grade
Units Required	*Freshman Year*	*Sophomore Year*	*Junior year*	*Senior Year*
Mechanical Drawing 1–8	Mech. Drawing	Mech. Drawing	Mech. Drawing	Mech. Drawing
Distributive Education			D.E. 1–2 Work 1–2	D.E. 1–2, 3–4 Work 1–2, 3–4
Music 1–8	Band Orchestra Voice	Band Orchestra Voice as assigned	Band Orchestra Voice as assigned	Band Orchestra Voice as assigned
Driver Education (No Credit)			Driver Education for age 16 and over	Driver Education age 16 and over
Physical Education required (No Credit)—Boys for 8 Semesters, Girls for 3 Semesters	Physical Ed. 1–2	Physical Ed. 3–4	Physical Ed. 5–6	Physical Ed. 7–8
Military Training (No Credit)	Military T. 1–2	Military T. 3–4	Military T. 5–6	Military T. 7–8

code was mocked in good humor during "Anti-Ivy Day."[20] On this occasion, students broke routine, donning shirts without button-down collars and leaving their Villager sweaters and circle pins at home.

Perhaps no other development served to symbolize Tee-Jay's commitment to college preparation more than the creation of Advanced Placement courses in the late fifties. The groundwork for these courses was laid by a special committee of teachers from Richmond Public Schools and the University of Virginia.[21] This group made it possible for outstanding Tee-Jay graduates attending the University of Virginia to take special examinations in subjects where they had completed advanced work in high school. If they passed, the students received college credit and were allowed to skip introductory classes. The committee reviewed and approved the content of advanced high school courses in English, mathematics, history, science, and foreign language.

While conventional wisdom links the emergence of AP courses to the launching of Sputnik in 1957, the work of the joint curriculum committee indicates that the Tee-Jay faculty was already thinking of ways to increase the rigor of their most challenging courses by the time the Soviet space program achieved its initial success. By the fall of 1957, college-level AP courses had been introduced in world history, trigonometry-algebra, and chemistry. AP physics was added in February of 1958. Students were told that they could sit for Educational Testing Service examinations in May if they desired college credit for their work.

Advanced Placement courses became Tee-Jay's hallmark. After attending a 1958 Yale conference for high schools with AP programs, Bill Brock proudly noted that Tee-Jay was the only high school from the South that was represented.[22] Calculus, English literature, and foreign language courses eventually were added to the AP curriculum. While the number of offerings dropped in later years, Tee-Jay still boasted more AP courses than other Richmond high schools.

To support students aspiring to take AP courses, "accelerated" courses for sophomores and juniors were introduced in the fall of 1958.[23] As a result, ability grouping, which had been introduced on a limited basis in the thirties, was expanded and fully institutionalized. The same year also saw the return of German and the addition of Russian to the list of foreign language offerings.

Tee-Jay's first Russian teacher deserves special mention, since he was a living lesson in Russian history.[24] Igor Aleksandrovitch Yacenko was born in pre-Bolshevik Russia, served as a cavalry captain in the czar's army, and later fought with the White Russians against the Bolsheviks in the Crimea. He escaped to Yugoslavia, where he studied and practiced mining engineering. When Yugoslavia was taken over by Communists after World War II, he taught himself English and came to the United States. After teaching at the Army Language School in California, he became an American citizen and moved to Virginia. A seasoned world traveler, Yacenko was also one of the first persons in Russia to pilot an airplane.

With the development of AP, accelerated, and other challenging courses like Russian, it might be expected that non-college-bound students received little attention at Tee-Jay. Such was not the case, however. A concerted effort was made by the Tee-Jay faculty to assist students who planned to enter the workforce after high school. The Business Department, staffed by seven teachers, offered course sequences leading to secretarial, clerical, and book-keeping careers. Demand for Tee-Jay business majors by local employers exceeded supply.[25] Students also were able to take a full series of mechanical drawing courses and gain on-the-job retailing experience through the distributive education program. In 1962 the Distributive Education Department added programs in fashion and advertising. Students interested in military careers participated in the Cadet Corps. Occupational guidance and job placement assistance were available from both the Business and the Guidance Departments.

The Guidance Department began in September 1934 as a college advisory service staffed on a part-time basis by history teacher Bessie Motley.[26] Two years later she switched to full time and was joined by Mary Jordan, who continued to teach mathematics part of each day. The Guidance Department operated out of the teachers' lounge with one full-time counselor and various part-time teacher-counselors until the fall of 1945, when room 212 was partitioned into a suite of guidance offices. The Guidance Department's interest in non-college-bound students steadily grew during the thirties and forties. A systematic study of the placement needs of these students was undertaken in 1941, and Guidance Week provided an annual occassion for information on vocational opportunities to be shared. By 1958 the Guidance Department consisted of three full-time counselors and a secretary.

To say that a concerted effort was made by the Tee-Jay faculty to address the needs of the non-college-bound is not to say, however, that every student had a successful experience. Table 3.5 contains data compiled by the school district on "pupil eliminations" at Tee-Jay from 1946 through 1963. While many eliminations resulted from students moving away or transferring to another school, a small number each year left school because of "indifference" and "conduct" problems. Of particular interest is the tiny number of dropouts attributed to "lack of ability." Tee-Jay faculty believed that practically all of their students were capable of graduating from high school. It also should be noted that in 1951–52, when 99 out of 1,682 Tee-Jay students left school before graduation, 311 of John Marshall's 1,626 students were listed as "eliminations." That this year was no aberration is demonstrated by the 1956–57 statistics, when Tee-Jay again lost only 99 students (out of 1,806), while John Marshall reported that 296 out of 1,609 students left school. John Marshall's figures reveal a school increasingly resembling a contemporary urban high school, while the data on Tee-Jay show a pattern more characteristic of suburban high schools.

The final curriculum changes to affect Tee-Jay before desegregation involved mid-year promotions and graduation requirements. The Richmond School Board voted in May of 1958 to eliminate mid-year promotions. The Board hoped to cut costs by eliminating low-enrollment half-year courses and to facilitate scheduling. Students who failed required courses henceforth would be compelled to attend summer school or retake an entire course. The faculty began to convert semester courses into single, year-long offerings.

In February of 1959 the Richmond School Board approved the recommendation of a committee on high school requirements that called for the eighth grade to become an integral part of high school. Graduation requirements, as a result, were increased from sixteen to twenty-three Carnegie units. Eighteen units had to be earned in grades 9 through 12, thereby effectively ending the sixteen-credit high school minimum requirement introduced in 1943. The number of diploma options was reduced from four to three, as students could no longer earn a vocational diploma. The three remaining alternatives were college preparatory, business, and

TABLE 3.5
Pupil Eliminations at Thomas Jefferson High School, 1946-1963

Reasons for Leaving School

Years	Moved Away	Went to Work	Went to Private or Out-of Town School	Military	Indifference	Marriage	Personal Illness	Home Duties	Conduct	Lack Of Ability	Other	Total Eliminations	Avg Daily Enrollment	% Of Eliminations
1946–47	50	50	13	8	20	10	11	0	0	0	9	171	1804*	9.5
1947–48	36	50	7	11	25	7	9	1	4	0	2	152	1811*	8.4
1948–49	38	40	5	6	1	10	15	1	0	0	11	127	1766*	7.2
1949–50	35	32	7	5	15	6	7	1	2	0	17	127	1737*	7.3
1950–51	17	45	15	13	4	14	12	3	0	3	11	134	1659	8.1
1951–52	22	18	19	5	8	6	6	0	0	1	14	99	1682	5.9
1952–53	36	25	9	3	13	10	10	0	5	0	11	122	1744	7.0

Years	Moved Away	Went to Work	Went to Private or Out-of-Town School	Military	Indifference	Marriage	Personal Illness	Home Duties	Conduct	Lack Of Ability	Other	Total Eliminations	Avg Daily Enrollment	% Of Eliminations
1953–54	7	29	45	3	46	2	3	0	2	0	21	158	1801	8.8
1954–55	30	20	9	4	0	12	4	0	5	0	18	102	1835	5.6
1955–56	34	26	6	5	14	6	7	1	2	1	7	109	1887	5.8
1956–57	14	17	11	10	9	7	10	3	3	8	7	99	1806	5.5
1957–58	25	12	7	6	7	15	12	1	20	0	14	119	1869	6.4
1958–59	30	22	13	11	6	11	12	0	15	0	13	133	1986	6.7
1959–60	39	18	20	16	2	8	16	1	9	0	5	134	2057	6.5
1960–61	20	15	7	10	16	15	6	0	7	0	34	130	1664	7.8
1961–62	3	27	3	10	23	5	7	1	3	0	41	123	1472	8.4
1962–63	25	16	23	5	35	10	18	1	5	0	8	146	1467	9.3

TABLE 3.6
REVISED (1959) THOMAS JEFFERSON HIGH SCHOOL
CURRICULUM

DIPLOMA	Academic	Business	General
Subjects	Units	Units	Units
English	5	5	5
Mathematics	4	3	3
United States History (Grade 8)	1	1	1
World History and Geography	1	1	1
Virginia and United States History	1	1	1
Government and Economics	1	1	1
Laboratory Science	3	3	3
Foreign Language (3 units in the same language)	3	0	0
Health and Physical Education or Military	1	1	1
Additional Units for Specific Program	0	3 to 5	3 to 5
Electives	3	2 to 4	2 to 4
TOTAL	23	23	23

general diplomas. The justification for these changes reflected the Board's growing concern for curriculum differentiation and programs for the very brightest students:

> The new requirements would "continue and increase the emphasis" on opportunities for academically talented students and would provide the appropriate programs for "slow learners" and physically handicapped students.[27]

In comparison to earlier requirements, the new course requirements for each of the three diplomas represented an increased emphasis on academic subjects (see table 3.6). All high school graduates now had to complete an extra semester of social studies (economics) and two extra years of science. All three years of science in the new program had to involve laboratory work, whereas previously only one year of laboratory science was required and that exclusively for college preparatory students. Students in other diploma programs were not required before 1959 to take any laboratory science (see table 3.3). The foreign language requirement for the college preparatory diploma was increased from two to three years. With the exception of one less mathematics course and no foreign language requirement, students working toward business and general diplomas were expected to cover the same "fundamentals" as students in the college preparatory program.[28]

THE ORGANIZATION OF STUDENT LIFE

William H. Whyte helped to characterize the postwar period in America as the "age of organization"—a time when formal organizations and group commitments were regarded as keys to a sense of belonging and meaning in life.[29] Whyte put the prevailing belief succinctly when he wrote, "Man exists as a unit of society. Of himself, he is isolated, meaningless; only as he collaborates with others does he become worthwhile, for by sublimating himself in the group, he helps produce a whole that is greater than the sum of its parts." To confirm Whyte's observations, one need look no further than the organization of student life at Tee-Jay. Virtually every aspect of student activity was organized and governed by rules, regulations, expectations, and norms. Students were exhorted to achieve and exhibit good behavior not just for themselves, but for the sake of their homeroom, class, team, school, and community. In a very real sense, Tee-Jay in the late forties and fifties functioned as a boot camp for the "organization man."

If the organization of student life at Tee-Jay could be envisioned as a solar system, the sun's place would be occupied by the Student Participation Association, the first such organization in a Richmond high school. The purpose of the Student Participation Association was to promote "active participation by all members of the student body in affairs pertaining to the student life at the school."[30] Around the Student Participation Association orbited the class organizations (freshman, sophomore, junior, and senior classes). Homeroom organizations, in turn, revolved around each class organization.

At the heart of Student Participation were the Senate and House of Representatives. Made up of the five officers of the Student Participation Association, five senior senators, five junior senators, five sophomore senators, one freshman senator, the presidents of the classes, and any state or district officers, the Senate assembled daily for a class period to handle business items and convened formal meetings once a week. Besides serving as a forum for the discussion of school problems "from the student point of view," the Senate provided "direction" for all the standing committees chaired by senators.[31] Committees included the Honor Council and Character Committee (to be discussed later), the Board of Coordination, and the Club Affiliation Committee.

The Club Affiliation Committee consisted of the president of every school club and society. Among the group's responsibilities were the exchange of ideas related to student activities, assistance in starting new organizations, and coordination of meeting times and locations for all clubs and societies. The Club Affiliation Committee approved all proposed club activities and handled applications for the Club of the Year Award.

The Board of Coordination was created to promote better understanding and cooperation among various organizations and between students and faculty. Composed of the officers and sponsor of the Student Participation Association, the sponsor of the House of Representatives, the presidents and sponsors of the senior, junior, and sophomore classes, the chair of the Club Affiliation Committee, and representatives from the Cadet Corps, music groups, boys' and girls' athletics, and the literary and business staffs of all publications, the Board of Coordination drafted the calendar of school events each term, making sure to avoid scheduling conflicts. The board also directed the American Field Service foreign-exchange program.

Homerooms were guaranteed a voice in school affairs through the House of Representatives. The president of each homeroom sat in the House and shared the concerns and suggestions of their classmates. In addition, these representatives were expected to report to their constituents on the plans and activities of the Student Participation Association and choose each year's cohort of cheerleaders.

Though modeled after the bicameral legislature of the United States, the Student Participation Association was primarily an advisory, rather than a lawmaking, organization. As a 1952 *Jeffersonian* article noted,

> Since Tee Jay does not have student government, but only student participation, the Senate is not empowered to make laws, and it can only make suggestions to the administration. These suggestions are almost always approved, however.[32]

The organization of student life at Tee-Jay reinforced the belief that adults were the ultimate source of authority, but that students had an obligation to make their feelings known. On occasion, some students might complain that their elected representatives constituted an elite or that their views were not represented well, but for the most part the Student Participation Association seemed to function as an effective outlet for student concerns and as a positive force in school life. If students were dissatisfied with some aspect of their school experience—be it an overabundance of homework or the scheduling of a dance—they knew that a proper process for expressing their grievances existed.

Tee-Jay students were particularly proud when their school was chosen to host the 1962 convention of the Southern Association of Student Councils. The selection was regarded as evidence that the organization of student life at Tee-Jay was worthy of distinction.

EXTRACURRICULAR INVOLVEMENT

Tee-Jay's administrators and teachers worked hard and played hard, and they expected the same of their students. The ideal of the well-rounded student required, in fact, that students develop interests apart from their academic pursuits. A rich variety of extracurricular opportunities were available to Tee-Jay students during the postwar period. These included athletics, performing arts, publications, clubs, service organizations, and honorary societies.

Male athletes at Tee-Jay could choose to participate in football, basketball, baseball, track and field, and tennis, while female athletes selected from field hockey, basketball, and tennis. Although Tee-Jay never sustained a reputation in the postwar period as a sports powerhouse, the school enjoyed its share of success. In 1952 the school not only registered its first football victory over John Marshall in six years, but won its second state championship (the first was in 1943). In tennis, Tee-Jay players were dominant state-wide, stringing together eleven seasons without a defeat between 1947 and 1958. So talented were the Tee-Jay netters that they regularly played college tennis teams—and won. Field hockey and girls' basketball consistently boasted winning seasons.

The performing arts were represented by the preparatory and concert orchestras, Cadet Marching Band, A Cappella Choir, Girls' Glee Club, Boys' Glee Club, preparatory choirs, and the Pep Club. Tee-Jay musicians frequently were selected to perform with the Richmond Symphony Orchestra. Annual productions included Junior Stunt Night, the Senior Class Play, and an operetta. Tee-Jay students also published a newspaper (the *Jeffersonian*), a yearbook (*The Monticello*), and a twice-yearly literary magazine (the *Declaration*). The newspaper and yearbook routinely won awards in regional and national competition. Opportunities for students to engage in charitable activities and pursue areas of special interest in greater depth were available through a variety of service organizations and clubs. These included the following:[34]

Junior Red Cross (60)
Future Teachers of America (27)
Future Nurses Club (37)
Biology Lab Assistants (15)
Chemistry Lab Assistants (17)
Science Club (15)
Business Education Club (38)
Bookkeeping Club (23)
French Club (24)
Latin Club (17)
Spanish Club (55)
Forum (24)—social studies club
Christian Youth League (24)
Stage Crew (19)
Harry A. Woody Club (21)—service club for boys
Key Club (29)—Kiwanis-sponsored boys' leadership group
Y Teens (94)—Social and service club for girls.
Tebahoes (17)—Girls' athletic club
Hi-Y (21)—Service club for boys
Library Staff (32)

Honorary societies each year tapped outstanding writers (Quill and Scroll) and drama students (Thespians) as well as scholars (National Honor Society). These organizations elected officers, undertook special projects, and held elaborate induction ceremonies. On any given afternoon following school, Tee-Jay's corridors and classrooms were likely to be buzzing with club meetings, rehearsals, and special projects. Pep Club members might be in the halls painting posters for an upcoming game, trying hard to avoid being run over by the track team as they completed indoor laps. *Jeffersonian* staffers would be rushing to edit proofs for an upcoming issue, serenaded by the A Cappella Choir practicing in the auditorium. After-school activities permitted casual interaction among faculty and students, a time when formal barriers dropped a bit to allow adults and teenagers to work together. The "normal" relationships that might have been hard to nurture during class were allowed to develop in the late-afternoon world of extracurricular activities. Teachers and students stepped out of their roles and became, if but for a few hours, human beings with similar drives, feelings, and frustrations.

Extracurricular activities were very popular at Tee-Jay during the postwar period, in part because of the absence of alternative sources of entertainment. So many after-school options, in fact, were available to students that at least one teacher complained that students no longer dropped by just to "chat" after school.[34] The commandant of a shrinking Cadet Corps in the early sixties attributed the decline to stiff competition from other student activities.[35] Even students sometimes voiced concern. Editorials periodically appeared in the *Jeffersonian* decrying the tendency of some students to join clubs and service groups solely for the purpose of accumulating "participation points" so that they could earn a Student Participation Certificate at the end of their senior year.[36] When a Richmond journalist asked high school students in 1962 whether they believed schools had taken on too many responsibilities outside the field of academic learning, Ginny Southworth, a Tee-Jay senior, responded:

> I feel that many schools have taken on too many extra-curricular activities. However, schools have realized this and are de-emphasizing the extras in favor of academic learning.
>
> For example, they now limit the number of activities in which any one student may participate, and many activities

require a certain grade average as a prerequisite for participation. The increasing difficulty to meet college entrance requirements has made academic achievement the most important part of high school.

Perhaps there are too many other responsibilities, but schools do not encourage students to become involved in enough of them to interfere with their classwork.[37]

One of Ginny Southworth's senior classmates, Bob Gray, offered a less critical view, one that probably came closer to capturing the prevailing sentiment of Tee-Jay students and faculty:

American schools try to develop the whole person, not just his mind, and I don't believe they have gone too far beyond academic work yet.[38]

To encourage students to participate in extracurricular activities, a point system had been proposed by students and adopted by the faculty in 1937. Activities were grouped into four categories and assigned point values based on the time required and the level of responsibility. Students who earned a specific number of points qualified for special recognition. When concerns arose in the mid-forties that students might be more interested in the accumulation of points than conscientious participation, a study group of students and faculty sponsors met and offered some recommendations for improving the point system. As of the fall of 1946, sponsors were asked not only to assign points for student participation but also to grade the quality of participation by awarding students an A, B, or C.[39] Students could not earn a Student Participation Certificate if they had received more than two C grades. In this way it was hoped that students would focus on doing a good job in a few activities, thereby creating opportunities for greater numbers of students to play leadership roles in extracurricular activities. Periodically, adjustments were made in the points assigned to particular activities in response to student complaints regarding inequities.

CULTIVATION OF CHARACTER

The ideal of the well-rounded student dictated that students embrace certain core values as well as meet academic requirements, participate in extracurricular activities, and function effectively as members of the school community. Some of these core values already have been addressed—healthy competition, respect for adult authority, civic responsibility, and balanced interests (as opposed to narrow specialization). Such values were promoted by formal mechanisms as well as exhortation and example. Contests among homerooms and classes, recitation of the School Pledge at assemblies, the point system, and the Student Participation Association represented some of the ways character development was encouraged. Three additional mechanisms will be discussed in this section—the Honor Council, demerits, and the Character Committee.

Tee-Jay's commitment to the cultivation of character was hardly unusual during the postwar period. In fact, Virginia's State Board of Education adopted a policy statement in 1951 which spelled out the responsibilities of all public schools in the area of moral development:

> Along with the classroom courses, the child must be taught by precept, example, and experience the importance of moral standards and the meaning of good citizenship. Regardless of the extent to which other agencies meet their responsibilities for such training, schools in a democracy cannot escape this obligation. Public Education has failed unless, in addition to mental development and knowledge of facts, its pupils go out with a mold of character which will help them to meet their responsibilities to their country and to their fellow men.[40]

What perhaps was unusual about Tee-Jay, however, was the lengths to which its faculty and students went to promote good character. The Honor Council was a good example. Formed in February of 1957 to encourage honesty, the Honor Council advised the administration in cases of cheating and other infractions of the Honor Code. The Honor Code was contained in the following pledge, which initially applied only to students who joined the Honor System and received an honor card:

I will strive to be honest with myself and with others in thought, in word, and in deed at all times.

I will not cheat on any test, examination, or other classroom activity by giving or receiving information.

I will not condone stealing or vandalism in any form and will conduct myself at all times as a good representative of the school.

I will endeavor to fulfill all responsibilities delegated to me and to uphold the ideals of Thomas Jefferson High School as stated in the school pledge.

When Tee-Jay students attended the Southern Association of Student Councils Convention in November of 1957, they proudly discovered that Tee-Jay was the only member of the association to boast an honor system.[41] Students from other southern high schools reported that their classmates did not support the idea of such a system. Nancy LaPrade, a junior senator from Tee-Jay, noted, "The other schools didn't see how Tee Jay could have so much school spirit and unity."[42]

A standardized procedure guided the operation of the Honor Council. This procedure was described in the *Jeffersonian*:

When a student's honor card has been revoked because of his failure to comply with the Honor Code, the case is brought before the Honor Council. It considers the circumstances and gives a decision concerning reissuance.

The details of the case are written on an envelope in which is enclosed the offender's honor card. To avoid partiality, the student goes by a number, not his name.

The Honor Council then decides what should be done with the card, not to the student.[43]

The existence of the Honor Council and its carefully crafted operating procedures, of course, did not eliminate student conduct problems. Between September 1961 and March 1962, for example, "approximately 20 violations" of the Honor Code were heard by the Honor Council.[44] The violations, which represented an increase over the *total* number of cases heard the previous year, included six incidents in which "cheat notes" were used during tests, two forged hall passes, two forged parental signatures on tests, two cases involving copied homework, and one case of copying from another student's paper during a test. Recommended sanctions entailed zeroes on school work, parent interviews, after-school detention, and, in certain cases, exclusion from school honors.

Besides Honor Code violations, Tee-Jay students committed less serious offenses. Periodically the *Jeffersonian* contained articles decrying such problems as rudeness during assemblies, running in the halls, and smoking in the restrooms. In the fall of 1961 a concerted effort was made to toughen the policies governing student conduct.[45]

The demerit system was revised at this time by a student-faculty committee. "Conduct notices" henceforth would be given for discourtesy, misconduct, and violations of class rules. One hour of after-school detention had to be served for each conduct notice. Five conduct notices resulted in a demerit, a visit with the assistant principal, and five hours of detention. Five demerits led to a two-day in-school suspension. Additional revisions involved absences from school. Any student who missed more than fifteen days of school in a semester automatically received a failing grade in all subjects, unless the administration granted an exception.

The Honor System also was adjusted in 1961 to combat a perceived rise in cheating. For the first time, *all* students were required to participate in the Honor System. Previously, only students who chose to obtain an honor card were subject to the Honor Council's judgments. Students not only had to pledge to be honest themselves under the new system, but to report any students seen cheating. The Honor Council was granted greater powers to punish offenders. Second offenses could result in a recommendation to suspend. Instead of adjudicating cases without knowing the name of the accused, the Honor Council was allowed for the first time to order individuals to appear before it.

In addition to the Honor System and the demerit system, the Character Committee existed to promote responsible behavior among Tee-Jay students. Each homeroom sent a representative to the Character Committee to discuss problems and exchange ideas concerning how to further the values embodied in the Honor Code.[46] Programs dealing with value-related issues were developed for homeroom representatives to share with their classmates.

As the faculty and students of Tee-Jay worked to improve the character of individuals, the character of the society in which they lived was being tested and reshaped in ways that eventually would affect them all profoundly. In the final section of this chapter, the events leading up to the desegregation of Richmond Public Schools will be briefly recounted.[47]

SHADOWS ON THE HORIZON

Few of those who taught or studied at Tee-Jay in the spring of 1954 could have predicted the full impact of the momentous decision handed down by the United States Supreme Court on May 17. In *Brown v. Board of Education*, the nation's highest court unanimously ruled that the segregation of white and black students was unconstitutional. Subsequent years witnessed various efforts by state and local governments, initially in the South, to subvert or block the full implementation of the *Brown* decision. The determination of the federal government to thwart these initiatives and end racial segregation in public education received its first major test in the fall of 1957. President Eisenhower dispatched troops to Little Rock, Arkansas, to protect black students involved in the integration of Central High School.

Tee-Jay students, of course, were not oblivious to events in Little Rock. An editorial in the October 11, 1957, *Jeffersonian* foreshadowed the tone of moderation which would characterize Tee-Jay's own response to desegregation several years later:

> Southerners, indeed Americans as a whole, have rarely been so rocked by the beginning of a school year as they have this year with the opening of Central High School in Little Rock, Arkansas.
>
> The events causing the discussions, excitement, and even mob hysteria are briefly cited:
>
> - In accordance with a pre-prepared, agreed-upon gradual integration program, a group of Negro students were scheduled to enter the school.
> - Governor Faubus of Arkansas called out the National Guard to prevent Negroes from entering to avoid violence. As Governor, he does possess this power.
> - Federal District Court ordered the Governor not to prevent the laws being carried out.
> - Governor Faubus withdrew the National Guard from the school.
> - With city policy and state troopers on hand the Negroes attended classes at the school but were taken out before mobs had gathered outside the school.
> - President Eisenhower sent in paratroopers, and under their supervision the Negroes went to classes. The President does possess this power, as he is enforcing the orders of the Federal Court.

- Arkansas legislature may plan for action to close the school and re-open it under private control.

Students in this school and other schools can set an example by keeping a level head, staying informed, and discussing the issue intelligently. The ignorant and extremists of both sides are causing much of the conflict.

The answer to this problem in Little Rock and the overall situation in the South can be found through only one medium—time.[48]

Politicians and state officials in Virginia did not always share the even-handed views expressed in this editorial. Their initial response to the threat of federal intervention was "massive resistance." This policy, first mentioned by Senator Harry Flood Byrd on February 24, 1956, called for unprecedented actions by the Commonwealth of Virginia. All local student requests to attend a school other than the one to which they had been assigned had to be referred to the state's Pupil Placement Board. As Robert Pratt points out, "Although not explicitly stated, it was clearly understood that the primary function of the Pupil Placement Board was to maintain segregated schools."[49] Just in case the Board failed to carry out its implicit function, the General Assembly passed a law requiring Virginia's governor to close any school that was threatened with integration and remove it from the public school system. In addition, the state was authorized "to provide private-school tuition grants from public funds to parents in any district where the public schools were closed to prevent integration."[50]

When twenty-two black students applied for admission to Warren County High School in September of 1958, the school became the first to be closed under Virginia's massive-resistance laws. Schools in Charlottesville and Norfolk soon followed. Four months passed before a three-judge federal court ruled in *James v. Almond* that Virginia's school-closing law violated the Fourteenth Amendment. On February 2, 1959, twenty-one black students entered previously all-white schools in Norfolk and Arlington, thereby concluding the era of massive resistance.[51]

Richmond's public schools never closed during this period, though Robert Pratt cautions against interpreting this fact as evidence that local officials supported school integration. He maintains that Richmond officials were as committed to segregation as their counterparts elsewhere, but that they learned from the experiences of other school divisions that defiance of the Supreme Court was foolhardy.[52] The strategy of choice in Richmond, according to Pratt, was to foster the illusion of compliance by admitting a few "token" black students to formerly all-white schools. School Board chairman, and later Supreme Court justice, Lewis F. Powell, Jr., expressed this strategy of "containment" succinctly when he declared in 1959 that "public education will be continued in our city—although every proper effort will be made to minimize the extent of integration when it comes."[53] Given the pattern of residential segregation in Richmond and the domination of city government by whites, Powell's declaration was hardly an idle promise.

The official end of segregated schooling in Richmond came on September 6, 1960, when two black girls entered the eighth grade at Chandler Junior High School without incident. The two students actually had been allowed to transfer schools by the state Pupil Placement Board on the grounds that they lived closer to Chandler than to the nearest black school. This action represented the first time the Pupil Placement Board approved the requests of black students to transfer to a white school.

During the 1961–62 school year previously all-white schools in Richmond admitted twenty-nine more black students, while denying admission to twenty others. The containment strategy was challenged in court at this time as eleven black parents initiated a class-action suit against the Richmond School Board. Eventually a court of appeals ruled in favor of the plaintiffs and reprimanded the school board "for publicly shirking its responsibility while privately sanctioning the segregationist policies of a placement board."[54] The process which would allow integration efforts to proceed in earnest thus had been set in motion. Eight years would pass, however, before the courts finally ordered busing.

On Sunday, September 2, 1962, five days before the beginning of the fall semester, an editorial appeared in the *Richmond Times-Dispatch*. Entitled "Virginia's Story Gets Across," the piece appeared to congratulate the state and particularly its capital city for leading the nation toward productive race relations. In a fit of what some readers might have regarded as sheer hubris, the author cited a recent *Washington Post* article entitled "Richmond Quietly Leads Way in Race Relations:"

What so impresses the writer in the Washington paper is the fact that Richmond's race relations are good, and always have been good; that the Negro vote is becoming important here; that Negroes may stop at our leading hotels and dine at several of our principal restaurants; that about 130 Negro children will attend previously all-white public schools here this year; that Richmond led the South in bus desegregation and employment of Negro policemen, and so on. This is all a part of the evolutionary race pattern in Richmond.[55]

It would appear from the editorial as if the forward-looking city fathers of Richmond always had intended to integrate, even without a "gentle nudge" from the Supreme Court and federal authorities. The notion that Richmond was different from other places—a key element of local culture—thus received additional reinforcement. Over the years a myth of moderation had developed which held that Richmonders avoided the intemperance and excess of other communities.[56]

If philosopher Jean-Paul Sartre's claim that people eventually become what they pretend to be is valid, then Richmond may have been well served by the myth of moderation. The desegregation of the city's schools occurred without any of the rancor or violence that shook cities like Birmingham and Boston. This peaceful, though painfully gradual, process included the enrollment of one black girl at Tee-Jay on September 6, 1962.

PART 2

The Struggle to Preserve Excellence

Excellence can never be taken for granted. Those associated with Tee-Jay came to understand this nostrum in the days and years following desegregation. In the three decades after the first black student enrolled, the school confronted a series of daunting challenges. Initially, the challenges focused on the preservation of academic excellence amidst demographic changes and student unrest. Eventually, threats involved the very survival of the school. The next three chapters identify critical incidents in school history between 1962 and 1994 and the responses they engendered. Initial desegregation. Court-ordered busing. Competition from alternative schools. Declining enrollment. Closure threat number one. Reorganization into a "complex." Closure threat number two. The Governor's School. Closure threat number three. Each of these challenges offers an opportunity to examine how a well-established high school responds to social and political change and to understand better the contemporary context of urban education. Was Tee-Jay able to make the necessary adjustments without losing the very qualities which had caused it to gain widespread respect in the first place? Ultimately the answer to this question may hold a key to the fate of high schools like Tee-Jay across the nation.

CHAPTER 4

Giving Proper Direction to Change

"Education must not only adapt itself to change, it must anticipate change, and in many cases attempt to give proper direction to that change." These words were spoken by H. I. Willett to a *Jeffersonian* reporter in the fall of 1964.[1] Willett—superintendent of Richmond's schools, former national Superintendent of the Year, and during his lifetime the only superintendent ever featured on the cover of *Time* magazine—offered his remarks in response to the advent of educational television, but they might have been equally appropriate as a description of how Richmond Public Schools—and Tee-Jay in particular—responded to school desegregation. Schools typically do not create social change, but once such change begins, they must be prepared to accommodate it and guide it in constructive directions. What constituted a "constructive" direction, of course, was by no means clear in the early days of desegregation. Various interest groups, for example, held different opinions concerning the proper course for public schools. From 1962 until 1970, the prevailing view of influential Richmonders was that freedom of choice represented the most appropriate district-wide response to desegregation. At the school level, the response of Tee-Jay's administration and faculty was business as usual. Court-ordered busing in 1970, however, compelled both Richmond Public Schools and Tee-Jay to consider different strategies in order to "give proper direction" to change.

THE EARLY DAYS OF DESEGREGATION AT TEE-JAY

On September 6, 1962, Tee-Jay enrolled its first black student, a ninth grader who previously had attended Westhampton Junior High. Little fanfare and no disruptions or ugly protests marked the event. If the young woman experienced overt harassment or blatant rudeness, it was not common knowledge among her classmates.[2] Still, the experience of being the only black person among

1,672 students must have been a lonely and intimidating one. The fact that she was a lowly freshman in a system where status arrogated to upperclassmen probably only compounded her isolation and insecurity. Margaret Campbell, a teacher, recalls that the young black woman was "quiet and dignified." When Bill Brock said to her one day, "I hope you are happy here," she responded politely, "I am not here to be happy."

On September 6, 1963, an editorial entitled "More Riots and Violence" appeared in the *Richmond Times-Dispatch*. The piece recounted a litany of tragedies in the Deep South, including the recent murder of Medgar Evers and the bombings of a black leader's home in Birmingham. Blame for the tense atmosphere was laid at the feet of Governor George Wallace and Martin Luther King. The day the editorial appeared, Richmond commenced its fourth year, and Tee-Jay its second year, of token integration without incident.[3] Of Richmond's more than 26,000 black students, 312 were enrolled in white schools.[4] Six of these students attended Tee-Jay along with 1,658 white students. John Marshall's 1,398 students, meanwhile, included 68 blacks.

On June 9, 1965, Johnnie Squire, Tee-Jay's first black graduate, received his diploma in ceremonies at the Mosque. He was not listed in the May 21, 1965, *Jeffersonian* as one of the seniors who would be attending college in the fall. Tee-Jay's first black teacher arrived the next September to teach physics and earth science, but she remained only a year. The following year three black teachers—Edna Davis, Henry C. Jones, and James Edward Wallace—became members of the faculty. At the time Tee-Jay boasted a faculty of seventy-seven, twenty-six of whom held master's degrees.

The number of black students at Tee-Jay gradually increased throughout the sixties. On the eve of court-ordered busing in the spring of 1970, the yearbook pictured 122 blacks among Tee-Jay's 1,592 students.[5] While roughly 8 percent of the Tee-Jay student body was black, over 70 percent of Richmond's 42,719 students were black.[6] Throughout the next two decades both percentages climbed. By 1992, almost nine of every ten students in the Richmond Public Schools were black.

The Rise and Fall of Freedom of Choice

Policymakers with short memories may be tempted to think that the idea of school choice was born during the Reagan-Bush years.

While the term may have become "politically correct" at this time, school choice was very much an issue in Richmond and other cities facing desegregation during the sixties. Richmond's so-called "freedom of choice" plan was adopted in March of 1963 as a response to a court order requiring the school board to abolish the system of feeder schools and dual attendance zones.[7] Under this system, white elementary schools "fed" white junior high schools which, in turn, sent students to white high schools. Black schools followed a similar pattern. When the court found this arrangement to be "patently discriminatory," the school board offered to circumvent much of the red tape of the State Pupil Placement Board and provide more choice of school assignments to Richmond students. While at least one board member understood "freedom of choice" to mean the removal of *all* barriers to integration, Superintendent Willett maintained that the plan entailed choice "within limits."[8] Robert Pratt concluded that the plan allowed the school board to retain "such broad discretion in the matter of assignments that it was able to resist any uniform policy which might result in wholesale integration."[9]

Displeased with "freedom of choice," Samuel Tucker and Henry Marsh, the two attorneys who had challenged dual attendance zones and feeder systems, sued to overturn the school board plan. On March 16, 1964, District Judge John Butzner upheld "freedom of choice." The Supreme Court eventually heard the case and, on November 15, 1965, ruled that Judge Butzner "had erred in approving a desegregation plan for Richmond without addressing assertions of racial bias in faculty assignments."[10] The Richmond School Board developed a revised "freedom of choice" plan which included provisions for faculty as well as student integration. This plan remained in effect until 1970.

Under the new plan all parents with children in public schools received a form, beginning in the 1966–67 school year, which asked them to indicate the school they wished their children to attend. The only official constraints on choice were the suitability of the school's curriculum and the availability of space. Parents were given thirty days within which to file a school preference form.

Initially, black parents and teachers were reluctant to "cross over" to white schools. Advocates of integration clearly were disappointed. Educators and civil rights workers tried to find out why more blacks were not participating. Complaints of subtle forms of racial harassment were heard from some of the black students who had broken the color line.[11] Other blacks openly admitted their preference to remain in familiar territory. Pratt reasoned, though, that the "greatest obstacle to school desegregation under freedom of choice was residential segregation."[12] Most blacks in Richmond did not live in neighborhoods with easy access to white schools. Black parents who wanted their children to attend schools like Tee-Jay had to provide their own transportation.[13]

The future of Richmond's freedom-of-choice plan dimmed in 1968 when the Supreme Court ruled in the case of *Green v. County School Board of New Kent County*. New Kent, a small, rural county east of Richmond, had adopted a freedom-of-choice plan in August of 1965 in order to remain eligible for federal funds. The New Kent Plan, like its Richmond counterpart, led to token integration, but most black students remained in all-black schools. Calvin Green, a New Kent resident, sued the school system on the grounds that the freedom of choice plan left largely intact a dual school system. In its 1968 verdict, the Supreme Court declared New Kent's plan unconstitutional and thereby "removed from blacks the onus of initiating school desegregation and placed it with local school boards."[14] Two years later, following the demise of Richmond's freedom-of-choice plan, Calvin Green joined the Tee-Jay faculty as a science teacher and coordinator of science programs for West End schools. This would not be the only time that a member of the Tee-Jay faculty would be linked to a landmark civil rights case.

On March 10, 1970, a motion was filed in Richmond seeking relief in light of the recent Supreme Court verdict in *Green*. Enrollment data as of May 1, 1970, indicated that three of Richmond's seven high schools were entirely black; one was 99.3 percent white; one was 92 percent white (Tee-Jay); one was 81 percent white, and one was 68 percent black.[15] The only high school with a greater percentage of white students than Tee-Jay was Huguenot High School. Originally part of the Chesterfield County Schools, Huguenot was involved in an annexation move on January 1, 1970, that increased Richmond's size by twenty-three square miles. Of greater significance politically was the fact that annexation changed the racial composition of Richmond from 52 percent black and 48 percent white to 42 percent black and 58 percent white.[16] The portion of Chesterfield County added to Richmond was predominantly white.

District Court Judge Robert Merhige, Jr., informed the Richmond School Board on June 26, 1970, that it would need to develop a new plan for desegregating its schools. The plan proposed the following month was still regarded as unsatisfactory by Judge Merhige, but in light of the impending opening of school, he permitted the plan to proceed for the time being and ordered a more acceptable plan to be submitted within ninety days. The interim plan called for school pairing, pupil assignments, majority-to-minority transfers, greater faculty integration, and some busing. The advent of busing and related changes would present Tee-Jay with a new set of challenges. The school's response will be addressed in later sections of this chapter.

It is likely that Tee-Jay unintentionally played a role in the political and legal drama that unfolded in Richmond during the sixties. White Richmonders believed their schools to be among the region's finest. Tee-Jay represented the system's capstone institution, a school "among the finest high schools in the Southeast."[17] The claim was made that Tee-Jay sent as large a percentage of its graduating classes to college as any high school on the East Coast.[18] Such outstanding credentials served as eloquent testimony to the fiction of "separate but equal." As fine a high school as was Armstrong, it could not compare to Tee-Jay in terms of resources, honors courses, teachers with advanced degrees, facilities, extracurricular opportunities, and a host of other factors. In creating a high school without local parallel, those associated with Tee-Jay during its formative years unwittingly helped undermine the foundations of school segregation in Richmond. Whether the remarkable school they created would survive desegregation, and if so, in what form, are the central questions of this and the subsequent chapter.

Business as Usual

What was going on at Tee-Jay in the sixties as the future of public education in Richmond was being deliberated in the courts? In some respects, what did not happen was of greater significance than what did. Unlike the desegregation of some of its sister high schools around the country, no angry protests or violent confrontations greeted Tee-Jay's first black students. Nor did any mass exodus of white students ensue. No special programs or remedial classes were created to accommodate black students. The handful of blacks who attended Tee-Jay in the sixties were not isolated in separate courses or subjected to blatantly lower expectations.

If Tee-Jay students were preoccupied about anything during the early sixties, it was the threat of nuclear war, not desegregation. The Cuban Missile Crisis in 1962 overshadowed all other events and left Richmonders wondering whether they would fall prey to a "first strike," given their proximity to the nation's capital and the military installations of Hampton Roads. A bomb shelter—the icon of the period—was built in Tee-Jay's basement in February of 1963.[19] Food and water supplies for a two-week period were stored in the facility. The assassination of John F. Kennedy later in 1963 deflected attention once again from school integration. Tee-Jay students who attended school on November 22, 1963, never will forget the distraught announcement over the intercom or the sound of taps as members of the Cadet Corps lowered the school flag to half mast.

While Richmond school officials did not become obsessed with the challenges of desegregation, neither did they act as if it were no concern at all. When Superintendent Willett addressed the annual convocation of Richmond teachers and administrators on September 4, 1963, he focused on four sensitive issues facing educators. They included the need (1) to provide students with a thorough knowledge of economics, (2) to stimulate greater student creativity, 3) to develop a prudent approach to handling beliefs and religion in school, and (4) to accommodate "changing images" of minority groups.[20] On the last issue, Willett opined:

> Minority groups in our country and the peoples of the undeveloped countries of the world are no longer willing to think only in terms of certain freedoms and rights, "creature wants," and higher standards of living for their children—they want these things now for themselves as well as for their children. Too often they fail to recognize the preparation and responsibilities that must go hand in hand with freedom. . . .
> The basic problem facing the schoolteacher will be how education can be used in creating individual and national images by which and through which people will be motivated to develop their full potential and to act on reason rather than emotion.[21]

Teachers at Tee-Jay during the sixties do not recall that black students were systematically excluded from academic opportunities or discriminated against in any planned way, but neither do they remember any organized efforts by white students or faculty to exhibit unusual sensitivity toward the newcomers or recognize the uniqueness of their culture and background. Whatever demonstrations of special caring or disdain marked the early days of desegregation at Tee-Jay took place on a personal basis between individuals and remained largely outside the public arena. One teacher, for example, recalls a coach saying that he might be compelled to allow black students to join his teams, but he did not have to play them. Recollections of this sort were the exception, not the rule, however.

If there was an official response to desegregation at Tee-Jay in the sixties, it was "business as usual." This observation does not suggest, however, that Tee-Jay stood still during this period. Adjustments were made in some curriculum content and instructional methods. The first signs of student unrest regarding adult authority surfaced. New faculty were hired, and overcrowding resurfaced as an issue. By and large, however, the essential elements that made Tee-Jay special remained in place. These elements included the school's mission, culture of excellence, organizational structure, opportunities for student involvement outside of the academic program, and relations with the community. Like a latter-day exemplar of the Confucian ideal, Tee-Jay managed change within the general constraints of its traditions. When change occurred, it tended to reflect planning and thought rather than impulse and careless reaction.

School mission and culture. The ideal of the well-rounded student continued to guide the efforts of the Tee-Jay faculty during the sixties. That this student was presumed in most cases to be bound for college also carried over from pre-desegregation days. No concerted effort was made to expand vocational offerings or moderate the school's precollegiate orientation.

Tee-Jay's mission continued to be well served by its culture. Among the most persistent aspects of this culture were high expectations for all students and a belief in the benefits of organization.

High expectations were manifested in various ways. Teachers expected students to work hard, whether they were enrolled in honors or regular courses. Students in different ability-level courses undertook different assignments and used different textbooks, to be sure, but they all were apt to complain about hard grading, difficult work, and too much homework. Tee-Jay offered few remedial programs or special alternatives for students who found the regular curriculum daunting.[22] When students proposed exam exemptions for those with A averages in courses, teachers voted down the measure by "a vast majority."[23] End-of-semester exams were perceived by teachers to be more consistent with Tee-Jay's culture than an early vacation.

Opinions vary as to how black students fared prior to 1970. Several teachers recalled that some "honor roll students" from black high schools struggled with essay questions and certain courses, but other teachers noted that Tee-Jay's first black students had little problem meeting the school's high expectations. The explanation that usually accompanied the latter observation held that Tee-Jay's black students prior to 1970 came from relatively well-to-do families.

Conduct and character, as well as academic performance, were subject to high expectations, as they had been before 1962. Requirements for the Honor Roll, for example, included not only a minimum of two As and no grade below a B, but also a satisfactory conduct and attendance record with no demerits, unexcused absences or tardies.[24] Testimony to the absence of gratuitous grades and slack discipline at Tee-Jay is the fact that only between 4 and 5 percent of the student body usually earned Honor Roll status during a given grading period.

The Honor System and the Character Committee functioned throughout the sixties to instill respect for appropriate behavior. Despite turmoil on many college and high school campuses during this period, Tee-Jay managed to avoid serious disturbances or widespread student unrest. There were some signs, however, that students were less willing than in past years to accept certain policies and practices without question. For example, a student editorial in the winter of 1964 attacked inconsistencies in teachers' grading procedures.[25] The following year students expressed outrage at efforts to censor the Senior Class Play, "The Man Who Came to Dinner."[26] Faculty members insisted on eliminating all expressions using the words "God" and "sex." "For God's sake" became "for Pete's sake," while "sex-life" inexplicably was transformed into "hand-washing life." Complaints were also heard about the absence of books such as *The Grapes of Wrath* and *Catcher in the Rye* in the library.[27] While Tee-Jay students in the sixties probably were more inclined to voice criticism of authority than their predecessors, their views were delivered in a sufficiently respectful manner to engender no alarm among the faculty and administration. The same could not always be said after 1970.

The only serious disciplinary concern during the sixties involved the use of illegal drugs by some students. Teachers recalled, toward the end of the decade, encountering sporadic indications of drug use, including lethargy, dilated pupils, unresponsiveness in class, and excessive absenteeism. No one who was interviewed, however, characterized the problem as pervasive.

Faith in the benefits of organization was another hallmark of Tee-Jay's culture that persisted during the sixties. Student life continued to be guided by the Student Participation Association and its network of homeroom organizations, committees, and school-wide governing bodies. Faculty business revolved, as before, around powerful departments and the Faculty Senate.

The only time that the Student Participation Association came under fire—besides the perennial complaints about how many Student Participation points were allocated to particular activities—occurred in 1968. An editorial in the *Jeffersonian* expressed concern over Tee-Jay's bicameral legislature, claiming that the Senate possessed greater authority than the House.[28] It seemed that a law originating in the Senate was referred directly to the administration for approval, while a law originating in the House first had to gain approval in the Senate before being forwarded to the administration.

Faculty and administration. Much of the credit for the continuity of culture and mission at Tee-Jay in the sixties must go to veteran teachers and administrators. While these years brought greater teacher turnover than previously, a cadre of senior teachers, many of whom were department heads, remained, as did Bill Brock and his assistant principals.[29] Department heads routinely interviewed prospective teachers and recommended who should and should not be hired, thereby ensuring some degree of continuity between new and veteran faculty.

Senior teachers often functioned as "priests" and "priestesses," to use the terminology of organizational culture.[30] They embodied the school's memory, invoking stories to familiarize newcomers with the school's traditions and pointing out "how things are done around here." Tee-Jay's professional gerontocracy made its presence felt in other ways as well. Fred Bateman, currently Superintendent of the Chesapeake (Virginia) Public

Schools, recalls with fondness being mistaken for a student and banished from the teachers' lounge in his first year at Tee-Jay. He was twenty-seven at the time!

Many of the teachers who joined Tee-Jay's faculty in the sixties noted how "traditional" was much of the teaching. While it is true that a visitor dropping in on many classes likely would encounter a lecture, seatwork, or discussion, some instructional innovation did occur. Educational television made its debut in 1964, problem- or inquiry-based teaching was attempted in various science courses, and theme English was initiated. Convincing some veteran teachers of the need for instructional change remained a challenge, however—particularly given the past record of success compiled by their students.

The notion of "success" most often conveyed by those who taught at Tee-Jay in the sixties involved top-level achievement. For example, great pride was taken in the fact that Tee-Jay produced more National Merit Scholarship semifinalists between 1965 and 1970 than any high school in the Richmond area except Henrico County's Douglas Freeman High School.[11] When the *Jeffersonian* chose to spotlight academic success in the sixties, its reporters invariably focused on the highest achievers—prizes won at regional linguistic competitions; awards at chemistry contests; students selected for the Virginia Junior Academy of Science; perfect scores on the Scholastic Aptitude Tests (of which there typically were four or five); winners in the Westinghouse Talent Search. Rarely if ever cited as an example of success was the struggling student who made impressive gains to move from behind-grade-level to grade-level performance or the likely dropout who succeeded in graduating.

Among Tee-Jay's new faculty members in the sixties were several black teachers. They did not always feel a part of the close-knit professional family that had evolved over the years. While newly hired white teachers typically recalled Tee-Jay as a "caring place," their black counterparts sometimes remembered feelings of isolation. Interestingly, these pioneer black teachers eventually came to be regarded as cherished members of the pre-1970 faculty that continues to gather in August for lunch and reminiscence.

Academic program. In the late fall of 1962, students from Tee-Jay, John Marshall, and George Wythe discussed the curricula of their schools on a local radio program.[32] The Marshall and Wythe representatives focused on their schools' new certificate programs, which afforded opportunities to take a prescribed course of study for students who did not intend to complete high school or earn a diploma. Patsy Jones, Tee-Jay's representative, chose to highlight her school's AP chemistry and European history courses and accelerated courses in French and Spanish.

Although the pride of the Tee-Jay academic program in the sixties remained the AP, honors, and accelerated courses, some excitement was generated over the addition of new courses and the updating of existing courses for less gifted students. Much of the curriculum reform that took place at Tee-Jay reflected nation-wide interest in having students *apply* their "book learning." The Science Department, for example, added "curriculum study" courses in chemistry, biology, and physical sciences.[33] Students in these courses spent up to 80 percent of their time in the laboratory seeking their own answers to questions of common interest. In Ann Hancock's biology classes, for instance, students learned about bacteria by exposing sterilized petri dishes to bacteria-infected air in different parts of the school. Among their findings was the fact that the bacteria count in the cafeteria jumped dramatically after lunch was served—a discovery that students with a sense of humor doubtless took full advantage of.

The "laboratory" approach even invaded Tee-Jay's venerable English Department. A visit to the English Composition Laboratory at Grimsley High School in Greensboro, North Carolina, impressed Nancy Gary, chair of the English Department, with the value of providing students with two-hour blocks of time in which to write themes.[34] Characteristically, however, Gary added that she felt the quality of Tee-Jay's writing was just as good as Grimsley's, despite having no lab period! The following fall at Tee-Jay, experimental theme English courses were paired with biology, history, and government courses. On alternating Fridays students in theme English spent two periods working on compositions. Theme readers were employed to review and critique the compositions.

Toward the end of the decade the Science Department scored a coup by acquiring the first planetarium in any Virginia high school. Located in room 401, the traditional haunt of the student Senate, the planetarium allowed the Science Department to offer classes in astronomy.

The Mathematics Department continually updated its offerings during the sixties. A course in probability and statistics was launched in January of 1963. The only course of its kind in Virginia at the time, probability and statistics involved three days of films by a Harvard professor and two days of discussion and problem solving every week.[35] A noncredit slide rule course also was introduced. Two years later Richmond's first high school course in computer programming was added, along with a course called "Independent Study" which provided selected students with opportunities to pursue mathematical topics in depth.[36]

Curriculum reform was not limited to college preparatory courses. The Business Department made a concerted effort to update its offerings in the hopes of appealing to college-bound students. An editorial in the school newspaper in the spring of 1963 announced,

> Although approximately 600 students are enrolled in business courses now, the Business Department is anxious for more college-bound students to take a new course in personal typing and for boys interested in data processing to take basic accounting.[37]

By the mid-sixties, Tee-Jay's few vocational offerings also were being augmented. The two Distributive Education coordinators, Walter Jennings and Barbara Gouldin, developed pre-employment training centers that allowed over one hundred students annually to prepare for jobs. Their efforts bore fruit, as the number of students enrolled in Distributive Education rose from 40 in 1963–64 to 130 in 1964–65.[38] In the fall of 1965, vocational office training and practical nursing were added to the Tee-Jay curriculum. Students in these programs spent half the day in classes and the other half receiving on-the-job training. Practical nursing was available only to senior girls, however.

For reasons that are unclear, reading courses were expanded in the mid-sixties. While some reading courses were remedial in nature, others focused on speed reading and comprehension.[39] There was no indication in interviews with former teachers that the appearance of remedial reading was linked directly to desegregation. What is certain, though, is that Tee-Jay would have offered even more reading courses had space been available.[40]

By 1965 the school was sufficiently over-crowded that Mary Jordan, head of the Guidance Department, doubted that a free room could be found each period to enable reading to be available all day. Table 4.1 shows enrollment figures for Tee-Jay, John Marshall, and Armstrong from 1962 through 1975. While Tee-Jay did not reach the numbers it had enrolled in peak years before desegregation, enough students were in attendance to create cramped quarters. Overcrowding remained an issue throughout the sixties. When in 1968 the Richmond School Board appointed a committee of college professors and teachers to conduct an assessment of the quality of the "educational system" in the city's schools, the group investigating Tee-Jay reported that, while the school's programs were "outstanding," lack of classroom space prevented a greater variety of courses from being offered.[41] Dr. Rufus Tonelson, professor of education at Old Dominion University and head

TABLE 4.1
Enrollments at Selected Richmond High Schools:
1962–1975

Year	Tee–Jay	John Marshall	Armstrong
1962–63	1,672	1,441	2,251
1963–64	1,757	1,465	2,344
1964–65	1,748	1,490	1,976
1965–66	1,769	1,515	1,986
1966–67	1,732	1,515	1,986
1967–68	1,737	1,606	1,953
1968–69	1,758	1,540	1,823
1969–70	1,701	1,501	1,802
1970–71	1,537	1,557	1,622
1971–72	1,328	1,866	1,520
1972–73	1,233	1,864	1,593
1973–74	1,010	1,564	1,236
1974–75	1,100	1,537	1,273

of the team, went on to observe, however, that Tee-Jay "retained its high position in rank of academic achievement."[42]

Despite space limitations, Tee-Jay offered more curriculum "units," or distinct courses, than most schools in the state. To help offset the shortage of classrooms, Bill Brock created "zero period." This early morning session was available for special courses that might require more time than regular courses. The *Report of the State Superintendent of Public Instruction* for 1969–70 indicated that Tee-Jay's 123.5 curriculum units surpassed such high schools as Armstrong (92), Henrico County's J. R. Tucker (82), and Norfolk's Granby (77.5), though these schools boasted larger enrollments than Tee-Jay. John Marshall, with 140 units, was one of the few schools to exceed Tee-Jay, due to its substantial number of vocational courses.

When the Center for Southern Education Studies at George Peabody College for Teachers published a fact book, *High Schools in the South*, in 1966, Tee-Jay's academic program appeared truly exceptional in comparison to its sister institutions in the region. Only 30 percent of Southern teenagers attended high schools offering at least fifty courses.[43] More than three-quarters of the high schools in the region offered forty or fewer courses. Other findings that might have caused Tee-Jay students to count themselves fortunate included the following:

- Fifty-seven percent of high school students had no opportunity to take an art course. (Tee-Jay offered Art Fundamentals, Arts and Crafts, Jewelry, Fine and Commercial Arts, and Advanced Drawing and Painting.)
- Thirteen percent of high school students attended schools that did not offer a foreign language. (Tee-Jay students could study French, German, Latin, Russian, and Spanish.)
- Fourteen percent of high school students had no access to music instruction. (Tee-Jay offered four years of instruction in band, orchestra, and voice.)

Virginia's schools, along with those of North Carolina, generally were superior to schools elsewhere in the South. Even within Virginia, however, Tee-Jay's offerings were impressive. In 1969, for example, only 17 of the 490 public secondary schools and 68 private secondary schools in the state offered advanced chemistry.[44] Tee-Jay was 1 of the 17. In addition, it was the only school with an astronomy program.

Besides its rich academic program, Tee-Jay continued to boast an extensive number of extracurricular opportunities throughout the sixties. In 1963, a chapter of Future Business Leaders of America was formed and the Debate Club was revived. Special community service projects increased in popularity. In 1967, one such project organized by the student Senate sent several Tee-Jay students to Richmond's East End to help tutor elementary students in reading. If students had idle time on their hands, it was through no fault of the Tee-Jay faculty.

A Special School

While some teachers looked back on the period from 1962 to 1970 as a slightly less "glorious" time for Tee-Jay than the preceding era, others made no such distinction. Of the sixties, one teacher, for example, wrote:

> Tee-Jay was a special school because faculty, parents, and students worked together to maintain excellence. Requirements were strict: homework must be done; book reports must be turned in; team athletes had to maintain passing grades; the honor code was strictly enforced. Traditions which had worked in past years could still be followed. Lockers could be searched; prayers could be offered; vulgar or disrespectful speech or conduct could be forbidden.
>
> Looking back, many of us can, a bit wistfully, echo the words of Charles Dickens: "It was the best of times."

While change had indeed come to Tee-Jay in the sixties, in most cases it was carefully planned change. New programs were not thrust upon the school. Tee-Jay teachers prided themselves on their knowledge of the latest curriculum developments. That the school's academic offerings were enhanced between 1962 and 1970 was, therefore, no surprise. What did not change during this period was as important as what did change, however. School organization remained largely untouched. The culture of high expectations, competition, and student involvement persisted. No serious move was made to challenge ability grouping, advanced courses, or the college preparatory focus of most departments. Faculty, administration, students, and parents continued to be committed to the ideal of the well-rounded student.

In hindsight, the fact that Tee-Jay changed remarkably little during the turbulent sixties might be regarded as a key to the school's success during the first years of desegregation. Success, at this point in time, did not mean simply remaining open—as it would later. Instead, success referred to Tee-Jay's ability to preserve academic excellence. A central ingredient in the formula for success involved the retention of white students. While white students in other places were opting in large numbers to attend private schools or transfer to suburban high schools, those in Richmond's West End generally preferred to attend Tee-Jay. They did so because that which they and their parents had come to expect of the high school continued to be found there. In June of 1969, the last graduation before court-ordered busing included 433 Tee-Jay seniors. Richmond's five private and parochial schools—Benedictine, St. Christopher's, St. Catherine's, Collegiate, and Marymount—together only graduated 339 students.[45] The numbers would soon begin to shift.

While the claim can be made that Tee-Jay faculty and administrators did not make enough effort to accommodate black students in the sixties, their business-as-usual approach might be deemed defensible today. Considerable research during the seventies and eighties condemned the practices of lowering expectations for disadvantaged students and placing them in special remedial programs.[46] While well intentioned, such efforts often served to ensure that these students remained behind other students. Black students at Tee-Jay generally were held to the same high standards as white students. Whether Tee-Jay would be able to continue business as usual after the advent of court-ordered busing is the subject of the next section.

THE END OF TOKEN DESEGREGATION

On August 17, 1970, Judge Robert R. Merhige, Jr., ordered the Richmond Public Schools to implement an interim desegregation plan requiring the busing of approximately 13,000 students. Exactly two weeks later, on Monday, August 31, Richmond schools opened for the fall semester. Teachers and administrators who lived through the period recall the confusion and hard work. The headline on the first page of the September 1, 1970, *Richmond Times-Dispatch* doubtless provided them with a temporary measure of satisfaction—"Opening Day Peaceful, with Little Boycotting." The days to follow, however, would cause them to realize the enormity of the challenges facing them.

The Depression, World War II, the Cold War, early days of desegregation—Tee-Jay had confronted each of these challenges in a deliberate and thoughtful manner. The events of August 1970 unfolded so quickly, though, that there was no time for a carefully measured response. Overnight the school was told to accommodate hundreds of new students—predominantly black—and dozens of black teachers transferred from other Richmond schools. Close on the heels of these challenges came others—belated student activism, competition for top students from public alternative schools, and white flight. "Giving proper direction to change" under such circumstances would test the strength of Tee-Jay's culture and traditions as well as the mettle of its teachers, administrators, students, and parents.

A Year Like No Other

Martin Erb, a white senior at Tee-Jay, shared his thoughts about the 1970–71 school year with a reporter from the *Richmond News Leader*. "The main thing I've seen change this year is everybody's attitude—the kids don't feel as pressured to come to class on time because they feel like the whole year this year is an exception."[47] Few would have disputed his assessment.

The end of "freedom of choice" and the commencement of court-ordered busing resulted in a major shift in the racial composition of Tee-Jay's student body. Approximately 45 percent of Tee-Jay's students now were black.[48] Unlike the smaller contingents of black students prior to the fall of 1970, this larger group reflected a wide range of abilities, including substantial numbers of students with academic deficiencies. Alma Lowance, head of the English Department, estimated that one out of every ten freshmen had "serious reading problems."[49] She added,

> The large majority of them are Negroes who previously attended all-Negro schools. This is really not a high school problem—it should have been caught much earlier—I think many of these children have received social promotions rather than knowledge promotions.

Dr. James Tyler, an asssistant superintendent with Richmond Public Schools, and later superintendent, observed,

> I'm sure that the program [at Tee-Jay] is not relevant for a lot of students and that they are bored because they don't understand what's going on."[50]

Not only did the racial make-up and ability level of the student body change dramatically, but the distribution of students across grade levels shifted. The interim desegregation plan called for the abolition of junior highs and the formation of middle schools. As a result, Tee-Jay enrolled the largest freshman class in its history. Overcrowding resulted, compelling Tee-Jay to operate a seven-period day with each teacher responsible for five periods of instruction plus additional assignments. Virtually every room in the building was in use as a classroom every period. Laboratories had to be used for regular instructional purposes.

Dealing with changes of this magnitude would have been challenging enough for a well-established faculty, but the interim desegregation plan also called for major teacher transfers in order to achieve racial balance among the faculty. In the spring of 1970, on the eve of busing, Tee-Jay housed a faculty of eighty-seven, thirty-four of whom had taught at the school in 1962 when the first black student arrived. Four of the eighty-seven teachers were black. The following fall, roughly half the faculty were black. One of the individuals who chose to retire rather than risk being transferred from her beloved Tee-Jay was librarian Clyde Carter. In his farewell letter to her, Bill Brock captured not only Carter's exceptional talents, but the special nature of the school she had served for twenty-two years:

> Dear Miss Carter:
>
> On behalf of all of us at Thomas Jefferson I want to thank you for your great contribution to our school and for the help you gave our boys and girls, teachers and principals over the years. You and your colleagues set the tone for this school, and its high reputation for excellence and integrity is the result of your dedicated efforts.
>
> The library is the heart of the instructional program. You made it so by building up an outstanding collection and introducing young men and women to these treasures with graciousness and warmth . . . a sort of extra dividend to the pleasures of reading.

You are a professional. I never knew a person better read, more modern, more up to date in the trends and fashion or more solidly grounded in the "good books." We at Tee-Jay were fortunate to have had so well informed and so wise a guide. In the uncertain days ahead we can count on a firm base in the library. Thank you very much.

Come to see us and keep us up to date on what is good reading; then we won't miss you so much.

Very truly yours,

William W. Brock, Jr.
Principal

By the fall of 1971, only a dozen of Tee-Jay's faculty of 59 had taught at the school in 1962. These Tee-Jay veterans, as well as newcomers, had to learn to work with different students and colleagues. Newcomers meanwhile had to cope with strange surroundings and a new culture. Small wonder that the mother of a tenth grader said her daughter felt that her teachers seemed "more serious" and "not as happy and light-hearted" as the previous year.[51]

One source of stress for faculty and administration involved scheduling students and planning for the new school year. The 1970–71 school annual captured some of the stressful nature of the opening of school in the following passage:

> Less than a week before school opened, administrators faced the problem of setting up a schedule for both students and faculty who had not yet been assigned. When the pre-school planning days began, the Thomas Jefferson faculty was fifty percent new. Teachers who had been in the school for many years had been transferred to schools that formerly had been all black. The same applied to the black teachers. In four days, the faculty and administrators working together had scheduled the students; moved the books; organized the classrooms; and prepared to meet students. The task was almost impossible, yet it was done. Not all the problems were solved, for it took weeks to reduce teaching loads to achieve a more realistic pupil-teacher ratio. In the pre-school planning the teachers and administrators devel-

oped a mutual respect and understanding that remained throughout the year.[52]

While the challenges noted above provided an opportunity for teachers and administrators to bond, not every new teacher felt that he had entered a supportive environment. Dr. Calvin Green, for example, recalled, "A few people at Tee-Jay knew I was Green of *Green v. New Kent,* so some attitudes were visible when I arrived." He further noted that some white male students had trouble taking chemistry from a black teacher. Several of these students withdrew from Tee-Jay.

Student behavior problems no doubt contributed to the faculty's frustrations. In one incident, two white teachers were assaulted by two black students. Other incidents involved fights between white and black students and unprovoked attacks. Less serious discipline problems increased as well. Tardiness, disrespect for authority, and vandalism caused teachers and administrators to devote more time and energy to discipline than at any previous time in the school's history. Their efforts to establish order reflected considerable uncertainty, particularly when circumstances required disciplining a student of another race. Black teachers from previously all-black schools were tentative about reprimanding white students, and white teachers felt similarly unsure about how to deal with black students. George Martin, a black senior who attended Tee-Jay before busing, told a newspaper reporter covering the "story" of discipline problems in Richmond schools in 1971:

> The kids are getting away with things they didn't get away with last year and the teachers' not knowing how to cope with discipline in a new situation has added to the problem.[53]

Some observers claimed that the situation warranted stricter discipline than Bill Brock and his assistants were willing to mete out. One assistant principal was Morgan Edwards, Brock's eventual successor and Tee-Jay's first black administrator. Edwards previously served as assistant principal at Armstrong High School. His assessment of the situation pinned primary blame on "30 to 50 students" who were "constant discipline problems."[54] He estimated that roughly half of these problems stemmed from the frustration of lacking the ability to do well in a challenging academic environment.

For some students, the destabilizing effect of court-ordered busing and related problems proved too much to bear. By March of 1971, eighty students had left Tee-Jay—forty-four having dropped out or been suspended, twenty-three transferring to other public high schools in Richmond, five enrolling in private schools, and eight going to public schools in other cities.[55] Students were not the only ones to depart. Some of Tee-Jay's most respected teachers decided to leave at the end of spring semester. Mary Maddox, head of the History Department and a veteran of thirty-two years at Tee-Jay, recalled her last day. As she was gathering up three decades worth of instructional materials and memorabilia, someone shot out the light in the corridor outside her classroom. This incident confirmed for her the wisdom of the decision to retire.

Despite the loss of valued faculty, students, and perhaps, innocence, the 1970–71 school year cannot be judged to have been bereft of redeeming features. To the faculty were added some talented new teachers. As Dr. Calvin Green pointed out, Tee-Jay's reputation as Richmond's outstanding academic high school meant that black teachers chosen to transfer to Tee-Jay had to possess "the best available academic credentials." Academic success continued, as exemplified by the selection of four seniors as National Merit Scholarship semifinalists. In athletics, despite a small turnout for the team, Tee-Jay's harriers won the Capital District Cross Country Championship, setting a record for the lowest score and launching what would become a dynasty of champions coached by Jim Holdren. Bill Brock, in reference to the year, believed that Tee-Jay's students had "risen to the challenge" of full integration "to a remarkable extent."[56] The conclusion to the school yearbook probably offered the most constructive postmortem, however, for a year like no other:

> By bus and car, students came from across the city to Thomas Jefferson which was the target. By June 1971 the group was more united and a sense of student loyalty became evident. We face another year with more confidence and the belief that we can solve our problems through unity and cooperation.[57]

Rising to the Challenges

Bill Brock credited Tee-Jay's students with rising to the challenge of court-ordered busing. Administrators and faculty also deserved recognition for trying to accommodate large-scale change. The early seventies presented the Tee-Jay faculty and administration with three distinct, though related, challenges. First, the arrival of large numbers of low-achieving black students meant that adjustments in curriculum and instruction would be needed. Too great a shift in emphasis from academics to remediation, however, would risk the loss of support of many white parents. Preventing white flight therefore became a second challenge. The third challenge did not stem from busing, but from the fact that the sixties finally caught up with Tee-Jay. Students of the early seventies— black and white—were not as inclined to compliance and deference to authority as their older brothers and sisters. Teachers and administrators consequently found themselves spending more time dealing with student behavior. Examples of how Tee-Jay responded to these three challenges are presented in this section.

Meeting the needs of black students. Once the initial traumas of court-ordered busing had passed, teachers and administrators turned their attention to the needs of their students. Since little consideration was given to altering Tee-Jay's mission or allowing the school to slide into the status of an ordinary urban high school, the path was reasonably clear, if somewhat steep. Newly arrived black students must be helped to fill in the gaps in their content knowledge and skills so that they could meet the expectations of a top-flight academic program. Black parents, after all, had not fought for school integration so that their children could receive a second-rate education.

By the second year of court-ordered busing, Tee-Jay had begun to implement a variety of strategies to meet the needs of low-achieving black students. One of the boldest moves involved Bill Brock's insistence that Tee-Jay's "best teachers" had to teach at least one "basic" course. "They didn't always like it, but they did it," Brock noted. Ida Wanderer recalled that she required her general mathematics classes to complete daily homework assignments and a test at the end of each week. Basic courses were no excuse for low expectations. Wanderer indicated that her students appreciated the fact she treated them like real students instead of "dummies."

When students encountered difficulties, they were encouraged to seek out teachers for tutorial assistance. Brock required every teacher to be available for tutorial assistance at least one period a day. Learning centers in language arts and mathematics were created in 1972 and staffed by full-time teachers.[58] Students typically utilized the centers during their study halls. Among the special equipment on hand were computers and speed readers.

Because reading deficiencies played such a key role in the academic problems of many of Tee-Jay's new students, Project Read was launched in the fall of 1971.[59] Intended to help ninth graders make the adjustment from middle to high school, the program focused on improving reading skills in specific content areas. Students for whom Project Read was deemed necessary were assigned to the same five teachers for their core academic courses. These teachers received special training, coplanned their courses, and met periodically to assess the progress of their students. Reading growth was tracked systematically using "continuing progress cards." Community volunteers were enlisted to provide students with tutorial help.

In one of the rare cases where efforts to accommodate the needs of low-achieving students resulted in a significant reduction in expectations, the elementary algebra course was lengthened from a one-year to a two-year course. More than any other subject, algebra was perceived as impeding the progress toward graduation and college of many of Tee-Jay's new students.

Besides these adjustments in curriculum and instruction, various efforts were made to facilitate the social integration of black students and make them feel welcome at Tee-Jay. After a year without school dances, the Senate recommended and Bill Brock approved an October dance to welcome new students. Prudence, however, led Brock to schedule the dance for an hour immediately after school rather than in the evening. A new service club, Student Organization for Black Understanding (SOBU), was created in 1971 to help both blacks and whites understand African-American culture and improve relations between the races.[60] The club, which arose from discussions among student leaders, originally was named Student Organization for Black Unity, but a majority of the Senate resented the exclusionary tone and "understanding" replaced "unity." Some black students felt the school administration had pressured the Senate to change the title.

Students also detected adult "interference" concerning the course in black history.[61] Black students who transferred to Tee-Jay in the fall of 1970 discovered that no course in black history was available, despite the fact they had signed up to take such a course. Bill Brock claimed that no teacher on his faculty was qualified to teach the subject. After vociferous complaints from a delegation of students, Brock relented and scheduled the course for the next school year. When only twenty students signed up and the teacher assigned to teach the course transferred to Maggie Walker, Brock considered canceling it. Once again, student intervention convinced the principal to change his mind. Brock promised to do what he could to prevent Doris Morris, another teacher able to teach black history, from being transferred. He insisted, though, that only juniors and seniors could take the course, maintaining that its content was too "mature" for freshmen and sophomores.

Brock's capacity to "win some and lose some," while all the while treating students and teachers with respect, helped prevent the tense early days of full desegregation from degenerating into rancor and disorder. He never dug in his heels or issued ultimatums that would have served only to incite resistance. Like a loyal captain, he refused to abandon ship in the midst of crisis. When he finally retired in June of 1976, Brock would take with him the satisfaction of knowing that he had steered Tee-Jay through turbulent waters and kept it largely on course.

Those who did not know Brock sometimes felt he could have been more innovative. In fact, the man's openness to new ideas was exceeded only by his reluctance to take credit for them. In the wake of full desegregation, Brock had been responsible for Project Read and the requirement that the most talented teachers offer basic courses and provide tutorials for struggling students. During his years at Tee-Jay he constantly sought out new ideas, travelling to Europe on a Fulbright Fellowship to visit experimental schools and touring schools in Melbourne, Florida, to examine nongraded education and meet B. Frank Brown. That he never acted on some of the new ideas which he found interesting was due less to an inherent conservatism than to his finely tuned sense of what his faculty and community would support. Brock realized that it was one thing to innovate in a school facing serious problems and quite another matter to introduce change in a successful school like Tee-Jay.

It is perhaps unfortunate that Brock never had an opportunity to try one of his boldest ideas. Just before he retired, he recognized that the focus of much opposition to contemporary public schools was crosstown busing, not desegregation per se. He believed that parents might be more supportive of public schools if they knew their children would not be switched periodically from one school to another, thereby risking dislocation and possible transportation problems. His answer—a K–12 school and assurances to parents that all thirteen years of their childrens' schooling could be completed at the same familiar location.

Brock retired in 1976 at the age of sixty-four. During his tenure, Tee-Jay's student body changed from all-white to 80 percent black.[62] Most of the black students came from Richmond's North Side, as the neighborhoods near the school remained predominantly white. Brock saw the percentage of Tee-Jay graduates going to college drop from a high of nearly 80 percent in the sixties to less than 50 percent.[63] Freely admitting some early misgivings about busing, he remarked, "We didn't know how it would work, and it meant an increased workload for everyone."[64] With characteristic enthusiasm, however, Brock went on to say,

> Integration is one of the main events of our time, and there was no better place to watch it than right here in the middle of it. I wouldn't have missed it.

Trying to retain white students. The second major challenge of the early busing era involved minimizing the loss of white students. With enrollments for high schools projected to decline as baby boomers matured, a West End high school with few white students surely would have been a likely target for closure. As the preceding paragraph indicated, efforts to prevent white flight were not particularly successful in a strictly numerical sense. Relative to most other schools in Richmond, however, Tee-Jay's 20 percent white enrollment in the late seventies seemed impressive.

Besides the white flight that typically attended busing for purposes of desegregation, Tee-Jay had to deal with two other enrollment-threatening developments. In the fall of 1972, Richmond Public Schools began to transfer special education students to Tee-Jay—a move ironically intended to help offset a sizeable drop in the school's enrollment (see table 4.1). The same year, the school system inaugurated its first alternative high school, Open High School. Five years later, a second alternative—Community High School—also opened. These developments affected Tee-Jay's ability to attract and retain bright students, white and black. Faculty and administration rightly sensed that the presence of bright students was a key, not just to preserving Tee-Jay's reputation and academic culture, but to the school's very survival.

The assignment of a handful of special education students might not seem, on the surface, to pose a problem for a large and well-established high school.[65] Taken in the context of other events, however, this move was interpreted by some observers as another signal that the instructional focus of Tee-Jay was changing. Public Law 94-142, which would mandate the "least restrictive environment for handicapped students," had not yet been passed. In the years before the implementation of this revolutionary bill in 1975, academically oriented high schools in the Richmond area usually did not house special education programs. It is likely, though difficult to prove, that the initiation of special education at Tee-Jay constituted the last straw for some parents who already harbored reservations about sending their children to a school "in transition."

The impact of Richmond's decision to open several alternative high schools, especially Community High School, is clearer. These schools competed directly with Tee-Jay for bright students who desired a more personal and, some would argue, homogeneous environment. The origins of Community High School, which advertises itself as the "first full-time alternative, four-year school in the nation for gifted students," are unique. Established in 1977 with funds from a private donor, the school receives its basic operating expenses each year from Richmond Public Schools. A volunteer advisory board of influential citizens annually raises more than $100,000 to provide enrichment experiences for Community High students. The school functions as a collaborative effort between Richmond Public Schools, local institutions of higher education, and the advisory board.

Since graduating its first class of thirty students in 1981, Community High has gone on to develop a national reputation. Through 1993, *every* graduate has gained admission to college and ninety-nine percent have actually attended. The Carnegie Foundation recognized Community High as 1 of 200 schools in the United States that promote educational excellence. In 1992 *Redbook Magazine* selected Community High as 1 of 140 top high schools around the nation.[66] The aspect of Community High that has particularly captured the imagination of national observers is the school's clientele. Community High boasts that a "majority" of its students come from "lower economic backgrounds."[67] A newspaper article on the school in March of 1992 indicated that "about 55 percent of the students are from low socioeconomic households."[68]

Community High annually receives up to 200 applications for 55 freshman slots. Enrollment in the spring of 1992 was 185 students, and the principal, Dr. Pamela Trotter-Cornell, indicated that "65 to 70 percent" were black. The average Scholastic Aptitude Test score for Community High students in 1991 was 1,045. Despite the "lower economic background" of many of their students, Community High teachers wage a battle familiar to Tee-Jay faculty in past years—dispelling the impression that the school is elitist.

A glance at Community High's program and policies might serve to confirm this impression, however. Virtually all offerings are honors or AP courses, and students routinely take seven courses a semester. The pace of instruction is rapid, and late work is not accepted. Nor is any grade below aC. The regular academic program is supplemented by a rich array of "mini-mester" classes and summer programs. All freshmen and sophomores, for example, spend four weeks in June and July studying science and the arts. Pamela Trotter-Cornell freely acknowledges that the curriculum is "driven by testing a lot." She goes on to observe that the school is characterized by a "conspiracy of expectation" which leads teachers to give students alarm clocks and pick students up at home to make sure they get to school on time.

Community High shifted venue several times before moving to Maggie Walker High School, near the campus of Virginia Union University. For reasons that are not entirely clear, the school then was relocated during 1990 in the West End, in the aging brick structure that once housed Westhampton Junior High School. Some individuals have speculated that the reluctance of many white parents to have their children attend school in a downtown black neighborhood compelled the move. The school's reliance on donations of white-run businesses and white benefactors may have seemed to necessitate some effort to accommodate the concerns of white parents, though their children made up less than half the school's enrollment. Besides, one alternative school—Open High—remained in the downtown area.

Locating Community High at Maggie Walker had threatened Tee-Jay's ability to attract bright black students. The alternative school's relocation to Westhampton posed a threat to Tee-Jay's efforts to recruit and retain bright white students. The success of Community High and its continuing ability to attract white students, despite enrolling a majority of black students, testifies to the fact that some white Richmonders are not opposed to desegregation as long as they perceive safeguards exist. These include a school location considered to be reasonably secure and a student body that is motivated to study and excel.

Community High exemplifies the spirit of free enterprise and consumer choice that some observers contend is the only salvation for public education. Urban school systems like Richmond's have evolved into a strange form of market economy. It is a cruel irony that the viability of these systems is often perceived to depend more on their ability to meet the needs of the few remaining white students than of their preponderance of black students. The reasoning goes as follows: most black students have little choice but to attend the city's public schools, but many of the remaining white students do have a choice. If school conditions are perceived to deteriorate too far, white parents either can move to the suburbs or seek private schooling. School systems that lose most of their white students fear that their ability to secure needed resources and political support from the white community, and particularly white power brokers, may be jeopardized. Realpolitik and a high-minded commitment to an integrated society must share the same bed.

Often, the chief "commodity" in this market economy is bright black students. Because the number of white students remaining in urban school systems like Richmond's is relatively small, schools that are likely to meet the needs of white students must also accommodate, by necessity, large numbers of black students. If a substantial proportion of these black students are perceived to be unmotivated to do well in school or conform to school rules, their presence may drive away some of the remaining white students. As a result, public schools that assure white parents that their children will go to school with motivated black students are far more likely to retain white students and, hence, the support of the white community. While the public school population of cities like Richmond is largely black, the power structure of the city remains largely in white hands. White support, in other words, is more than a preference; it is a practical necessity.

While Tee-Jay could not compete with Community High School's private endowment, selective admissions policies, instructional flexibility, and teacher-student ratio of one to fifteen, it did explore various ways of maintaining an academic focus and, therefore, increasing the likelihood of its attracting and retaining bright white and black students. One of the most interesting, and short-lived, of these efforts took place toward the end of the school's first year of full desegregation.

In February of 1971 the *Richmond News Leader* printed an article with the alluring heading, "TJ High May Become a 'Model'."[69] Prompted in part by parent complaints that their college-bound youngsters were "hampered by a slower classroom pace," Acting Director of Secondary Education Harold Gibson convened a group of secondary supervisors from various curriculum areas to consider ways of developing greater flexibility in Tee-Jay's curriculum and grading system. John B. Cary Elementary School and several middle schools already had created more flexible programs to accommodate a more diverse group of students. Gibson was quoted as saying, "We hope to have some interdisciplinary programs, some team teaching, and possibly a learning center approach in some areas." In addition, he said that thought was being given to replacing traditional letter grades with assessments based on behavioral objectives. Such a move was intended to benefit low-achieving students who might become discouraged by consistently low grades. College-bound students would still receive letter grades, though. A final suggestion involved dropping grade-level designations for certain courses so that "more proficient students could leave before the end of the semester and enter another course." Of all the proposals considered for the "model" school program, however, only some interdisciplinary teaching and learning centers in reading and mathematics actually were implemented. Formal status as a model school never was conferred.

In the final analysis, the strategy for attracting and retaining bright students that seemed most sensible was to preserve as much of the "old" Tee-Jay as possible. The "old" Tee-Jay, after all, was what presumably had attracted whites to the West End and kept large numbers of white students from transferring to private schools after initial desegregation. The "old" Tee-Jay and the qualities for which it stood also formed the basis for black complaints that segregation constituted unequal opportunity. Black parents had not struggled long and hard to gain access for their children to schools characterized by watered-down curricula and modest expectations. The chance to send their sons and daughters to schools like Tee-Jay was what the *Brown* decision had been all about.

The most obvious act of preservation was the retention of AP and honors courses. Without them, many who taught at and attended Tee-Jay felt that brighter students would have abandoned the school for private or alternative schools. Because of confusion and concern over who qualified for honors courses, criteria governing eligibility periodically had to be reviewed and reported. Throughout the seventies, the criteria changed only slightly. Students wishing to take honors courses still required parental consent, teacher approval, demonstrated competence in the communicative arts, good attendance, and evidence of good character as represented by adherence to the Honor Code ideals.[70] Much of Tee-Jay's academic curriculum also remained intact. As Bill Brock put it, "More important than finding new courses to offer here, we should find new ways to handle the courses we have now."[71] Brock went on to stress the importance of independent study as a way to provide students opportunities to progress at their own rate. Other elements of the Tee-Jay culture that were left intact included the Student Participation Association, the Honor System, the rich array of extracurricular activities, and the abiding commitment to developing well-rounded students. Tee-Jay actually lured some students away from Community High School because they disliked the single-minded focus on academic success, the intense pressure, and the absence of extracurricular opportunities.

Coping with a New Generation

Preserving those aspects of Tee-Jay that had helped it become an excellent high school was not easy in the years following court-ordered busing. Besides having to provide programs to assist large numbers of low-achieving students, teachers and administrators faced a generation of young people influenced by the activism, questioning of authority, and disillusionment of the sixties. For these individuals, tradition was anathema and change essential.

When *Jeffersonian* reporters in December of 1970 asked students whether they were "really getting an education" at Tee-Jay, most responses reflected some degree of discontent.[72] Paul Woodley said, "The courses are too set; you have to do everything a certain way." Dina Swartz added, "The school system needs improving. . . . Creativity should become more a part of school." The Cadet Corps came under attack from Mark Rosenbaum, who felt that students who wanted "to get together and play army" should not be able to earn a course credit.[73] Terry Dascher complained that her courses did not encourage "thinking on your own." Reggie Mitchell drew a bead on the administration, claiming that it "tends to be too regulatory and strict in students' activities." He went on to recommend that each student should be free to choose whether or not to take exams.

In the same issue of the *Jeffersonian* an anonymous student penned a particularly scathing indictment of his alma mater:

> At school the student faces innumerable pointless rules regarding personal habits such as smoking and necessities such as going to the bathroom. His time in class is spent being droned at in lecture after lecture, which teach him little worth knowing. Reward comes not for creativity or thinking, but for skillful regurgitation of mostly useless facts.[74]

Reluctant to ignore totally such strong feelings, Tee-Jay's teachers and administrators responded with a limited number of new initiatives. A few new courses were developed, including the aforementioned black history and "The American Experience," an interdisciplinary humanities course. Arts Week was developed as a spring opportunity for students to learn about various aspects of the fine and performing arts and demonstrate creativity. Minicourses were introduced, providing students with a chance once a year to suggest and sometimes teach subjects of particular interest to them. In the fall of 1971 the Senate drafted a Bill of Rights for students, thereby establishing the principle that adult authority had its limits.[75] At the same time, the Parent Teacher Association (PTA) was expanded to the Parents Teachers Students Association (PTSA). This move may have been prompted, in part, by a precipitous postbusing drop in PTA membership from 806 to 152.[76] To assist parents and students wishing to attend the PTSA, a bus was sent to North Side for the reconstituted organization's first meeting.

By the mid-seventies student activism was on the wane. So, too, was enrollment, interest in challenging courses, and commitment to college preparation. Increasing percentages of Tee-Jay students required academic assistance. At this point, Richmond

Public Schools also began to experience serious budget problems—problems which would put into question the very existence of Tee-Jay.

Assessing the Seventies

Few would argue that Tee-Jay had escaped the seventies unscathed. Critics of busing could, and did, point out that many of the bright students who might have attended Tee-Jay opted to go elsewhere. Faculty veterans of the "glory days" retired. Discipline problems were greater than during the pre-1970 period. Low enrollments made it harder to justify highly specialized courses. Most Tee-Jay students no longer went on to college. Instead of worrying about whether they would gain admission to the college of their choice, students fretted increasingly about just graduating from high school. Many extracurricular activities fell on hard times. The Cadet Corps folded in 1971, and the school's award-winning publications either ceased operation altogether or reduced their scope of operations.

Despite these setbacks, the decade cannot be written off as a total loss. With reference to the three primary challenges of the seventies, Tee-Jay had performed respectably, if not with complete success. A reasonably effective effort had been made to accommodate the needs of black students without severely diluting the quality of their education. Student unrest had been contained, allowing Tee-Jay to avoid the major boycotts, racial incidents, and disruptions to which other high schools fell prey. While a desirable racial balance had not been maintained, the school was able to keep 15–20 percent of its white students at a time when most high schools in the city had lost all but token white representation.

The transition from a predominantly white, suburban high school to a predominantly black, urban high school was made without the need for sweeping reorganization or the total abandonment of the ideals, mission, and high expectations for which Tee-Jay had become famous. Throughout the decade, Tee-Jay students continued to post successes, gaining entrance to first-rate colleges, winning awards in academic competition, graduating from high school to a greater extent than their counterparts in most city high schools, and scoring victories in athletics. Under the guidance of coach Dave Robbins, for example, the Tee-Jay basketball team won its third state championship in 1975. Soccer, tennis, and cross country teams also registered impressive seasons. At a time when many high schools in Virginia faced serious budget problems and declining enrollments, Tee-Jay managed to hang on to many of its specialty courses. For instance, in 1974 it was one of only sixteen high schools in the state to offer an Advanced Placement American history course and one of twenty-eight schools to offer a course in black history.[77]

In some ways, Tee-Jay actually had improved during the seventies. For those who believed that a vital part of every young person's education was learning to deal with diversity, Tee-Jay enrolled a more diverse student body—racially, socioeconomically, and ability-wise—and employed a more diverse faculty than at any previous point in its history. Students displayed a greater interest in the welfare of their community than had many of their predecessors. Bernard Craighead, a black Tee-Jay senior, and Tom Klein, a recent white graduate, manifested this spirit of constructive activism in 1972 when they ran for the Richmond City Council. Bright, committed young teachers joined the faculty throughout the decade, thereby ensuring a steady flow of new ideas and energy. At the same time, the continuity of values and beliefs so crucial to preserving Tee-Jay's academic culture was maintained by virtue of the continued presence of veteran teachers like Edna Davis, Russell Flammia, Kathleen Hancock, Jim Holdren, and Ida Wanderer. The departure of Bill Brock in 1976, an event which could have signalled a prolonged leadership vacuum, was handled smoothly, thanks to the cooperation of Tee-Jay's faculty and staff and the talents of his successor, Morgan Edwards.

Following in Brock's footsteps was a challenge. The fact that Edwards had served as one of his predecessor's assistant principals for six years allowed him to interact with parents and faculty and earn their trust before replacing Brock. Still, Edwards recalls that some people at first had "reservations" concerning the ability of a black man to assume the helm of Tee-Jay. A patient person, Edwards realized that the more people got to know him and see him in action, the more they would realize that his interests were the same as theirs—the welfare of students.

It did not take Edwards long to convince people that he was the right person for the job. The 1976–77 edition of the Tee-Jay yearbook carried the following assessment of Edwards' first year on the job:

More discipline was needed. For too long the classroom atmosphere had been too lax. Mr. Edwards realized this. With him came a renewed emphasis on school rules and their enforcement. The teachers and a surprising majority of the students supported him in this, most agreeing it to be high time that the wheels of discipline be set in motion again. . . . Also, because of these new rules, there seemed to be a boost in school spirit and a renewed strain of self-respect and respect for others. These results were so noticeable that teachers experienced a sense of satisfaction they had thought to be long lost. Since these improvements could be considered the results of Mr. Edwards' first year as principal, it only stood to reason that his second could be anticipated as being equally successful, with the fruits of the labors of the administration just as rewarding.[78]

Edwards inherited a faculty of sixty-four teachers plus three counselors and two assistant principals. Ten of his teachers were new to Tee-Jay. The faculty consisted of thirty white and thirty-four black teachers, nineteen men and forty-five women. Four reading specialists now were employed, as well as a learning center proctor, study hall proctor, and security officer. Still, the faculty also included teachers of Latin and German, astronomy, and a variety of AP courses. Whereas remediation prior to 1970 largely had been handled informally, if at all, with teachers arranging for struggling students to meet with them during free periods, Tee-Jay now sponsored a variety of special programs designed to provide systematic academic assistance. A phone call home no longer assured the cessation of discipline problems at school, as it normally had in earlier days, but order prevailed nonetheless and most students took their education seriously.

Reflecting on the first decade of full desegregation at Tee-Jay, Kathleen Hancock, one of Tee-Jay's best-loved teachers and a fixture in the History Department for thirty-six years, provided perhaps the most fitting tribute to the efforts of Morgan Edwards, Bill Brock, and her fellow teachers: "Tee-Jay never gave up." Successes might have been harder to come by and external challenges greater than in previous years, but few who were associated with the school were prepared to write its obituary. Their faith in and commitment to Tee-Jay would be sorely tested in the years to come.

CHAPTER 5

The Certainty of Uncertainty

If a Tee-Jay student or teacher during the "glory days" had been told that their school eventually would be threatened with closure, they would have been incredulous. Even during the first decade of integration, no one seriously believed that an organization as venerable as Tee-Jay might soon face extinction. By this time, Tee-Jay had become as much a part of the dream of opportunity for black parents as white. If concerns for the school existed, they involved the preservation of high standards and academic excellence, not organizational survival.

With the seventies, however, came an era of economic decline and taxpayer revolt. Coupled with the effects of a declining birthrate, these events spelled trouble for most public agencies, including school systems. Few schools—particularly aging urban high schools—were completely safe from sale, the wrecker's ball, or reassignment. How Tee-Jay as an organization coped with these uncertainties—and the many that would follow—is the focus of this and the following chapter.

The present chapter opens with the fiscal crisis that faced Richmond Public Schools in the late seventies and the advent of Plan G, a consolidation strategy for keeping all seven high schools open while cutting operating expenses. The next part describes the eventual demise of Plan G and the Save Our School campaign, a grassroots effort to keep Tee-Jay in business. The chapter closes with the aftermath of the campaign—a time when Richmond began to experiment with magnet programs in three comprehensive high schools, including Tee-Jay.

A COMPLEX SOLUTION

The mid-seventies was a period of growing anxiety for Richmond educators. Economic problems combined with declining student performance and public criticism to elevate concern. Richmond's dropout rate steadily increased during these years, from 8 percent in 1975–76 to 10 percent by 1976–77 and almost 11 percent in 1977–78.[1] In the fall of 1977 the school board approved Superintendent Richard Hunter's proposal that all seniors be required to pass ninth-grade reading and mathematics proficiency tests as well as tests of oral and written communication before receiving their diplomas.[2] The decision was prompted, in part, by the fact that nearly 12 percent of Richmond's seniors the previous year had failed to pass all the proficiency tests.

At the same time, school board member Jacob Orndorff, Jr., called for the creation of an academic programs committee. Expressing concern over the shrinking number of academic and honors courses for college-bound students, he stated that the "consensus among high school staff members is that small academic classes for college-bound students are the first casualties of budget cuts."[3]

The same issue of the *Richmond News Leader* that carried Orndorff's remarks also contained a feature story contrasting discipline problems in Richmond's public and private schools. Tee-Jay, the standard against which other schools had been judged a decade earlier, now found itself the target of negative comparisons:

> Like all the other Richmond public schools, Thomas Jefferson High School is a different world from Richmond's private schools and some of the public schools in Henrico and Chesterfield Counties.
>
> Eighty-six percent of the 1,173 students at Thomas Jefferson are black. Classes are large with limited individual help. Students there walk to class through long, locker-lined hallways and eat lunch in a cafeteria where most students still segregate themselves by race.
>
> St. Catherine's School has half the enrollment of Thomas Jefferson and only 11 minority students. When Mrs. Heroy walks to room 114 where she teaches senior English, she pads softly down a carpeted hallway and across a stone-floored arcade overlooking a well-kept lawn.[4]

The article also pointed out, in fairness to Tee-Jay, that its teachers were making a concerted effort to keep students in school and on task. Ruth Gibson shared the fact that she and her fellow Tee-Jay teachers spent time each evening at home phoning parents regarding their children's absences that day. Part of a new policy initiated by Morgan Edwards, these calls seemed to be reducing the level of absenteeism.

Questions about student competence in basic skills, decreasing interest in college, discipline problems, and absenteeism—such was the context of public schooling in Richmond when the first official mention of closing Tee-Jay was made by Superintendent Richard Hunter. At a special meeting on November 29, 1977, Dr. Hunter announced that the school board faced a "major dilemma" trying to justify the expenditure of the $29 million that was estimated to be needed to improve the city's high school facilities.[5] Since roughly $10 million of the total would be required to renovate Tee-Jay and Maggie Walker, these two schools topped the list for closure. It should be noted that closing just one high school was never mentioned publicly as an alternative strategy at this time, despite the board's acknowledgement that shutting down any high school—much less two—would be daunting. Privately, school officials admitted that it would be politically unwise to shut down a traditionally all-black high school without also closing one that had been all-white.

As deliberations on the school budget for 1978–79 continued into the winter, Tee-Jay and Maggie Walker remained yoked together, probable sacrifices to efficiency and cost cutting. Meanwhile, the school board and Dr. Hunter became locked in a fierce dispute with City Manager William Leidinger over the city's contribution to school renovation expenses.[6] Some observers felt that the capital improvement funds Hunter claimed had been promised by Leidinger were being diverted to Project I, a downtown development initiative. The affair caused questions to be raised regarding the commitment of influential Richmonders to the improvement of the city's public schools.

While the budget squabbles continued, support for Tee-Jay and Maggie Walker grew more vocal. Students from both schools addressed the school board concerning the importance of maintaining their alma maters. This would not be the last occasion when Tee-Jay students rallied to the defense of their school. Impressed by public support for Tee-Jay, Hunter asked Dr. Robert T. Frossard, assistant superintendent for secondary education, to oversee the identification of alternatives to school closure. The process of developing and debating alternatives consumed months of activity. In the meantime, Coalter Cabell Hancock, Tee-Jay's second principal, passed away on May 8, 1978, not knowing the fate of the school he loved so much and contributed to in so many ways. Not until April 11, 1979, in fact, would Superintendent Hunter declare unequivocally that a specific alternative to school closure had been selected.[7]

The chosen alternative was known as Plan G. It had been preferred over other options, including Plan A, which called for Tee-Jay and Maggie Walker to be converted to middle schools. Based on a similar plan in California, Plan G provided for the continued operation of all seven high schools, but as part of three multi-school "complexes," instead of as separate schools. Tee-Jay would join George Wythe and Huguenot, both high schools located south of the James River. Armstrong was paired with John F. Kennedy, while the third complex comprised John Marshall and Maggie Walker. Every high school would continue to offer a "basic curriculum," while certain high schools would focus on special programs. In this way, low-enrollment courses and programs could be continued. Arrangements were made to bus students between the schools in each complex. Not surprisingly, Tee-Jay was chosen as the site for many of the honors and AP courses in the Jefferson/Huguenot/Wythe complex.

Plan G occasioned considerable criticism from its very inception. So politically volatile was the plan that Superintendent Hunter quickly laid responsibility for its selection at the doorstep of his assistant superintendent, Robert Frossard. Frossard, when interviewed, claimed Plan G actually had been Hunter's idea. In any event, Frossard soon left Richmond Public Schools.

Years later Frossard, in reflecting on the adoption of Plan G, expressed the opinion that Richmond Public Schools had missed a wonderful opportunity by creating high school complexes. Declining enrollments meant that Richmond's high schools—had school officials been so inclined—could downsize, thereby providing more manageable facilities where students and teachers would be more likely to get to know each other. High schools of more than 1,000 students might offer a few more courses than smaller organizations, but they also were more apt to be characterized by discipline problems and impersonal relations between teachers and students. Frossard recalled that an administrator from Maggie Walker told him, on the eve of Plan G's implementation, that the recent drop in enrollment at his school (Maggie Walker fell below 1,000 students) finally had permitted the faculty and administration to "re-assert control, get to know the students, and begin working on quality education."

Plan G was justified in public as a way to achieve efficiency while preserving quality. The basis for the claim of quality centered on the preservation of AP and other low-enrollment courses. Numbers had dropped so precipitously in some schools that they no longer could afford to offer these courses. Some form of consolidation of services seemed the only way to ensure that college-bound students might still have access to higher-level courses in science, mathematics, and foreign language. Dedicated fans of high school athletics, particularly basketball, also argued that combining students from different high schools was the only way for Richmond teams to remain competitive with teams from larger suburban high schools.

In April of 1979, four months before Plan G was scheduled to go into effect, the *Jeffersonian* ran a pair of front-page articles on the pros and cons of complexes.[8] Alan Schwitzer, speaking for the strengths of Plan G, pointed out that Tee-Jay students would have access to a more modern chemistry lab than the one currently in use. He also noted that pooling talent across three schools would lead to higher quality extracurricular experiences. Possible disruptive effects of busing were minimized by the observation that many Tee-Jay students already traveled during the school day in order to attend technical programs or go to distributive education placements.

Danny Willis, in his rebuttal, warned of "hassle and confusion:"

> If students have classes in different buildings, they will have to be bused from one building to another during the school day. Not only does this waste time, it also adds the expense of busing the students from one building to another.
>
> It is inevitable that extracurricular activities will suffer. Will there be one newspaper and yearbook for the entire complex? If so, how will they be organized? I'm sure everyone is aware that there will be a problem organizing sports activities. . . .
>
> Plan G may be an attempt by the school board to save what's left of the Richmond School System, but it is obvious that this plan will cost more than it is worth and will be inconvenient for both students and faculty.[9]

A major controversy with Plan G concerned the particular combinations of high schools. In some ways the school board's choices made little sense. In terms of enrollment equalization and travel distance, Tee-Jay should have been grouped with Maggie Walker and John Marshall. Such a move would have created three complexes, each with approximately 2,200 students. Grouping Tee-Jay with Wythe and Huguenot resulted in a complex substantially larger than the other two. In addition, the distances between Tee-Jay, Wythe, and Huguenot were much greater than the Jefferson-Walker-Marshall alternative. Interschool travel promised to be even more difficult because only two bridges spanned the James River in the West End. Tee-Jay, Maggie Walker, and John Marshall, on the other hand, were all located west of Lombardy on the same side of the river.

How could such a flawed arrangement have been accepted? While no record of school board deliberations is available, considerable speculation by insiders supports the view that Tee-Jay was grouped with Huguenot and Wythe because these schools contained most of the white students left in Richmond's high schools. Fear persisted that linking Tee-Jay with Maggie Walker and John Marshall might result in Tee-Jay losing the small percentage of white students who still remained.

Whether the decision to group Tee-Jay, Huguenot, and Wythe was made out of an abiding commitment to the fading dream of integration is not known. What is clear is that, by the beginning of the new decade, integration no longer seemed to be a high priority for many Richmond educators. In a 1980 retrospective on ten years of court-ordered busing in Richmond, Allen McCreary, an education writer for the *Richmond News Leader*, wrote,

> Having tried dozens of desegregation techniques during the past decade, many city school officials now have other things on their minds.
>
> "We don't think about desegregation anymore; it just doesn't seem to matter," said A. Edward Ooghe Jr., principal of 88 percent black Ginter Park Elementary School, which serves an integrated neighborhood in North Side Richmond.
>
> "It seems like we're moving toward resegregation now—the desegregation was somewhere in between," he added.
>
> In many Richmond schools today, desegregation seems about as urgent a topic as a bunch of old photographs in an attic trunk.[10]

Dr. James W. Tyler, deputy superintendent under Richard Hunter and, later in the eighties, superintendent (on two separate occasions), tried to put desegregation into historical perspective:

> Desegregation probably was not as important as the end of Feudalism, the Crusades, or the Industrial Revolution. It probably was more important than whether the Yankees win the pennant or who gets elected president this year.
>
> There are not many things more important to a parent than where his child will go to school, particularly if it's somewhere across town.[11]

The Birth of JHW

The beginning of Richmond's fall semester in 1979 saw the appearance of a new acronym—JHW. Encompassing most of South Richmond and the West End, the Jefferson-Huguenot-Wythe complex required new forms of organizational integration and coordination. The principals of the three high schools reported to a complex principal, Dr. Robert Marchant. Similar academic departments from each school were combined under a single chairperson. Tee-Jay's Dr. Calvin Green, for example, was selected to head the twenty-two–teacher JHW Science Department. Besides evaluating science teachers at Tee-Jay and Huguenot, Green taught Advanced Placement physics at Tee-Jay and Advanced Placement chemistry at Huguenot. Science teachers at Wythe were evaluated by Green's associate department chair. Students were bused between the three schools to take courses unavailable at their home school. Huguenot and Wythe students seeking most Advanced Placement and certain honors courses thus traveled each day to Tee-Jay. The main reason Advanced Placement chemistry had to be taken at Huguenot was the outdated laboratory facilities at Tee-Jay. Additional students commuted between schools in the afternoon for extracurricular activities. Each complex supported a single team in each sport. Similarly, yearbooks, literary magazines, bands, and other activities were consolidated.

On the eve of the opening of school, district officials insisted that Plan G would "have little effect on the daily experiences of students."[12] They noted that no attendance areas had been altered, and that a relatively small number of students actually would be involved in intracomplex busing. The initial estimate for the JHW complex was that 241 out of 3,543 students would take to the roads during regular school hours.[13] The estimates for the Walker-Marshall and the Kennedy-Armstrong complexes were 150 and 50 students respectively. It was difficult to imagine substantial savings resulting from such a modest effort, particularly in light of the need to appoint an additional principal to head the JHW complex.

The State Department of Education, on December 11, 1979, officially recognized each Richmond complex as a single high school, seemingly bringing an end to Tee-Jay as a distinct educational entity. School colors, mascots, and publication titles were changed. The Tee-Jay Vikings gave way to the JHW Trojans, while the Monticello yearbook became the Odyssey. Officially, Thomas Jefferson High School was referred to as the "Jefferson Building." JHW yearbooks did not indicate which building in the complex served as each student's "home." June found seniors from the Jefferson, Huguenot, and Wythe buildings graduating together in a single ceremony.[14]

High schools with proud traditions, distinct cultures, and rivalries based on years of athletic and academic competition might not be expected to respond to merger without a struggle. A small number of students taking a few courses at another high school was one thing; the loss of school name and identity quite another. Armstrong and Kennedy coordinated activities least of all the high schools. Buses running between the two East End schools often carried no more than three or four students. Maggie Walker and John Marshall opted to divide operations by grade level, Walker taking the ninth and tenth grades, Marshall the eleventh and twelfth grades. As a result, little coordination of services aside from extracurricular activities took place in the Marshall-Walker complex. Many observers felt that the JHW complex achieved a higher degree of coordination than the other two complexes, but that achievement, in reality, was relatively modest.

A host of predictable problems attended the operation of the complexes. For example, many seniors, particularly those who wished to attend college, complained about the creation of a single class ranking for each complex. This change meant that college-bound students, of whom Tee-Jay and Huguenot accounted for the largest numbers, had to compete for class ranking with larger numbers of students taking non-college-preparatory courses. The odds of receiving a lower rank thus seemed much greater. Students from Wythe and Huguenot claimed that Tee-Jay students had an unfair advantage because they had easier access to AP and honors courses, both of which carried greater weight in class rankings. Wythe students worried that their rankings might suffer because they were competing with Tee-Jay and Huguenot students, who boasted the highest eleventh-grade reading scores of Richmond's seven comprehensive high school buildings.[15]

Teachers and administrators found little in the new arrangements about which to exult. They complained that distinguishing between unwanted strangers and visiting students from other buildings in the complex was extremely difficult. Many teachers disliked being evaluated by chairpersons from other buildings. Claims were made that certain chairs favored their old colleagues over new ones. The strain was so great for Ida Wanderer, in fact, that she left Tee-Jay and took a position at Virginia Commonwealth University. As head of the JHW Mathematics Department, she was spending more time dealing with petty squabbles than the improvement of instruction and student achievement.

In June of 1983 the first class of students with four years of experience in the JHW complex graduated. Tee-Jay students, however, still referred to themselves as "first of the Trojans." In an effort to stimulate enthusiasm for the new organizational arrangement, the yearbook staff opened the *Odyssey* for 1983–84 with the following upbeat message:

> We came together, physically—in 1979 when our Complex first started. But, spiritually we were still separated. Old spirits still flickered, symbolizing an ever-present resistance to change. Like the best of our country's athletes, politicians, and statesmen, we were rivals in our own cause, reaching for the gold, seemingly united to our spectators.
>
> But, in the Olympic year 1984, the Trojan torch was lit by a new generation—a generation who knew only of Trojans. And Trojans they were from start to finish. The truce of Jefferson's Vikings, Huguenot's Falcons, and George Wythe's Bulldogs was clearly evident.[16]

During the 1984–85 school year, at the request of the school district, a "self-study" of the JHW complex was undertaken. The results of this comprehensive review of school purpose, curriculum, organization, and programs by a team of forty-one visiting educators appeared to endorse the complex concept and provide a green light for continued efforts to integrate programs and coordinate services.[17]

The self-study opened with an overview of the community served by the complex. Half of the JHW parents were high school graduates, and one in five had attended college. Fifty percent of male parents were employed in skilled or semiskilled occupations, while 60 percent of female parents worked as housewives or in skilled or semiskilled occupations. The Visiting Committee noted that many students lived in single-parent households. Eighty-three percent of the JHW student body was black, 13 percent white, and 3 percent Asian-American. These aggregate figures had not varied significantly since the beginning of the complex, but the Huguenot building saw a decline in white enrollment from 22.1 percent to 9.6 percent. The number of Asian-American students at Huguenot rose from 0 to 6 percent. This shift meant that Tee-Jay, with roughly a 15 percent white enrollment, now had the largest percentage of whites of any of Richmond's seven high school buildings.

Of the JHW seniors to graduate in 1984, 49 percent planned to go on for some form of postsecondary education. Of the 3,276 students enrolled in JHW for 1983–84, 10.4 percent withdrew from school. Most of these students dropped out because of "low achievement." Based on SRA and district competency tests, 44 percent of the students in the complex read at or above grade level. Roughly 1 student in 5 possessed an IQ in excess of 109, while 34 percent possessed IQs below 92.

Tee-Jay's clientele clearly had changed since the "glory days," but not as much as its sister buildings. The Jefferson building still catered primarily to the middle class. Not only had Tee-Jay retained the support of some middle-class white parents, but it had attracted substantial numbers of young black professionals. This latter group sometimes disagreed with the beliefs and politics of Richmond's traditional black power brokers. They often preferred, for example, to live in the integrated West End rather than Richmond's traditional black strongholds. In addition, they felt no special allegiance to Armstrong High School, the alma mater of many of the city's black elite. Tee-Jay received an added boost when Charles Robb became Governor of Virginia in 1982. He and his wife chose to send their two daughters, Lucinda initially and later Cathy, to Tee-Jay, rather than a closer public high school or a private school.

Since 1970, retaining white students had been a continuing challenge for Tee-Jay, but particularly so in the early eighties, when an incident involving a Tee-Jay teacher and the *Richmond Times-Dispatch* focused attention anew on the consequences of desegregation. A synopsis of the affair, which eventually reached the state judicial system, was provided in the introduction to the appellate court's decision:

> Some parents of public high school students were unhappy with the class behavior of a particular teacher. One of the parents approached the administration of the school and attempted to have the teacher removed. When he was unsuccessful he contacted a newspaper reporter and told him about the situation. The reporter interviewed a number of students and their parents about the teacher and about classroom incidents. The reporter contacted the school superintendent, the teacher in question, and other teachers. They all refused to discuss the specific complaints. Plaintiff teacher refused to respond at all, despite the reporter's statement that it would look bad for her if she did not. On the Sunday prior to the beginning of school [August 16, 1981] the newspaper published a front page story about the difficulty parents had in getting the school system to remove incompetent teachers. Plaintiff was the only teacher singled out for particular scrutiny. Former students and their parents were quoted at length. They complained about the teacher's lack of preparation, her absences, and her behavior toward students. Only a few quotations from the administration and other teachers supported the teacher's competence. Plaintiff sued the newspaper, the publisher, and the reporter, and was awarded $1,000,000 in compensatory damages and $45,000 in punitive damages by a jury.[18]

The fact that the teacher, Vernelle Lipscomb, was black and the parents who tried to have her removed were white caused many to regard the incident as racially motivated. That the Richmond newspapers were at the center of the controversy came as no surprise to some longtime observers of race relations in Richmond. Two decades earlier, the Richmond newspapers had backed "massive resistance." Subsequently, they opposed virtually every step toward school integration, in the process elevating editor James J. Kilpatrick to the status of patron saint of segregationists. Of these newspapers, Supreme Court Justice Thurgood Marshall would say:

We put some trust in the decency of man. . . . I'm afraid we assumed that after a short period of time of one to five years the states would give in [on resisting desegregation]. We did not, however, give enough credence to the two Richmond newspapers, the Richmond Times-Dispatch and the other one [Richmond News Leader] . . . who were determined that they would build up the type of opposition that would prevent the states from voluntarily going along [with desegregation].[19]

When interviewed, Lipscomb, who has remained on the Tee-Jay faculty, maintained that the real source of parental complaints had been a low grade given to one of her students. The student's father was a prominent Richmond physician. Lipscomb believed that he would have been less likely to contest the grade if it had been given by a white teacher. Her greatest solace in the protracted case derived less from the financial award, which was reduced by the appellate court, than from the fact that many of her white students and their parents rallied to her defense. Lipscomb wondered why the newspaper reporter whose unbalanced coverage prompted her to file suit in the first place had made no effort to contact these individuals. Lipscomb's case eventually was won on the grounds that teachers cannot be considered "public officials." As a result, they are free to recover damages for defamatory falsehoods relating to their conduct on the job. The Richmond newspapers claimed, unsuccessfully, that teachers are prohibited, by virtue of their status as public officials under the so-called New York Times rule, from suing the press unless malice is involved.

Getting positive press coverage—never a problem prior to desegregation—became increasingly difficult for Tee-Jay. Even before the Lipscomb case, in fact, Morgan Edwards had complained that reporters seemed to be interested primarily in racial incidents, declining student achievement, and other problems. He related the following story to illustrate his point:

I actually had reporters who would call and ask if anything was happening. What they meant by that was—Was anyone getting shot? Not whether good things were going on.

So, I decided to have a little fun with a reporter one day. He called and asked what was going on. I said that there were rumors of something big happening at 1:00 p.m. I knew that would get their attention. When the reporter showed up at 1:00, we were having a National Honor Society induction!

I guess the reporter had hoped for a riot. He stormed off. We never did get coverage of the National Honor Society ceremony.

Returning to the self-study of JHW, the Visiting Committee read various materials prepared by the complex faculty and administration and interviewed a number of teachers and students. The result was a fifty-one-page report containing dozens of "commendations" and "recommendations."

Under the heading "Staff and Administration," for example, the Visiting Committee commended JHW for working together to provide leadership and guidance for the total school program, establishing an atmosphere conducive to learning, and modelling appropriate "student decorum, dress, and attitudes."[20] Considering that JHW consisted of 3 building principals, 6 assistant building principals, 167 full-time teachers, 17 part-time teachers, 13 full-time guidance counselors, 5 full-time and 1 part-time media specialist, 4 in-school suspension coordinators, 1 educational specialist in charge of the Tee-Jay planetarium, 6 security specialists, 2 full-time and 1 part-time nurse, and other support staff, these observations represented no small accomplishment.

Fourteen recommendations regarding "staff and administration" were offered by the Visiting Committee. As the list below indicates, several concerns surfaced in the self-study regarding the role of department chair, parental involvement, teacher development, and building maintenance.

1. The staff and administration should develop and implement an organized program designed to encourage parental involvement in the total school program.

2. The administration should implement in-service programs for all teachers designed to enhance skills and techniques of effective teaching.

3. Consideration should be given to the establishment of a Foreign Language Department as a separate department with its own department head and associates.

4. Efforts should be made to insure that all teachers are teaching classes for which they are fully endorsed.

5. An evaluation should be made of the instructional leadership responsibilities of department heads and associates.

6. The staff and administration should make a concentrated effort to protect instructional time from interruptions as

stipulated in Standard D of the "Standards for Accrediting Schools in Virginia."

7. Efforts should be made to provide appropriate supervision of the custodial staff.

8. Provisions should be made for employing substitutes in the event of custodian absence.

9. The administrative staff should establish a schedule for the timely repair and replacement of equipment.

10. The administrative staff should ensure that all students are provided with the appropriate textbooks.

11. The administrative staff should provide department allocations, subject to budgetary limitations, which allow the purchase of needed instructional materials and supplies.

12. Department heads should be involved, in a timely manner, in the budgetary process to include both the preparation and expenditure of departmental allocations.

13. A procedure should be established to keep departments aware of the status of individual budget requests.

14. The staff should be encouraged to consider the advantages of affiliation with and participation in subject area professional organizations.[21]

When the Visiting Committee turned their attention to the JHW curriculum, they were pleased to find "correlation, cooperation and planning within departments and between buildings."[22] The existence of educational programs for students of all academic levels also was commended, as was the "school environment," which reflected "an atmosphere of serenity and calmness." As for suggestions, the Visiting Committee urged the Huguenot and Wythe buildings to emulate Jefferson by adopting a seven-period day, "in order to offer students a greater selection of electives, curriculum choices and student activities."[23] In addition, they called on department chairs to assume leadership in preparing citywide examinations to ascertain whether "what is being taught is being tested." This recommendation doubtless was influenced by growing national concern that students were taking standardized tests covering knowledge to which they had never been exposed in class. The Visiting Committee also called on the JHW complex to offer a half-unit of economics, as stipulated in Virginia's "Standards for Accrediting Schools," and to infuse career education into "all curriculums."

Overall, the self-study revealed that JHW's programs generally were in compliance with state accreditation standards and the principles of effective schooling. As of November of 1985, therefore, it appeared as if the complex had received an important external vote of confidence. Within three months, however, the Richmond School Board accepted a new student assignment plan that would mark the end of the complex system. What had happened to cause this sudden shift in policy?

The major impetus for the reversal appears to have been Judge Robert R. Merhige's approval, in April of 1985, of a neighborhood school plan that effectively ended crosstown busing in Richmond. The self-study was already well under way when school officials began to draft this plan. Merhige's decision was not based on the fact Richmond had achieved a desirable level of integration. In fact, as the *Richmond News Leader* noted, Richmond was "still a city of segregated neighborhoods, especially those where children live."[24] Of sixty-nine census tracts, fifty-one were made up of more than 75 percent school-age children of one race. Only eighteen tracts could be considered racially mixed. When in July of 1986 Mehrige eventually relinquished court control of Richmond's schools and declared the school system "unitary," he acknowledged:

> The court finds . . . that, although it would be desirable to have greater balance than currently exists in the percentages of whites and blacks in Richmond public schools, such balance is not constitutionally required. As the Supreme Court has noted, there is no substantive constitutional right to a particular degree of racial balance or mixing.[25]

The court's endorsement of a return to neighborhood schools was not the only reason, however, why newly installed Superintendent Lois Harrison-Jones recommended abandoning the seven-year-old experiment with complexes. Despite the encouraging report of the JHW Visiting Committee, the complexes had failed to achieve their original purpose—cost reduction. In addition, between-school travel had grown wearisome and inconvenient, and many students and teachers longed for a return to the simpler days of single facilities. Robert Pratt wrote of Plan G's demise:

During its years of operation, Plan G remained controversial and unpopular. Critics argued that the plan was a fiscal failure, and that the notion of utilizing all facilities was expounded by administrators too timid to face the reality that eventually some schools would have to be closed. The students, supposedly the intended beneficiaries of the plan, never fully embraced it. Many of them disliked the idea of "their" school being merged with another; nor were they thrilled about the shuttle-bus rides that were now a part of their school day. They began to feel, as did their parents, that their school identity had been lost and that their traditions had been destroyed.[26]

The plan that called for a return to neighborhood schools and an end to complexes did entail one casualty. Maggie Walker High School was scheduled for closure, and arrangements were made for Community High School to be located in the Walker building. While Tee-Jay supporters breathed a sign of relief at this news, some must have wondered whether their school might be next. Declining school enrollments and budget problems, after all, had become trademarks of the Richmond Public Schools. It would not take very long for such fears to be confirmed.

Assessing the Impact

To what extent had seven years of merger with Huguenot and Wythe High Schools undermined what remained of Tee-Jay's traditions and special culture? The school had entered the complex years with its AP and honors courses largely intact, though dwindling in enrollments. These courses remained in 1986. In fact, their status actually may have improved as a result of receiving additional students from Wythe and Huguenot.

Tee-Jay began the complex years with the second highest percentage of white students of Richmond's seven comprehensive high schools. By 1986 Tee-Jay had surpassed Huguenot as the high school with the largest percentage of white students. The fact that Governor Charles Robb's, Lieutenant Governor Douglas Wilder's, and influential attorney Harold Marsh's daughters had opted to attend Tee-Jay certainly helped the school's image as a place where a quality education for whites and blacks still could be obtained.[27] Perhaps this explains why Tee-Jay's student population remained very stable during the complex years. Eighty-nine percent of Tee-Jay's seniors in 1984 had attended high school at the Jefferson building for all four years, compared to 79 percent for Huguenot and 74 percent for Wythe.[28] Morgan Edwards recalled that, during his twenty years at Tee-Jay, the school produced the student with the highest academic average in Richmond every year but one.

The seven-period day gave Tee-Jay students access to a greater variety of courses and extracurricular activities than their counterparts in other city high schools. This provision meant that the ideal of the well-rounded student remained alive and reasonably well at Tee-Jay.

Throughout the complex years, in subtle and sometimes obvious ways, Tee-Jay staff and students had acted to preserve their building's distinctiveness. The Jefferson building, for example, always had goals over and above those for its two sister buildings. The 1984 *Odyssey* described one such goal:

> A goal was set by the Jefferson Building principals for the highest level of achievement possible. It was decided that the seven-period day would be continued, but with a special emphasis on better use of time spent in study halls. A "one lunch period" was put into effect to prevent the loss of lunch and class time by travelling students. A stricter attendance policy was devised to encourage students to make it to school on time.[29]

When Tee-Jay returned to the status of a separate comprehensive school, faculty and students were elated and quickly went to work on a variety of school improvement efforts. Extracurricular programs, particularly in band and music, were rebuilt. The lilting chords of harp music filled the halls during fourth period as Mary Jane Smith guided students toward proficiency in that challenging instrument. A Junior Reserve Officer Training Corps (ROTC) was initiated. Science teacher Larry Volk induced large numbers of once-tentative students to tackle difficult labs and special projects. The results of this renewed commitment quickly became apparent. Four Tee-Jay students won the citywide Math Bowl and placed high in a statewide contest at Virginia Commonwealth University. Thirteen Advanced Placement history students commenced a two-year project to have their school declared a state and national landmark. Students in Advanced Placement physics and history undertook "The City Project," a year-long endeavor requiring them to study the relationship between science and government by "rebuilding" a small town on Virginia's Eastern Shore. Science students volunteered to work with physicians, dentists, veterinarians, teachers, physical therapists, and play directors in order to observe the practical applications of scientific theories.

School pride could hardly be concealed when writers for the 1988 yearbook reflected on the advent of Richmond's "Effective School Plan" the previous year:

> 1987 was the year of the "effective School Plan." The dominant themes became "All Can Learn" and "Striving for Excellence." Five correlates prevailed as the year progressed: strong instructional leadership, high expectations, emphasis on basic skills and academic achievement, a safe and orderly school climate, and continuous assessment of pupil progress. Teachers and students alike listened to this system-wide plan and pondered the "novelty" of it. After all, hadn't these *always* been priorities with Tee-Jay faculty and students![30]

SAVE OUR SCHOOL

"Thomas Jefferson Emerges As School Most Likely to Close." The front page headline in the *Richmond News Leader* of March 23, 1989, may have been expected by those who closely followed the deliberations of Richmond's school board, but the words shocked and upset Tee-Jay students, faculty, alumni still living in the Richmond area, and parents who expected to send their children to the school. Three years before, the reaffirmation of "neighborhood schools" by the school board had been regarded as Tee-Jay's new lease on life. Didn't the West End "neighborhood" deserve a high school like other sections of the city? What events had transpired during this brief period of time to produce such a startling reversal?

What did not happen between 1986 and 1989 may have been more important than what did happen. The financial situation of Richmond Public Schools did not improve, nor did enrollments increase. The circumstances that had led to the complex experiment, in other words, still remained. Maggie Walker's life as a comprehensive high school had ended in 1986, but school officials still believed that another high school needed to be shut down. Possible candidates included Armstrong, Kennedy, and Tee-Jay. Armstrong and Kennedy were geographically close, and their student bodies could be consolidated relatively easily. But Kennedy was one of the city's newest facilities, while Armstrong, though an older building, represented Richmond's last traditional all-black high school. A school with a proud tradition and a powerful group of alumni, Armstrong boasted many graduates among the leadership of Richmond Public Schools. For these individuals, Tee-Jay hardly evoked pleasant memories. The recollection of George Jones, a Richmond administrator, probably was typical:

> When I was a student at Armstrong [in the fifties] many of the books that we used came from Thomas Jefferson, and no attempt was made to conceal the fact that we were getting hand-me-down books because the "Thomas Jefferson" stamp was still in the books. The first Latin book I ever used was one that had been thrown out by Thomas Jefferson, with several pages torn out. That kind of thing was quite common.[31]

That Tee-Jay may have lacked friends in high places in the school system was not the only reason why it topped the list of possible closures. The school was, after all, the oldest high school in Richmond, and it needed substantial improvements, including asbestos removal and air conditioning. Relatively few of Tee-Jay's students actually resided in the West End—the neighborhoods west of the Boulevard. In addition, the demise of Maggie Walker in 1986 seemed to make the closure of a formerly all-white high school a political necessity. In many ways, therefore, Tee-Jay appeared to be the logical choice.

The timing also seemed right for closing Tee-Jay. The school system once again was in transition. Superintendent Lois Harrison-Jones, a staunch supporter of neighborhood schools, left Richmond to assume a high-level position with the Dallas Public Schools. Dr. James W. Tyler, a long-term administrator with the school system and superintendent from 1984 to 1985, came out of retirement to serve as interim superintendent while the board conducted a search for a new district leader. Tyler opted not to be a candidate. As a result, he was free to initiate a proposal to close Tee-Jay without having to live with the consequences. Tyler, indeed, took the position that Tee-Jay was not truly a "neighborhood school," since only 126 students lived close enough to walk to school.[32]

The *Richmond News Leader* endorsed Tyler's plan to close Tee-Jay. On March 24, 1989, two days following the announcement that Tee-Jay was the most likely candidate for closure, the newspaper printed an editorial entitled "Taps for TJ:"

Anyone tempted to think public service is easy hasn't followed the debate over Richmond's schools. Costs must be controlled, expenditures reduced. Enrollment in the city's public schools continues to decline. Therefore it makes sense to close schools and buildings, to consolidate certain programs in other buildings.

Deciding that something must be done is simple. The hard stuff comes when trying to decide which buildings to close, which schools to eliminate. Any proposal will draw protests—as officials for the Richmond schools are learning.

The school administration proposes to close either John Kennedy or Thomas Jefferson High Schools. Of the two, TJ (Or TeeJay) seems the logical candidate for closing. Its physical plant is much older than Kennedy's. And although the geographic area it serves includes many of the city's western neighborhoods, relatively few of its students come from the West End. If it is closed, the students will be transferred to other high schools. The school's building, however, could remain open—becoming the base for various specialized programs.

TJ's parents, students, and staff oppose the plan—for understandable reasons. Many Americans identify with their schools. A culture that worships adolescence holds sacred the symbols of youth. "Be True to Your School" is more than a beach tune. For better, or more likely for worse, it is a hymn. Class rings and class reunions, school decals and bumper stickers, cheerleaders and mascots: All reflect the devotion many people feel for their schools. (Often, though, one's feelings for his school intensify *after* he leaves it.) It makes no difference whether such devotion is good, bad, or neither. It is a fact.

Although closing TJ would disappoint students and alums, it would cause the least disruption. School officials estimate significant savings would result. TJ owns a treasured place in the city's educational history, but, sadly, its day is done.[33]

Less than a month later, another editorial concerning Tee-Jay appeared in the *Richmond News Leader*. This editorial reflected yet another reversal by the school board, one that, much to the newspaper's dismay, resuscitated the high school. The editorial, entitled "Anybody Home?," constituted a scathing indictment of the school board's unwillingness to make tough decisions. It opened as follows:

Because it would not agree on which of Richmond's six high schools to close, yesterday the city School Board voted to close none. Which prompts us to wonder whether, at the board, anybody besides the chairman is home.

Superintendent James Tyler had recommended closing 59-year-old Thomas Jefferson—a school (a) operating at only two-thirds capacity and (b) drawing only 126 of its students from west of the Boulevard. He said: "TJ is probably the least adequate building to house a senior high-school program."

And the board's commendable chairman, Leroy Hassell, agreed. But Hassell could not carry the ball alone—without other board-members in there doing some blocking and tackling.

Closing TJ would save half-a-million dollars annually; indeed, the board's requested budget for next year was based on closing at least one high school—as the board voted in December to do.[34]

Why had the school board suddenly shifted its position on closing Tee-Jay? The primary reason appears to have been an unprecedented campaign to keep the school open waged by students, faculty, alumni, and friends of the school. Following the distribution in February, 1989, of a school-district report entitled "Recommended Changes in Building Utilization," Tee-Jay supporters realized that the closing of Tee-Jay was part of a major cost-cutting initiative. Besides closing Tee-Jay, the plan also called for declaring surplus Maggie Walker, Blanton House, Hickory Hill School, Chandler Building, Navy Hill Building, and Grace Arents School. Eliminating the use of Tee-Jay as a comprehensive high school was estimated to save $483,459 a year.[35] Tee-Jay would be used to house programs previously located at Maggie Walker and Chandler. As shown in figure 5.1, John Marshall would pick up 126 Tee-Jay students, while Kennedy would receive 661 students.[36] Figure 5.2 indicates the school attendance boundaries and high school enrollments as of 1988–89.[37] Ironically, Tee-Jay's traditional archrival, John Marshall, would become the high school serving Richmond's West End if the new plan was implemented. To allow Kennedy to absorb many former Tee-Jay students, current Kennedy students living south of the James River would be reassigned to Armstrong and Wythe.

Mobilizing quickly, Tee-Jay supporters formed a grassroots organization called Save Our School (SOS). Among the most energetic organizers of SOS was Russell Flammia, a history teacher at Tee-Jay. Flammia had graduated from Tee-Jay in 1962, earned a

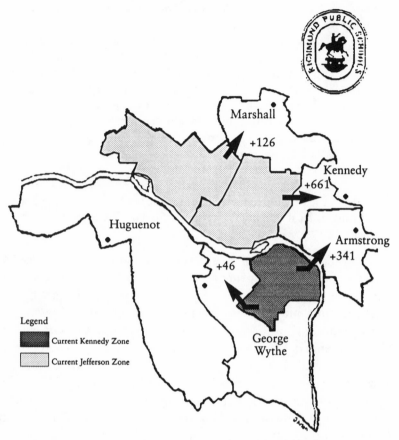

Richmond Public Schools Department of Planning and Development

FIGURE 5.1
1989–90 Proposed Changes to High School Zones Resulting from
Closing the Thomas Jefferson High School

bachelor"s degree at Frederick College, and returned to teach at
his alma mater in 1966. Flammia and colleagues like Jim Holdren
and Kathleen Hancock refused to forget what Tee-Jay had been
and still could be to the young people of Richmond. With the help
of influential Richmonders like Harold Marsh and Beverly Burton, fellow teachers, and students, Flammia and Jane Hastings,
another Tee-Jay faculty member, convened meetings, issued news-
letters, and gathered information to undercut the district's case for
closing Tee-Jay.

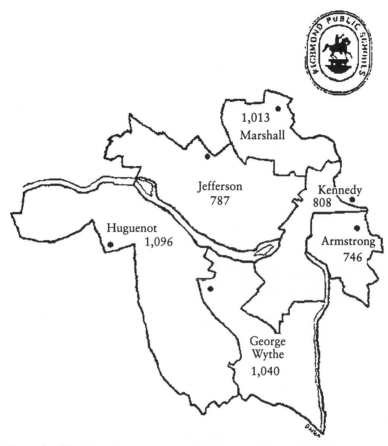

Richmond Public Schools Department of Planning and Development

FIGURE 5.2
1988–89 High School Zones

Among SOS's many arguments for keeping Tee-Jay open were the following:

- Closing Tee-Jay would constitute a reversal of the school board's stated goal of returning to neighborhood schools.
- Closing Tee-Jay "would discriminate against West End residents who must consider the accessibility of a continuum of school facilities (elementary, middle and high schools) when planning their children's education and deciding where to live in the Richmond area."[38]

- Tee-Jay offered more Advanced Placement courses than any other high school in Richmond.
- The cost of asbestos removal at Tee-Jay was far less than for many Richmond schools.[39]

Louis Timok, assistant principal, added to these arguments when interviewed by a newspaper reporter:

We have the only 13 (college level) AP (advanced placement) physics class in the city, the only 13 Advanced Placement history class in the city, and the only Keyette and Tri-Hi-Y clubs in the city. We offer the only advanced drama class, the only art photography class and the only television production class in the city.[40]

Science teacher Larry Volk noted,

Computer utilization at TeeJay is the largest in the city. We also have the most computer courses offered including computer concepts, basic programming, and PASCAL. We are the only high school that has competed in state computer competitions for the past two years.[41]

A key part of SOS's argument involved comparing the relative costs and benefits of closing Tee-Jay, Armstrong, and Kennedy. When Tee-Jay supporters reviewed district statistics on actual school membership and "present use capacity," they discovered the "percent utilization" figure for Tee-Jay was greater than for Armstrong or Kennedy (see table 5.1). Given the close proximity of Armstrong and Kennedy, Tee-Jay supporters wondered why the school board had not proposed absorbing Armstrong into Kennedy. Such a move also would have entailed less student dislocation than closing Tee-Jay, not to mention preserving the comprehensive high school with the best racial mix of Richmond's six comprehensive high schools. Had the school board abandoned the dream of integration? Did they believe that West End white parents would allow their children to be bused to John Marshall or Kennedy?

SOS was not the only group to question the wisdom of closing Tee-Jay. The Richmond Youth Council of the National Association for the Advancement of Colored People presented a report to the school board on March 22, 1989, proposing that Armstrong be closed.[42] The reasons for keeping Tee-Jay open matched many

TABLE 5.1
High School Membership and Building Utilization
September 1988

High School	Sept. 30 Membership	Present Use Capacity	Percent Utilization
Armstrong	746	1,215	61.40
Huguenot	1,096	1,189	92.18
Jefferson	787	1,177	66.86
Kennedy	808	1,580	51.14
Marshall	1,013	1,295	78.22
Wythe	1,040	1,465	70.99

of those raised by SOS. For example, the report noted that 1,174 students would be displaced if Tee-Jay closed, as opposed to 1,155 if Kennedy closed and 1,133 if Armstrong closed.[43] The report also tried to shift the focus of debate from economic concerns by maintaining that the greatest problem facing Richmond's schools involved keeping young people in school. It went on to suggest that further disruptions in the schooling of Richmond's young people was not the answer. The report constituted a dramatic acknowledgement by the civil rights group that the time for busing in Richmond had passed:

> We have silently watched as the school system has uprooted and displaced the young people in its attempts to solve the problems endangering the school system. From busing to achieve racial equality to the consolidation of schools into complexes to finally return to the idea of neighborhood schools. The students in the Richmond Public Schools have undergone many changes in recent times. Now that the youth of Richmond are finally in their respective neighborhood schools, there is a movement to close some of those schools and the cycle begins once again.[44]

Besides the NAACP Youth Council's report, hundreds of letters in support of Tee-Jay were sent to newspapers, school board members, and Tee-Jay administrators. Morgan Edwards, for example, received the following letter from one West End resident:

February 28, 1989

Dear Mr. Edwards:

As a taxpayer and a parent, I need to say that I find the proposal to disband Thomas Jefferson High School to be an
extremely unsatisfactory proposal. I cannot overemphasize the
importance of maintaining T.J. as a traditional High School,
serving the Central Richmond area (West End/Fan), and I ask
that the proposal be reconsidered.

We came to this area school because of its academic excellence and because of the *programs* it has to offer which were not
available in the other City schools. . . .

I feel *real estate* would be affected by an exodus of families
who might have found adequate middle school provisions in
Central Richmond (Hill & Binford) but would not have access
to a nearby High School. There has already been a mass exodus
from the city to the counties (because of busing), I would hate to
see it continue.

Consider further: not only does T.J. provide 10 *special education* classrooms, it is also the only High School equipped for
the handicapped. To modify another school for such use would
be an un-necessary duplication of expenditures. . . .

Louise Lipscomb, the mother of a 1988 Tee-Jay graduate, sent
this letter to interim superintendent Dr. James Tyler:

March 6, 1989

Dear Dr. Tyler:

I have been very disturbed to see the recommendation that
the school administration should close Thomas Jefferson High
School's regular academic program.

I protest this decision because I know it would cause a great
loss to the Fan neighborhood where I have lived for more than
twenty years and sent my children to the Richmond Public
Schools which were available to us. . . .

My son, Thomas Lipscomb, is a 1988 graduate of Thomas
Jefferson. He began his education at William Fox School where
he learned reading, writing, and arithmetic from a wonderful
group of teachers led by a fine principal. Then he moved to
Albert Hill Middle School and entered an advanced program
that allowed him to start taking high school level subjects while
still in middle school. Because of this advanced program plan,
Thomas was, by his senior year, eligible to take all 13 Advanced
Placement courses. Thomas Jefferson provided him with these

advancement [*sic*] placement courses in calculus, English, physics, French, and history.

My son found a number of very able teachers at Thomas Jefferson, especially during this junior and senior years in the school. Because of his hard work and their good teaching, he achieved significant honors—He was the only student in all of Richmond schools, both public and private, who was a National Merit Scholar in 1988. The University of Virginia invited him to enter there as an Echols Scholar. His mother held her breath when he left Thomas Jefferson for the Big University, thinking that her little boy would have a hard time adjusting academically in that much more complicated environment. Furthermore, she worried because Thomas had signed up for advanced classes in calculus, physics, English composition, and ancient and medieval history. She needn't have—His lowest grade for first semester was a B+ in physics. . . .

Tee-Jay teachers added their voices to the chorus of criticism concerning the school's closure. Jane Hastings, for example, focused part of her February 28, 1989, letter to the *Richmond News Leader* on the importance of neighborhood schools in light of the abortive complex experiment:

But there was a positive lesson we learned from this failure: the re-emergence of neighborhood schools. I teach at Thomas Jefferson High School; the re-birth of school bonds, long dead during the Jefferson-Huguenot-Wythe days, is a welcome change. The students hang around after school, becoming a part of activities again at their neighborhood school. At night, public transportation routes allow our students and parents without cars to come to school events. Ask our principal; he has been overwhelmed by the positive parental involvement since the neighborhood concept was reinstated two years ago.

Do we really want to doom listless students to another cycle of non-participation at another cross-town bused-to strange building in an unfamiliar neighborhood? Couldn't we, just once, figure out a way to cut costs without sacrificing the positive experiences that involve students and their families in a neighborhood school?

While letters such as these and the NAACP Youth Council report played an important role in causing the school board to reconsider the idea of closing Tee-Jay, perhaps nothing had a greater impact on their plans than the march staged by Tee-Jay students and faculty on March 22, 1989. Described in the introduction, the march commenced at Tee-Jay after lunch and ended at City Hall, where the school board had scheduled a special hearing on school closures. Anticipating a packed board room, Tee-Jay students arrived four hours early in order to secure as many seats as possible. In the end, spectators and supporters of other high schools who were unable to get inside the chambers had to watch the hearings on closed-circuit television monitors set up in hallways. The *Richmond News Leader* reported that almost fifty people spoke, and all but one asked the school board to reexamine the alternatives to closing Tee-Jay or Kennedy.[45] West End parents complained that there was little point in paying high taxes if they could not provide their children with neighborhood schools. Predictions of another exodus of West End families from Richmond Public Schools were heard. Tee-Jay student Nsenga Burton opposed school closure because Tee-Jay was "the academic leader of all Richmond high schools" and boasted unduplicated community service programs.[46] Burton went on to decry the "political motivation" behind the closure threat and to point out that students did not appreciate "being used in a power struggle."

The notion that closing Tee-Jay was motivated by "politics" was one of the most frequently heard criticisms during the late winter and early spring of 1989. A headline in the April 13, 1989, *Richmond Times-Dispatch*, in fact, revealed that even Tee-Jay's principal, Morgan Edwards, believed the school board was acting for reasons other than the best interests of students. "Bid to Close Jefferson Is Political, Chief Says" headed the article pitting Edwards against his superiors in the school system. The courageous administrator stated,

> It's a political ballgame so you eliminate logic when you play politics. We only hope the board will see fit to make a decision that will benefit citizens and students of Richmond. . . . The only logical approach is to have a school in every section of the city.

Whether Edwards's opposition to Tee-Jay's closure figured in his decision to step down as principal the following year is not known.

On April 18, 1989, the school board met in regular session and voted six-to-one not to close any comprehensive high school.[47] While the primary factor in the board reversal clearly seemed to have been the extent of public opposition, board chair Leroy Hassell noted that Board members themselves had been unable to agree on which high school should be closed as far back as December, when they decided that one of the six facilities needed to be shut down. In reporting the board's decision, Hassell took time to commend all the students who advocated for their schools, noting that they had behaved responsibly and communicated effectively. Later, Morgan Edwards would express a similar opinion:

> Everything was done in a fine manner. There was no belligerence or threats of violence. We studied the plan and found problems with it. We talked to Board members. We invited Board members to the school to talk to students.

Such conduct was what people had come to expect of Tee-Jay students and faculty. And they did not disappoint. No collection of supporters from the "glory days" could have performed any more admirably than these latter-day advocates. In a fitting finale to a year of surprises, plunging spirits, and emotional peaks, Lieutenant Governor Lawrence Douglas Wilder, soon to be the nation's first popularly elected black Governor, addressed Tee-Jay's graduating seniors on June 15, 1989:

> Of course, for Thomas Jefferson High School, today marks a particularly significant watershed in the long and proud history of this school and its people: its students, alumni, teachers and administrators—among whom is my own daughter Lynn, a graduate of this fine school and one of those individuals who helped place my name in nomination at the Democratic Convention last Saturday.
>
> Indeed, because of the efforts of so many dedicated people here today, there *will* be other graduating classes of Thomas Jefferson; there *will* be Friday night football games; there *will* be alumni who—like yourselves—will look back on their years at Thomas Jefferson with a fondness and warmth that mere words cannot describe.
>
> When threatened with the prospect that your school would be closed, the Thomas Jefferson community—students, parents, teachers, and others—rallied to save an institution that has meant so much to so many persons in the years since its doors first opened.[48]

History is fascinating because it is full of ironies. The image of hundreds of students, mostly black, marching in orderly fashion down Broad Street to protest the threatened closure of a high school that three decades earlier epitomized white elitism could hardly have been more striking. These students had barely begun to savor their victory, however, when the prospect of a new challenge for Tee-Jay surfaced.

Even before the board officially reversed its stance on school closure, Richmond school officials had applied for a $2.5 million federal grant to create a magnet school at Tee-Jay.[49] The two-year grant would permit the school, if it were allowed to remain open, to develop a variety of offerings in the area of international studies. Assistant Superintendent for Secondary Education Lucille Brown justified such a magnet school "because of the thrust of the commonwealth of Virginia to expand its economic base."[50] If the grant was awarded on June 30, 1989, Tee-Jay could become the Thomas Jefferson Magnet School for Governmental and International Relations in September.

THE ATTRACTION OF MAGNETS

Richmond was not the first city to explore the possibility of converting comprehensive high schools to magnet schools. In fact, it was relatively slow to give serious consideration to this innovation. By 1989, when school officials applied for a federal grant to support Tee-Jay's conversion, cities such as Houston, New York, and Kansas City had been experimenting with magnets for years. The federal government began promoting magnet schools in the seventies under the Emergency School Aid Act (ESAA). The intended purpose was "to help segregated school districts develop desegregation plans that not only guaranteed educational equity for poor and minority students but would provide *all* students with a vastly improved education."[51] The Magnet Schools Assistance Program (MSAP) replaced ESAA as the impetus for magnet school development in the next decade, thereby sustaining the federal government's commitment to "voluntary integration."

Of magnet schools, Mary Haywood Metz has written:

> Magnet schools have stirred considerable interest in the United States. They are racially mixed public schools which draw students on a voluntary basis by offering educational innovations

which are attractive to parents. They appeal to many educational constituencies by simultaneously creating desegregation without mandatory busing and an opportunity to blow a fresh breeze of educational innovation into city school systems.[52]

The assessment of magnet schools by two urban education scholars, however, is less positive:

> Several cities have also tried to keep their remaining middle-class students and reduce class and racial segregation within urban school districts by implementing selective academic and/or magnet schools. For the most part, however, the creation of these schools has produced ambiguous results. Although some of them have been able to provide "islands" of quality education, in many cities they have also functioned to increase class distinctions within city school systems.[53]

The school board's willingness to permit school officials to seek federal assistance for a magnet school at Tee-Jay, in retrospect, might seem to be yet another example of policy reversal. A basic feature of magnet schools, after all, is the recruitment of students from all sections of the school system. These schools, therefore, could be regarded as incompatible with the "neighborhood schools" policy adopted by the Richmond Board in 1986.

While such an interpretation of the district's application for federal magnet school funds is possible, an alternative explanation is simple opportunism. The school board and their administrative staff seemed prone, especially during the late eighties, to grasp at any straw that might provide fiscal relief. The prospect of a $2.5 million grant was sufficiently attractive to the financially strapped school system that policy consistency might be set aside.

Whether concurrent threats to close Tee-Jay jeopardized the school's chances of winning the magnet school grant is unknown. In any event, the grant was not awarded to Richmond Public Schools. That the school system continued to pursue the idea of magnet schools, despite the lack of outside funding, seems to suggest that opportunism alone cannot explain the district's interest in high school options. It should be added, however, that no evidence exists that magnet schools were viewed by district officials as a deliberate effort to undermine the neighborhood schools policy. Perhaps the best explanation for the district's initiative is the fact that Richmond's new superintendent, Dr. Albert L. Jones, took a personal interest in magnet schools as a mechanism for "restructuring" the school system.

Previously deputy superintendent in Wichita, Kansas, Jones became superintendent of Richmond Public Schools on July 1, 1989. Soon thereafter he called for the creation of a magnet school task force to be chaired by Virginia Commonwealth University professor Dr. John Pisapia. The task force presented its recommendations to the school board on January 3, 1990.[54] Among the thirteen recommendations was a proposal that three magnet "programs" be initiated in the fall of 1990. The task force specifically asked that the experiments be referred to as "programs" rather than "schools" until they had grown sufficiently large to justify the latter term. Tee-Jay was targeted for a magnet program in governmental and international relations, while Kennedy and Wythe were designated as sites for math/science computer-based technology and visual and performing arts programs. The intention was for each magnet program to coexist with the regular comprehensive high school program. Efforts were to be made to allow nonmagnet students to participate in magnet courses and activities.

Besides endorsing these recommendations, Dr. Jones accepted the task force's suggestion that each magnet program be phased in over a four-year period, beginning with one hundred ninth-grade students per program in 1990–91. Each year thereafter, one grade level would be added until a full four-year program was in existence at all three high schools. On the all-important question of funding, the task force urged that magnet programs be paid for out of regular district funds, which presumably would become available as a result of "redirecting current resources and increasing the cost effectiveness of the system."[55]

By the time the task force delivered its report on January 3, 1990, no doubt existed that the superintendent was committed to launching magnet programs the following fall. In fact, promotional brochures already had been printed by January 3! In addition, Dr. Jones had met with various political and business leaders to gain support for the magnet programs and secure financial backing. Richmond corporations like Ethyl, Philip Morris, James River Corporation, and Reynolds Metals, each with extensive operations abroad, took particular interest in Tee-Jay's proposed international relations focus.[56]

It is interesting to note that the original promotional material on Richmond's magnet programs specifically denied that the impetus for the new programs involved a desire "to draw more white students to Richmond schools."[57] One brochure indicated that,

> In most cities, magnet schools have been created as part of a desegregation plan for that very reason. In other areas, they are strictly for students with special aptitudes in the school's theme. . . . In Richmond, neither is the case.
>
> The magnet schools should attract students from surrounding areas, and will allow for a distribution of students without regard to where they live. However, the magnet concept represents a restructuring of how education is delivered and made meaningful to students. This remains regardless of the racial characteristics of the school system.

Did such a statement imply that Richmond no longer was concerned about school integration? Might the adoption, first of neighborhood schools, and now of magnet programs, signify that the existing demographics of the school system had been accepted as immutable? Or was the wording of the brochure simply a ploy to take the spotlight off integration while the school system quietly attempted to build the types of academic programs that could reattract white parents from the city as well as lure back suburban emigres?

Whatever the actual motives of school officials, the fact was that many parents, white and black, found the new magnet programs attractive. Kennedy filled all one hundred slots in its math/science/technology magnet program, while Tee-Jay attracted sixty students, including "about 30 white students who previously had attended private schools" and a number of students from suburban school systems.[58] Besides coursework in English and social studies, the "core offerings" from which students in the program could select their course of study included global science, various mathematics courses stressing "global applications," and a wealth of foreign language courses (see table 5.2). Mary Maddox would have been proud of the emphasis on international perspectives and the overt rejection of parochialism.

A brochure distributed to would-be magnet students indicated that the program was designed to "increase understanding of different cultures, to create proficiency in one or more foreign languages, to expose students to governmental and international careers, and to instill basic skills useful in higher education and in

TABLE 5.2
Core Program for International and Governmental Studies

Academic Area	Grade 9	Grade 10	Grade 11	Grade 12
English	Cross-Cultural Studies in English	World Literature	American Literature	English Literature
Social Studies	Comparative World Cultures	World History and Geography	Virginia and US History	Virginia and US Government
Foreign Language	French I Spanish I German I Russian I Italian I Latin I	French II Spanish II German II Russian II Italian II Latin II	French III Spanish III German III Russian III Italian III Latin III	French IV Spanish IV German IV Russian IV Italian IV Latin IV
Science	Global Science Biology	Biology BSCS Chemistry	Chemistry	
Mathematics	Basic Algebra with Global Applications Elementary Algebra with Gobal Applications Geometry	Elementary Algebra with Global Applications Geometry Intermediate Algebra with Global Applications	Algebra/Geometry Intermediate Algebra with Global Applications Trigonometry	

Academic Area	Grade 9	Grade 10	Grade 11	Grade 12
Physical Education	Health and Physical Education	Health and Physical Education		
Other Requirements	Computer Literacy Grade 9 or 10			

global careers." To these ends, students were required to complete a four-year course of study in a foreign language, four years of global studies and language arts, three years of mathematics and science, and a concentration in one area of specialized study. The latter possibilities included "International Business and Technology," "Foreign Language and Culture," and "International and Governmental Studies" (see table 5.3). Additionally, all magnet students were expected to participate in "cultural experiences, field trips, and international events and tours.

To head the new Tee-Jay, now called the Thomas Jefferson High School Center for Comprehensive and International Magnet Programs, Albert Jones hired Gordon Hill, only the school's fifth principal in six decades. Hill's background and experience constituted a perfect blend for the high school's new identity. Prior to coming to Richmond, the affable and energetic Hill had served as an administrative assistant to the superintendent of a North Chicago school district. Before getting into school administration, he had served in the United States Diplomatic Service in London, Stockholm, and other European venues. His graduate work at Teachers College, Columbia University, afforded Hill an opportunity to study the politics of education, a concentration he came to believe would serve him well in the highly political atmosphere of Richmond Public Schools. Hill's commitments to integration and a global perspective were personal as well as professional, as symbolized by his interracial marriage to a Swedish woman and decision to live in an integrated Richmond neighborhood.

To serve as one of his two magnet program coordinators as well as an assistant principal, Hill selected Dr. Cassandra Fletcher, a black educator who also boasted extensive international experience. Fletcher had earned a Bachelor of Arts degree in Romance Languages and Literatures and African American Studies at Radcliffe, a Master of Arts degree from Georgetown University in Latin American Studies, and a Doctor of Philosophy degree from Florida State University in International/Intercultural Development Education. She had studied, worked, and lived in Europe, the Caribbean, and South America. In her words, "early exposure to the global community has convinced [me] that high school is the right place and time to implement a curriculum and educational experiences which will broaden students' views of world cultures, develop their understanding of global economics, instill a sense of commitment to development, inculcate a sense of

TABLE 5.3
Study Track Electives

	Grades 10 and 11	Grade 12
International Business and Technology	Keyboarding Applications Accounting International Business Economics Fundamentals of Marketing International Marketing II Chemistry Trigonometry	International Business Law International Business Management Business Computer Applications Office Systems International Marketing III and IV Chemistry and Chemistry AP Trigonometry Calculus
Language and International Culture (two years of a second foreign language are needed)	French I Spanish I German I Russian I Italian I Latin I Art Photography I International Art Band Choir Drama Food Management Occupational Foods	French II Spajish II German II Italian II Latin II Art Photography II Advanced Art Studies Band Choir Drama Photojournalism Family Living International Catering
International and Governmental Studies	Administration of Criminal Justice International Political Leadership International Law	American Foreign Policy and Diplomatic History Comparative Political Philosophy Intercultural Affairs

responsibility for the earth, and promote values of peace, freedom, and social justice."[59]

With talented leaders like Hill and Fletcher, strong community and business support, a superintendent committed to magnet programs, and an innovative curriculum, Tee-Jay's future as of the fall of 1990 looked bright. That the school had teetered on the brink of closure sixteen months earlier seemed remote, a bad dream from a bygone era. Teachers and students looked forward to a renewal of the Tee-Jay tradition of excellence, this time with a curricular focus that would have delighted the school's namesake.

CHAPTER 6

The Challenge of Coexistence

Students of human nature claim that with age comes complexity. So, too, perhaps with organizations. As Tee-Jay commenced its sixth decade, it was vastly more complex than it had been in the early years. Where once operated a single school with a relatively homogeneous student body, there now coexisted an urban comprehensive high school and a magnet program serving a racially and socioeconomically diverse clientele. Soon a regional Governor's School would be located at the same site, adding even greater complexity. Tee-Jay's teachers and administrators reluctantly acknowledged that complexity and coexistence had become keys to survival. Soon they would learn that even keys to survival can pose a threat under certain conditions.

The chapter opens with a brief account of the 1990–91 school year, the first year of the joint comprehensive high school/magnet program. The creation at Tee-Jay of the Governor's School for Government and International Studies is the focus of the next section. The chapter closes with the subsequent struggle to prevent the Governor's School from completely replacing Tee-Jay.

FROM SPOTLIGHT TO SHADOWS

For many of those who had worked and studied at Tee-Jay when it was a premier comprehensive high school, the advent of the magnet program in international and governmental studies was a mixed blessing. They acknowledged that the magnet program constituted a form of insurance, but only a short-term policy. In a November 1990 article on the new magnet program, Dr. Cassandra Fletcher was cited as saying that the comprehensive school would be phased out by 1993, leaving only the magnet program.[1] Fletcher was careful to add that "the administration is building on TJ's past reputation (distinguished alumni, trophies, etc.) to fashion a new school" and that she hoped the community would rally behind the effort. Two months later, the *Richmond Times-Dispatch* carried news of a phase-out at Tee-Jay, but this time the yet-to-open Governor's School was the impetus.[2] The article noted that the comprehensive high school would cease operation by 1994, but the fate of Tee-Jay's fledgling magnet program was not discussed. Tee-Jay supporters optimistically assumed that the magnet program, which by this time had gotten off to an encouraging start, would be safe—allowed to coexist with the similarly focused Governor's School. Within several months, however, these hopes, too, had all but died, the victim of intense political maneuvering.

The recent history of Tee-Jay is a chronicle of dramatically fluctuating expectations. No sooner did faculty and students breathe a sigh of relief than a new crisis arose to dampen spirits and deflect energies. Education is about change, but the process of individual change, interestingly, seems to benefit from a measure of organizational stability.[3] Trying to operate a comprehensive high school and a magnet program for urban youth is challenging enough without the added burden of battling to survive. It is a credit to Tee-Jay's reputation that so many teachers and students decided to stay around and fight for their school instead of requesting transfers elsewhere. Apparently they believed that Tee-Jay was worth fighting for.

Evidence of this commitment can be seen in the enthusiasm with which magnet program students and teachers addressed rising sophomores in June of 1991.[4] Their purpose was to interest members of the audience in enrolling in the magnet program, despite the fact that by this time the program, along with Tee-Jay itself, had been scheduled to cease operation in a few years. Ronnie Boodoo, a student in the ninth grade completing his—and the program's—first year, acknowledged, "The magnet program is a challenge for each one of us." He went on to note, "We learned a lot. The magnet program supports us in every way. We work in unity." Jean McClenney, a teacher in the magnet program, added, "We will take these kids as far as we can as long as we have them."

Despite the prospect of imminent closure that clouded much of the program's first year, magnet students still performed well. Preliminary assessments in the spring of 1991 indicated that the sixty magnet students had "better attendance, grades and class participation than non-magnet peers."[5] An article on Richmond's pilot magnet programs pointed out that Tee-Jay teachers and parents believed that the lower student-teacher ratio in the magnet program contributed to more positive student attitudes and greater self-esteem.[6] Half of the twenty-six Tee-Jay students who earned honor roll status in the fall of 1990 came from the magnet program.

As the new magnet program began to attract press coverage, teachers in the comprehensive high school sometimes sensed their contributions were being overlooked. They noted that magnet classes tended to be small, around fifteen students, and that resources provided by corporate and governmental sponsors afforded magnet students opportunities unavailable to others. For example, magnet students attended the annual stockholders' meeting at Ethyl Corporation and served as interns with the city council and Chamber of Commerce.

Defenders of the magnet program were quick to point out that students in the comprehensive high school could take magnet courses as long as space was available and that dignitaries visiting the magnet program often addressed the entire Tee-Jay student body. They also countered accusations of elitism by noting that student interest was the sole criterion for admission to the magnet program. Magnet students represented no specially selected group of talented students.

While the magnet program attracted more attention than the comprehensive high school and doubtless engendered some jealousies within the faculty, few Tee-Jay supporters could dispute the fact that the new program had helped to revive the school's image as an academic leader, a school with so much to offer that it once again justified a commute from the suburbs or transfer from a private school. Tee-Jay students could choose to take Italian, Russian, French, Spanish, German, or Latin. Japanese was scheduled to be offered in the fall of 1991. Field trips took students to the World Bank, the Saudi Arabian Embassy, the National Gallery of Art, and a private dinner with and lecture by former West German chancellor Helmut Schmidt. The "Computer Concepts" class allowed Tee-Jay students to communicate directly with peers in Florida, Canada, and France, as part of the innovative AT&T Learning Network.

The impressive accomplishments of Tee-Jay's magnet program during the 1990–91 school year only heightened incredulity that the school system actually intended to shut down Tee-Jay by 1994. Tee-Jay supporters, once again, were left asking, Why?

The answer to their query lay less in the realm of logic than the province of politics. At the March 19, 1990, meeting of the Richmond school board, Dr. Albert Jones expressed gratitude to Delegate Frank Hall and his fellow Richmond representatives for their assistance in securing funds from the General Assembly to help in planning a government/international magnet at Tee-Jay.[7] At the same time, he also mentioned that negotiations were under way with the Virginia Department of Education to obtain the designation of "Governor's School" for Tee-Jay. Jones went on to point out, "Such a designation will require regional participation (such as presently exists with the Math-Science Center)."[8] At the time, no one seemed overly concerned that this expanded vision for Tee-Jay actually might jeopardize the high school's future. An editorial in the *Richmond News Leader* several months later, however, pointed out that the case for closing Tee-Jay had been complicated by plans to locate a Governor's School at the site.[9] The newspaper supported closing Tee-Jay as a cost-cutting measure and moving the Governor's School to a different location.

On April 3, 1990, Superintendent Jones reported to the school board that negotiations regarding a Governor's School at Tee-Jay were continuing with the Department of Education.[10] Furthermore, he indicated discussing the matter with neighboring school divisions which might send students to such a regional magnet school. No mention was made of the possible impact of a Governor's School on the then soon-to-open Tee-Jay magnet program or the comprehensive high school and its more than 600 students. Whether Jones had already decided that Tee-Jay would be phased out in the event that a Governor's School could be placed at the site was not known. Governor's School director Dr. Steven E. Ballowe told a newspaper reporter in August of 1991, however, that Jones had spoken in terms of a regional school serving "up to 200 students" on a "part-time" basis.[11] If this were the case, Jones's modest vision for the Governor's School might not have required the eventual closing of Tee-Jay. The only time that Jones mentioned target enrollment figures for the Governor's School in a public school board meeting occurred on May 7, 1991.[12] On this occasion, he announced that the Governor's School for Government and International Studies would open in the fall of 1991 and enroll 100 ninth graders. He added that another 200 to 250 students would participate in special programs at the Governor's School. Perhaps this reference explains where Ballowe got his figure of 200 part-time students. Jones also was quoted in the board minutes as stating that "students currently attending Thomas Jefferson will continue to do so, including students in the magnet program" and that "the tenth, eleventh, and twelfth grade levels will offer a comprehensive educational curriculum."

Unfortunately, Dr. Jones did not remain superintendent long enough to clarify any discrepancies or misunderstandings over projected enrollment figures. A month later, in June, the school board voted four to three to remove Jones "without cause."[13] The *Richmond Times-Dispatch* claimed that Jones was "often perceived as an arrogant outsider by Richmond's closely knit public education community."[14] Other allegations concerned his mishandling of consulting contracts, salary overpayments, and late buses.[15]

Several insiders insisted that Jones had "promised" State officials and Richmond delegates that, if arrangements for a Governor's School at Tee-Jay could be worked out, the comprehensive high school would be shut down. Whether these individuals actually pressed for Tee-Jay's closure cannot be determined with any degree of certainty. One individual close to the superintendent felt strongly, however, that a "conspiracy" had long existed to rid the West End of its only comprehensive high school. The implication was that certain influential Richmonders preferred that the facility in this fashionable part of the city enroll talented students from various school divisions rather than large numbers of Richmond youth.

The possibility that behind-the-scenes promises to phase out Tee-Jay had been made began to seem more plausible when Albert Jones' successor, Lucille Brown, went on record as supporting the coexistence at Tee-Jay of the comprehensive high school, the magnet program and the regional Governor's School. A graduate of Armstrong High School and a veteran of thirty-four years with Richmond Public Schools, Brown had championed initial efforts in 1989 to launch a magnet program with an international focus at Tee-Jay. Opposition to her coexistence proposal quickly surfaced among a number of powerful Richmonders. Observers claimed that these individuals intended to hold Brown's "feet to the fire" so she would honor her predecessor's alleged "agreement." When the Governor's School opened in the fall of 1991, Tee-Jay consequently was not permitted to enroll a freshman class. For Tee-Jay advocates, the beginning of the end had begun—again. Before trying to sort out these complicated matters, however, some background information on the creation of the Governor's School is necessary.

A GOVERNOR'S SCHOOL COMES TO TEE-JAY

In the early eighties, states and local school districts throughout the country explored a variety of strategies for promoting educational excellence. One strategy, initiated by North Carolina and emulated by Virginia and other states, was the regional Governor's School. The basic idea was straightforward—bring together under one roof a specially selected group of bright, motivated students from various school systems and provide them with opportunities to concentrate on a specific area of study while meeting other graduation requirements. The ultimate goal was for graduates of these specialized "brain farms" to attend the best colleges and eventually enter the workforce, thereby helping the United States regain its competitive edge in the world economy. The perceived need for Governor's Schools implied that some observers no longer felt conventional comprehensive high schools were capable of producing the talent needed to go head to head with Germany and Japan.

The first Governor's School in the Richmond area was created in 1983 at Varina High School in Henrico County during the administration of Governor Charles S. Robb. State support for the venture, which concentrated on technology, declined in the late eighties; but the state continued to fund broadcasts of advanced courses from Varina to students throughout the commonwealth. When the idea of a Governor's School devoted to the study of government and international affairs was proposed for the Tee-Jay site, Governor Wilder and his Secretary of Education, James Dyke, expressed interest. Wilder later provided the following letter to open a promotional brochure on "his" Governor's School. It is interesting to note that no acknowledgement was made that the school was located at Tee-Jay.

Dear Friends of the Governor's School:

Having long encouraged our Commonwealth's students to learn about their contemporaries the world around, and having worked with legislators and educators to facilitate such interaction, I am delighted to participate in the opening of The Governor's School for Government and International Studies.

This school highlights many of the approaches being suggested and planned for Virginia's schools of the 21st Century. Such concepts as variety in school programs, active parental involvement, school-business partnerships, regional cooperation, international academic standards and building-based management are the foundation for study at this Governor's School.

It is pleasing, too, to see community service as a requirement for graduation. Governor's School students will one day become leaders in our state with a greater appreciation for giving, rather than always receiving. These principles are cornerstones for integrating Virginia and her people into a peaceful and prosperous world community.

As Governor of Virginia, I encourage every eligible student to apply for admittance to our new Governor's School for Government and International Studies, and I ask each parent to support its programs, faculty and student body. This center of education excellence can serve not only as a model for Virginia but as a lighthouse in shaping national and international programs.

With best wishes, I am

Very truly yours,

Lawrence Douglas Wilder

The description of the Governor's School that followed Wilder's introductory letter informed readers that the venture resulted from a partnership of nine school districts, including the cities of Richmond, Petersburg, Colonial Heights, and Hopewell, and the counties of Charles City, Chesterfield, Goochland, Hanover, and Henrico. Nothing was said about the initiative of Albert Jones or the leadership role played by Richmond Public Schools.

The goals of the Governor's School reflected the spirit of the seminal 1983 reform document, "A Nation at Risk." Emphasis was placed on a rigorous curriculum, high expectations, and innovative instruction. As the following mission statement indicated, the school intended to serve as a center for professional development as well as college preparatory studies.

The Governor's School for Government and International Studies provides opportunities for:

- international learning experiences including instruction by satellite transmission and other innovative approaches
- participation in academic studies through total immersion in foreign language
- learning activities conducted by representatives from worldwide academic and business communities
- mentorships, internships and seminars with local, state and national government officials as well as representative from foreign nations
- comprehensive, differentiated, interdisciplinary instructional strategies for gifted students
- acceleration and in-depth studies beyond the usual high school curriculum.

The Governor's School for Government and International Studies provides programs designed to help its students become:

- independent, life-long learners
- problem solvers with skills in individual as well as group problem solving
- skillful communicators with ability to listen, to write, and to speak clearly and effectively
- risk takers who are skillful in developing and maintaining interpersonal relationships
- creative contributors and critical consumers in society
- citizens who are socially and ethically responsible.

The Governor's School for Government and International Studies supports regional and national efforts to strengthen education through infusion of an international perspective across the curriculum by:

- serving as a center for curriculum development
- providing in-service opportunities for teachers throughout the international community to stay abreast in their fields of government and international studies
- offering outreach programs for other students designed to strengthen their achievement in government and international studies and to stimulate their interests in this field of studies
- serving as a model for private sector/public education partnerships.

While high school students in Richmond needed twenty-three units of credit to earn an advanced studies diploma and twenty-one units of credit for a regular diploma, Governor's School students were required to earn twenty-nine units of credit. The recommended course of study included the following distributional requirements:

English	4 units of credit
Math	3 units of credit
Science	3 units of credit
Social Studies	4 units of credit
International Languages	6 units of credit (4 units of one, 2 in another)
Health & PE	2 units of credit
Fine Arts or Practical Arts	1 unit of credit
Strand Electives	3 units of credit (may not overlap with above)
Electives	2 units of credit
Community Service	1 unit of credit
Total units of credit required	29 units of credit

Strand electives represented opportunities for independent research in a major area of concentration during the eleventh and twelfth grades. Strands included diplomacy and international relations, international business and technology, international language, science and international relations, and medicine and world needs. Community service entailed a minimum of 180 hours of service, typically accomplished during the ninth grade.

Upstairs, Downstairs

When the Governor's School opened in September of 1991, interactions among students, teachers, and administrators of the three units that now constituted the Thomas Jefferson International Center generally were courteous. Cooperation appeared to be essential, given the fact that the Governor's School, which occupied most of the top floor of Tee-Jay, had to share library, cafeteria, auditorium, and athletic facilities with its downstairs neighbors. Despite these links, or perhaps because of them, relations became increasingly strained as the year progressed.

One of the earliest sources of friction concerned rules and norms of conduct. Gordon Hill and his staff, like their predecessors, had devoted considerable time and energy to maintaining an orderly school climate at Tee-Jay. Given the diverse student body with which they worked and the concern for student safety voiced by Richmond parents, Tee-Jay staff members felt the need to emphasize "preventive" discipline. Hallways were patrolled regularly to reduce loitering and tardiness. Students were expected to dress neatly and deal with teachers in a respectful manner. In-school and out-of-school suspensions were used on occasion to handle serious cases of misconduct.

Governor's School students marched to the beat of a different drummer. Selected on the basis of aptitude, intention to attend college, and interest in academic subjects, these students were regarded by their teachers as responsible and capable of mature behavior. As a result, they were allowed a looser rein. Sometimes they were found on the lower floors going to and from the library or other centers of activity during class periods. They were not required to carry hall passes like Tee-Jay students. Their dress and appearance did not always match the expectations of the Tee-Jay faculty. Unlike their Tee-Jay counterparts, Governor's School students were allowed to eat in the halls.

Complaints about the conduct of Governor's School students arose at the same time that the realization began to strike Tee-Jay teachers and administrators that their school's days were numbered. Governor's School staff tended, therefore, to dismiss complaints from "downstairs" as "sour grapes." No formal mechanism existed to facilitate communication between the units, nor was one created in the face of mounting tension. Gordon Hill, in an interview with the author, was struck by the irony of the situation: "Here we are trying to teach about global affairs and international relations in our two schools and we don't even talk to each other from one floor to another!"

Another source of concern involved resources. During one interview, Gordon Hill pointed to Jonathan Kozol's recently published book, Savage Inequalities, which he had just read and shared with Tee-Jay students in an assembly program, and said, "Savage inequalities don't just exist between adjacent school systems. We have them here in the same school building." Besides the tuition paid by each sending district (approximately $3,100 in 1991–92), the Governor's School received a grant of $350,000 directly from the state. Despite these resources, the Governor's School periodically asked for nonreimbursed assistance from its host school. For example, requests were made for Tee-Jay to sponsor athletic teams in new sports like lacrosse. These sports were perceived to be of marginal or no interest to Tee-Jay students.

As understandable as it was that Tee-Jay staff would have been reluctant to cooperate with a school they believed was the cause of their own school's demise, it is regrettable that constructive interactions between the three units never developed fully. Students and faculty in the magnet program and the Governor's School, in particular, addressed similar, if not identical, issues and subject matter. All could have benefitted from greater coordination and sharing.

THE NUMBERS GAME

Inquiries regarding the projected size of the Governor's School, as indicated earlier, yielded a variety of responses. Besides the confusion concerning the figures used by Albert Jones in his original negotiations with the Department of Education, there were discrepancies in the numbers used by the Governor's School. For example, the original size of the Governor's School was supposed to be 300 students per grade, or a total of 1,200.[16] A school of this size, in a building officially designated to accommodate 1,500, would have left no room for a comprehensive high school or much of a magnet program for that matter. Soon after the opening of the Governor's School, however, the figures were shifted downward to 200 students per grade level, for a total enrollment by 1994 of 800.[17] The revision probably resulted from the somewhat disappointing size of the first Governor's School freshman class. In any event, Tee-Jay proponents reasoned that a smaller Governor's School meant a reprieve for at least one of Tee-Jay's two units.

Seventy students were enrolled as ninth graders in the Governor's School in the fall of 1991. The number was far fewer than many observers expected, but director Steven Ballowe insisted in an interview that the target for the first year of operation had been only 50 students.[18] He indicated that 700 students had applied, 120 students had been accepted, and fifty of this number had elected not to attend. A rumor that circulated at the time among Tee-Jay administrators, but which cannot be confirmed, was that Virginia Secretary of Education James Dyke was sufficiently concerned about the low enrollment to have paid a special visit to Ballowe in September to determine if anything could be done to boost numbers. With his boss running for president as a fiscal conservative and state coffers depleted, an embarrassingly modest return on the taxpayers' investment in the Governor's School could be ill afforded.

The make-up of the first group of Governor's School students was considered to be reflective of "the racial composition of the area" by the *Richmond Times-Dispatch*.[19] Others were less charitable. Of the 70 students, it is true that 66 percent were white, 21 percent were black, and 13 percent were from other ethnic groups.[20] Given the fact, though, that the school was created during the administration of the nation's first popularly elected black governor, it struck some observers as ironic that only 3 black males were enrolled. Concerned Richmonders wondered whether the tough admissions requirements would mean that relatively few blacks from the city would gain admission in the future. The first Governor's School cohort included 22 students from Richmond, but it is not known how many of these students were black.[21] Henrico County accounted for 20 students, Chesterfield County 16, and the remaining school divisions 2 each.

When the Governor's School prepared its promotional materials for the 1992–93 school year, a "transition schedule" was included. The schedule, which appears in table 6.1, reflected a school size of 800. In addition, slots for 160 Richmond International Magnet School students were included. The inclusion of Richmond magnet students appeared to represent a strategy to appease Richmonders who worried that students from the host district might be underrepresented in the Governor's School. In addition, the presence of these students created the illusion that a small part of Tee-Jay would survive the phase-out process.

It is worth noting that Tee-Jay teachers and administrators indicated they knew nothing of the "transition calendar" when it was published in the late fall of 1991. Ironically, optimism regarding Tee-Jay's future was beginning to run high at the time, thanks, in part, to an article in the *Times-Dispatch*. Readers of the December 18, 1991, newspaper who wished for Tee-Jay to remain open thought they had received an early Christmas present in the form of the following headline: "TeeJay May Get New Lease on Life." The article reported on a recent meeting of the Governor's School board, made up of the superintendents of nine Richmond-area school divisions, including Richmond's Lucille Brown. Agreement

TABLE 6.1
Transition Schedule

1991–92	12th Grade–Comprehensive		150
	11th Grade–Comprehensive		150
	10th Grade–Int. Magnet/Comp.		200
	9th Grade–Governor's School		70
		total	570
1992–93	12th Grade–Comprehensive		150
	11th Grade–Int. Magnet/Comp.		180
	10th Grade–Governor's School		80
	9th Grade–Governor's School		200+40
		total	650
1993–94	12th Grade–Int. Magnet/Comp.		180
	11th Grade–Governor's School		80
	10th Grade–Governor's School		200+40
	9th Grade–Governor's School		200+40
		total	740
1994–95	12th Grade–Governor's School		80
	11th Grade–Governor's School		200+40
	10th Grade–Governor's School		200+40
	9th Grade–Governor's School		200+40
		total	800
1995–96	12th Grade–Governor's School		200+40
	11th Grade–Governor's School		200+40
	10th Grade–Governor's School		200+40
	9th Grade–Governor's School		200+40
		total	960

Note: +40 = Richmond International Magnet School

was reached that Tee-Jay should be allowed to continue to operate as long as the numbers of Governor's School students remained relatively low. In the short run this decision meant that Tee-Jay could enroll a freshman class in September of 1992. As part of the previous phase-out process that began with the opening of the Governor's School, Tee-Jay had been prevented from accepting freshmen in the fall of 1991.

Had Richmond school officials once again changed their position on shutting down Tee-Jay? Or were they buying time in the hopes that support for Tee-Jay gradually would dissipate and fade away? While no record of district deliberations exists, it is likely that numbers spoke louder than words for central office administrators and most school board members. Not just the low enrollment figure for the Governor's School, but also the number of "no-shows" among Tee-Jay freshmen reassigned to other Richmond high schools. The *Richmond News Leader* reported on September 24, 1991, that "about 125 students who would have attended Jefferson are not enrolled either at Marshall or Kennedy."[22] The article went on to say that school officials believed these students had enrolled in private or county schools rather than accept reassignment. Tee-Jay supporters long had predicted that parents who expected their children to attend Tee-Jay would balk at sending them to other high schools in the city. Here was proof! The loss to the city of so many students resulted in reduced state aid for the financially strapped school system. There were other losses, as well. The students who abandoned the city school system rather than attend a high school other than Tee-Jay included many white students and students of above average ability. Richmond Public Schools could not afford to part with either.

A second factor that may have influenced school officials was the mobilization of community support for Tee-Jay. In May of 1991, when it first became known that no freshman class would be admitted, the Save Our School Committee 2 was formed to lobby the school board. With wisdom gained from earlier efforts to forestall closure, committee members wasted little time in making their position known. Lucille Brown had not been superintendent for a week when Tee-Jay representatives met with her to determine where she stood. They came away feeling that Brown was supportive of Tee-Jay's continued existence. Heartened by her reaction and later by the Governor's School's small freshman class, the committee planned to meet with each school board member to ask that both the comprehensive high school and the magnet program be preserved. Prominent Richmond lawyer Harold Marsh, whose son attended Tee-Jay and whose daughter had graduated from the school, helped plan the group's strategy, which was based on the belief that "there's room for everybody."[23] Marsh tried to strengthen his case by speculating publicly that there might be some "jurisdictions" that wanted to get rid of "city kids" at Tee-Jay.[24] The implication was that some suburban districts might not have wanted their students at the same site as a comprehensive urban high school.

That Marsh's speculation may have possessed a degree of validity was indicated by the concurrent mobilization of Governor's School supporters. Though new to Richmond, director Steven Ballowe was no stranger to school politics. Prior to assuming leadership of the Governor's School, he had served as superintendent of Hopewell City Schools. Ballowe believed that much of the opposition to closing Tee-Jay could be quieted by agreeing to allow 160 Richmond magnet program students to attend his school. Leaving little to chance, he also created an advisory group of Tee-Jay alumni who were committed to seeing the Governor's School replace their alma mater. Many of the members had attended Tee-Jay during the pre-busing "glory days." The wife of one committee member even served on the Tee-Jay faculty. The advisory group took the position that the reputation of Tee-Jay could best be served by allowing the Governor's School to replace it. It is interesting to note that when Russell Flammia, a Tee-Jay alumnus and history teacher, was invited to join the group, he declined, fearing the Governor's School might become "elitist." Flammia questioned the future of urban youth if high achievers continued to be syphoned off into special schools.

With the battle lines clearly drawn, Lucille Brown made an announcement that left both sides feeling good and bad. On the day after Christmas she announced that Tee-Jay would be allowed to enroll a freshman class in the fall of 1992, but that the freshman class would be limited to the magnet program.[25] She went on to say that "the magnet program at Thomas Jefferson and the Governor's School will coexist in the building until the Governor's School enrollment reaches a point that it needs the entire building."[26] While the stay of execution was only temporary, Tee-Jay supporters took satisfaction in having delayed the phase-out. They still could hope that the Governor's School would fail to attract sufficient students to justify complete takeover of the building, thereby losing the "numbers game." Rumors also began to circulate at this time that Henrico and Chesterfield County eventually planned to create their own magnet schools in international studies, thereby eliminating the two largest suburban contributors to the Governor's School. While these rumors were never confirmed, they served further to buoy the spirits of Tee-Jay supporters during the winter of 1991–92.

Governor's School supporters also claimed victory following Brown's statement. While the phase-out could take longer than originally planned, Richmond's new superintendent, who also served as the chair of the Governor's School board, appeared to have accepted the inevitability of Tee-Jay's closure. A token number of Richmond students might be guaranteed admission to a scaled-down magnet program, but they would be subject to the authority of the Governor's School administration. Tee-Jay's staff would be transferred and its name retired.

Governor's School supporters had little time to savor the good news before being faced with another turn of events in the increasingly curious saga. In early January of 1992, Lucille Brown publicly stated that the number of students who would be allowed to attend Tee-Jay's magnet program had not yet been determined.[27] Steven Ballowe immediately declared that the Governor's School board, with Lucille Brown presiding, had agreed to sustain only a small Richmond magnet program of forty students for each grade level. He cited the Governor's School brochure and its "transition schedule" (see table 6.1), which specified the number of magnet program students. Lucille Brown insisted, however, that "Richmond school officials" had not yet determined the number of magnet freshmen who would attend Tee-Jay in the fall. She apparently did not regard the decision of how many freshman magnet students to admit as a matter within the jurisdiction of the Governor's School board. "We're looking at the needs of the school district and we should have that figure in the not-too-distant future," declared the superintendent.[28] The "needs of the school district" apparently depended on recent predictions of enrollment increases and possible overcrowding in Richmond schools.[29]

Governor's School supporters were dealt another blow a month later when the future of Tee-Jay became linked to a broader discussion of Richmond's commitment to neighborhood schools. At the regular meeting of the Richmond school board on

February 4, 1992, Lucille Brown presented a neighborhood school plan that "proposed to reaffirm and support open enrollment and the model school concept while embodying the neighborhood concept."[30] She pointed out that students would be given the opportunity to attend school near their homes, thereby reducing travel time and expense. Boundary adjustments for most schools would have to be made, but she assured the board that these arrangements would not upset "the co-existence of the Governor's School and the magnet school."[31]

It now seemed as if the Governor's School might be on the defensive. With no other high school in Richmond's West End, the neighborhood school plan seemed to require the continued operation of Tee-Jay. Furthermore, for the first time Tee-Jay's magnet "program" was referred to as a "school." Could this mean that the comprehensive high school would give way to a magnet school, one still bearing the name of Thomas Jefferson?

The *Times-Dispatch* announced on February 14, 1992, that a public hearing on the neighborhood school plan would be held at City Hall on February 25. In addition, it revealed that the plan called for a 258-member freshman class for Tee-Jay. This number seemed a far cry from the Governor's School's concession of a 40-student freshman class. Sufficient confusion concerning the exact nature of Tee-Jay's future now existed to warrant the formation of a special "planning and coordinating committee."[32]

Evidence of a Governor's School counteroffensive surfaced at the hearing on the neighborhood plan. Two parents expressed confusion over the proposed attendance zones for Tee-Jay.[33] They requested that action on the zones be postponed until a "feasibility study" could be undertaken to determine "the appropriate enrollment." Further, they insisted that Richmond Public Schools honor its commitment to the Governor's School. Presumably this commitment required phasing out Tee-Jay.

Tee-Jay supporters were also on hand to speak in favor of the new attendance zones and continuation of both the comprehensive high school and magnet program. Obviously they had learned never to take for granted that their school's future was secure.

During the hearing's question-and-answer period, one person raised an issue which, up to that point, had not been voiced publicly. "What has happened to the commitment to integrated schools?" the speaker asked. "Returning to neighborhood schools will bring back segregation." Could circumstances have become so twisted that the preservation of Richmond's most integrated high school depended on a policy—neighborhood schools—that originally had been intended to forestall integration? Did some Tee-Jay supporters secretly hope that a new commitment to neighborhood schools might actually lead to Tee-Jay's reemergence as a predominantly white high school? While many black professionals had moved to the West End, Tee-Jay's "neighborhood" still remained largely white.

School board minutes indicated that Chairman Rayford L. Harris, Sr., responded to the query by stating that "the board is not diminishing, deleting, or curtailing the concepts of model schools, open enrollment, and choice." Lucille Brown added that nothing in the neighborhood school plan threatened to eliminate open enrollment. She also pointed out that "historically 95 percent of patrons have chosen schools close to their home." None of these answers seemed to address the original question.

Could the superintendent and school board support both neighborhood schools and open enrollment and survive politically? Based on newspaper reports of Lucille Brown's popularity, it appeared the answer might be "Yes."[34] One key to her initially positive reception probably was her tendency to tell people what they wished to hear and her sincere efforts to accommodate all sides of an issue. Such tactics eventually can backfire, however, when actual commitments must be made. As spring approached, the school district had to inform parents of eighth graders of their magnet program options under the open enrollment scheme. At the regular board meeting of March 3, 1992, Lucille Brown was asked by a board member to clarify the attendance zones for Tee-Jay.[35] Brown responded that *only* eighth graders from the two West End middle schools, Albert Hill and Binford, would be permitted to attend Tee-Jay's magnet program. Even if the càp of 258 freshmen was not reached through the intake of ninth graders from these two schools, no students from other Richmond middle schools would be allowed to enroll. Open enrollment, in other words, would pertain to every school in the city *except* for Tee-Jay! Stunned Tee-Jay supporters were left to contemplate yet another policy reversal and wonder whether the powerful Governor's School lobby had played a role in the process. When Lucille Brown failed to show up for a scheduled meeting with the Tee-Jay Parent-Teacher-Student Organization soon after the March 3 board meeting, it indeed seemed that forces were at work behind the scenes to undercut Tee-Jay's position.

One of the county superintendents on the Governor's School board reasoned at the time that a well-organized steering group had to be orchestrating lobbying efforts on behalf of the Governor's School. He cited the example of a recent unpublicized Governor's School board meeting where more than one hundred supporters of Tee-Jay's closure showed up. Obviously someone had tipped them off so they could arrange a mass show of support for a Governor's School free of the burdens of coexistence. Among the supporters who showed up were several corporate heads and even a speech writer for Governor Wilder. Several observers believed that two members of the Richmond school board had played key roles in leaking information about district plans for Tee-Jay to Governor's School representatives.

The morale of Tee-Jay teachers and administrators hit rock bottom during the spring of 1992. The impressive recruiting campaign they had prepared to take to every middle school in the city had to be scrapped. Even diehard Tee-Jay supporters like Russell Flammia considered bailing out. Gordon Hill tersely summed up the situation when he told this writer, "The dream has died." Hill's dream, when he came to Tee-Jay, had been to create an "integrated, cooperative, comprehensive, and effective high school."

Years of uncertainty, raised hopes, dashed expectations, and the sheer effort required to fight and teach at the same time had taken a heavy toll on the Tee-Jay staff. They had dealt with hard times and uncertainty in the past and discovered that sound reasoning, good organization, and community support were sufficient to persuade policymakers to preserve their school. Now they confronted a different and more perplexing problem. School system officials appeared committed to allowing Tee-Jay to survive, at least for a time, but not in any form that would permit the pursuit of educational excellence, much less the recapturing of past glory. A limited magnet program, unable to compete openly for students, hardly seemed worthy of the Tee-Jay tradition. Those who cared about Tee-Jay clearly would have preferred to go out with a bang rather than a whimper, if indeed they had to go out at all.

The coup de grace was not delivered until the summer, when school was out of session and Tee-Jay supporters had turned their attention to other matters. The last few years obviously had been instructive for district officials as well as their adversaries. The former apparently had learned that the latter were tenacious in defense of their school and capable of mounting community-based campaigns on short notice. In an act many regarded as cowardly, Gordon Hill was removed as principal of Tee-Jay in June of 1992. The newspaper article announcing the decision reported that observers felt Hill had fought too hard to save Tee-Jay, in the process incurring the anger of "regional school supporters and some board members."[36] The article failed to note that perhaps Tee-Jay was worth fighting for and that the kind of community-based support that Tee-Jay possessed in abundance and that Hill had tapped was precisely what urban school systems struggled to achieve. How could it be that the Richmond school system was willing to abandon a school with such a precious commodity?

THREE'S A CROWD

The August 2, 1992, issue of the *Richmond Times-Dispatch* contained a special public relations insert entitled "Discover Richmond." The insert was intended to apprise newcomers and remind long-time residents of Richmond's many attractive features. The section dealing with education boasted a large photograph of Tee-Jay, the only city school so pictured. The accompanying profile contained the following statement: "Wonderful example of art deco style; designed to symbolize the importance of education in the city of Richmond."[37]

Six decades after its opening, Tee-Jay had come to symbolize other things besides the importance of education. By the early nineties, Tee-Jay had become a symbol of the highly politicized nature of public schooling in Richmond. It also served as a dramatic example of how complex had grown the struggle for integration and educational excellence in the almost forty years since the Brown decision and the reforms inspired by Sputnik. More will be said of these matters and the meaning of the Tee-Jay experience in the concluding chapters.

Returning to the summer of 1992, a new principal was appointed to lead Tee-Jay during what could only be described as highly uncertain times. Dr. Edward H. Pruden, Jr., was a white administrator with considerable experience in Richmond Public Schools. Having received a B.A. from the University of Richmond and a doctorate from William and Mary, Pruden had served as an assistant principal at Wythe High School during the period of complexes, principal of Albert Hill Middle School from 1987 to 1990, and principal of Henderson Middle School from 1990 to 1992. Among the many rumors that circulated during July and August was the idea that Pruden had been selected to preside over the dismantling of Tee-Jay. Another rumor was that Lucille Brown would not be offered a new contract.

The latter rumor was put to rest in August when Lucille Brown was offered a new contract through June of 1995. By this time Gordon Hill had been reassigned to develop an alternative program for dropouts. Publication of test results for Richmond high school students in August showed that Tee-Jay's once lofty position among city high schools had been lost.[38] Table 6.2 contains the results of the Tests of Achievement and Proficiency (TAP), taken by all Richmond eleventh graders. The national norm is pegged at fifty. As the data indicated, Tee-Jay juniors were near the bottom in almost every category and far behind their counterparts in the two selective alternative schools, Open High and Richmond Community High.

These data could only add to the discouragement of Tee-Jay supporters and provide ammunition for those who opposed continued operation of the comprehensive high school and magnet program. Their effect was mitigated somewhat by the release earlier in 1992 of Virginia Outcome Accountability Project (OAP) data. The May OAP reports, which for the first time included comparative data reported on a school-by-school basis, indicated that Tee-Jay fared reasonably well in relation to Richmond's other comprehensive high schools.[39] For instance, Tee-Jay was second to Wythe in the percentage of eleventh-grade standardized test scores above the seventy-fifth percentile (see table 6.3). As for the percentage of eleventh-grade standardized test scores above the median, Tee-Jay fell behind Wythe, Marshall, and Huguenot, suggesting that while Tee-Jay's top students were among the best in Richmond, other students fared less well in comparison with their peers. Tee-Jay students accounted for fewer absences in excess of ten days than students elsewhere and a much lower percentage of dropouts, including minority dropouts. Performance on spring physical fitness tests dropped below that of students at Wythe, Kennedy, and Armstrong.

The 1992–93 school year began with Tee-Jay welcoming 450 students, including 150 freshmen, distributed in roughly equal

TABLE 6.2
Tests of Achievement & Proficiency for 1991–1992

High schools

	Reading	Math	Written expression	Using information	Basic composite	Social studies	Science
Richmond (overall)	43	42	61	47	48	49	42
Armstrong	34	37	57	39	41	38	35
Franklin Military	44	35	61	45	47	31	28
Huguenot	43	39	60	47	47	46	41
Jefferson	34	36	52	45	41	43	36
Kennedy	31	37	61	40	42	34	30
Marshall	39	42	56	41	45	43	38
Open High	80	68	81	76	78	77	76
Richmond Community	82	79	89	81	86	88	89
Wythe	42	45	61	46	48	63	45

Richmond Times-Dispatch, August 9, 1992, p. B-6

TABLE 6.3
Outcome Accountability Project
Results for Richmond High Schools, 1990–91

	Tee–Jay	Kennedy	Armstrong	Huguenot	Wythe	Marshall
Percentage of 11th Grade Standardized Test Scores (Virginia State Assessment Program) above 75th Percentile	14	2	2	10	16	7
Percentage of 11th Grade Standardized Test Scores above Median	38	28	27	39	51	40
Percentage of Students Who Were Absent 10 Days or Less	47	22	30	42	—	30
Percentage of Students Who Dropped Out of School	5	14	14	9	14	11
Percentage of Minority Students Who Dropped Out of School	4	14	14	8	13	10
Percentage of 9th and 10th Grade Students Who Passed All 4 Spring Physical Fitness Tests	27	39	37	14	53	10

numbers between the magnet program and the comprehensive high school.[40] The Governor's School greeted 280 students from twelve different school districts.[41] To accommodate its increased student body, the Governor's School took over almost the entire third floor and the choir and typing rooms on the second floor. Much to the dismay of Tee-Jay faculty members, the locks were changed each time the Governor's School moved into a new room. Two Tee-Jay science teachers who still used the upper floor were not even given a key to the faculty restroom, prompting one administrator to liken the situation to "apartheid."

Much about Tee-Jay had changed since the first dislocating effects of the complex system. Gone was the extensive system of student government and homeroom organization. Fewer extracurricular opportunities were now available. The highly stratified series of course offerings, including honors courses, had been streamlined, due in part to declining enrollment and smaller numbers of college-bound students. Award-winning school publications had fallen victim to budget constraints and changing student tastes. Mary Maddox's classroom had been converted into the "Behavioral Improvement Center."

To assume, though, that no semblance of the traditional academic culture of Tee-Jay remained would have been a mistake. Faculty and administration still exhorted students to do their best. Academic achievement continued to be highly valued and receive public recognition. Mature behavior was still a basic expectation, not a pleasant surprise as in many urban high schools. Students frequently were reminded that they had Tee-Jay's reputation to live up to. Teachers from the glory days would have been pleased to walk the halls that remained unlittered and free of graffiti. Tee-Jay's AP courses, though no longer filled to capacity, exceeded the number of AP courses in other Richmond comprehensive high schools. Teachers and administrators, like their predecessors, viewed their association with Tee-Jay with pride. In fact, nine years had passed, according to one administrator, since a faculty grievance had been filed.

If grievances, though, could have been filed against the school system for inconsistency, conflicting signals, and policy reversals, Tee-Jay teachers might have filled a school bus with complaints. The events that began to unfold in the fall of 1992 did little to eliminate the uncertainty surrounding Tee-Jay's future. October found the school board considering three options regarding the school's status. Their deliberations were prompted by new enrollment projections that indicated by 1995 there would be 725 West End students in need of a "neighborhood" high school.[42] By that time, the Governor's School was estimated to grow to 700 students.[43] One option was to relocate Tee-Jay. Another was to add a new wing to Tee-Jay at an estimated cost of $3.6 million in order to accommodate the increased number of neighborhood students. The third option involved constructing a brand new West End high school. On October 20, 1992, the school board—the makeup of which had changed significantly since four years before when it had supported eliminating the last West End high school—decided to back the third option. If approved by city council, this choice would mean that the Governor's School eventually would take over all of Tee-Jay. City Manager Robert C. Bobb slowed progress toward a new high school in March of 1993, however, when he said that the city would provide capital improvement funds to the school district only on two conditions: (1) that the city, rather than the district, controlled construction and (2) that no new school would be built until existing facilities had been modernized.[44]

While Tee-Jay supporters awaited the school board's response to the City Manager's proposal, a subplot worthy of William Faulkner started to unfold. The Governor's School, which had appeared to enjoy a secure future, now found its own status somewhat uncertain. The Governor's School board voted in February of 1993 to reduce its incoming freshman class of 204 to 120 students.[45] Opposed by the school's Parent-Teacher-Student Association and faculty, the move was justified by the board in terms of budget concerns and lack of space at Tee-Jay. It was unclear whether or not board members were trying to force Richmond Public Schools to declare its intentions regarding the future of Tee-Jay's comprehensive high school and magnet program. Henrico County superintendent Dr. William C. Bosher, Jr. was quoted, however, as saying, that "No matter how you look at it [the Governor's School], it's a high-cost program."[46] He went on to point out, "We can't step aside from budgetary constraints. But if we had more money tomorrow . . . I'd go after things like teacher positions and library materials." In other words, the Governor's School did not appear to be a high priority in light of scarce resources.

The decision placed Governor's School supporters in a position very familiar to their Tee-Jay counterparts. The spring of 1993 witnessed a campaign by students and parents to force the board to reinstate the original freshman class. Arguments that the Governor's School provided a special learning environment, one committed to high expectations and academic achievement, must have struck those who had struggled for similar reasons to save Tee-Jay as ironic.

In April the Governor's School board, borrowing a page from the Richmond school board, reversed themselves, agreeing to accept a full compliment of freshmen in the fall.[47] At the same time they heard a report from a Department of Education evaluation team that urged the Richmond school board to find "a permanent home" for the Governor's School by June 1, 1993. Richmond school board chairman, Clarence Townes, Jr., was quoted by a reporter as saying, "I'm certain we will try to comply."[48]

REPRIEVE

Try though they might, the Richmond School Board was unable to meet the June deadline. Problems began to surface in May when Tee-Jay students sought reassurances from Lucille Brown that their school would be allowed to remain at its present location. They prepared to march on City Hall, but the superintendent agreed to meet with them at Tee-Jay on May 25, 1993. When Brown failed to promise that Tee-Jay would continue to exist at its 4100 West Grace Street location, students walked out of the meeting and the school. The newspaper reported that most of Tee-Jay's 530 students were involved in the protest.[49]

Student frustration was due, in part, to Brown's comment that a decision would not be reached on the fate of Tee-Jay until the summer, rather than the original June 1 date. Students recalled that she had waited until school was out the previous summer to remove Gordon Hill as principal. They suspected a similar strategy accounted for the present delay.

Harold Marsh, who chaired a district task force charged with studying how to resolve space problems at Tee-Jay, did not allow June 1 to pass without reminding the school board that the previous December his group had recommended that an addition be built onto Tee-Jay to provide sufficient space for both the comprehensive high school and the Governor's School.[50] A group of roughly 300 people in the audience responded to Marsh's suggestion by standing in a show of support. His was not the only option under consideration, however. A four-member City Council–School Board Liaison Committee was studying the feasibility of relocating the Governor's School at Westhampton Elementary School, a move that would require extensive renovations to the aging facility. Community High School, which occupied most of Westhampton, would be moved to Maggie Walker High School, which stood vacant and also would require renovations. In an editorial on June 16, 1993, the *Richmond Times-Dispatch* expressed the hope that an arrangement could be worked out where both Tee-Jay and the Governor's School would continue to exist.[51]

The summer of 1993 was an anxious one for supporters of Tee-Jay and the Governor's School. A decision by the school board kept being pushed back. At its retreat in August, the school board heard from State Superintendent of Public Instruction Joseph Spagnolo, who urged them to "send a strong signal to parents and the community" that the city was committed to supporting the Governor's School.[52] On September 1, 1993, the newspaper reported that the City Council–School Board Liaison Committee would recommend that the Governor's School move to Westhampton and Community High School relocate to Maggie Walker. The committee also announced that the school systems that sent students to the Governor's School should share the cost of renovating Westhampton with Richmond Public Schools. On October 8, it was learned that the price for improving and expanding the facility would be $14.7 million. At the same time, the committee announced that renovating Maggie Walker and Tee-Jay would cost an additional $31.3 million.

Within a few weeks concerns over the plan began to surface. Officials with Henrico and Chesterfield County School Districts hesitated to help underwrite the cost of renovating Westhampton. Henrico County even refused to identify an incoming cohort of students for the Governor's School until the matter of the school's location was resolved.[53] In November the Governor's School board officially registered its opposition to the relocation of the school and insisted that the Richmond school board honor Albert Jones's pledge to phase out Tee-Jay and allow the Governor's School to occupy the entire building.

As 1993 drew to a close the future of the Governor's School seemed murky, while Tee-Jay's suddenly appeared bright. In its meeting on December 7, 1993, the Richmond school board voted six to one to continue dual occupancy of the Tee-Jay building if the Governor's School rejected relocation.[54] The board added that Tee-Jay would have first call on all decisions regarding the use of space.

Further indication that Tee-Jay's stock had risen in value came in the form of a letter from city councilman and former Richmond principal Roy West to the Richmond school board. In the letter West, who earlier had opposed Tee-Jay's continuation, expressed irritation at the intractability of the Governor's School board. He accused those associated with the Governor's School of adopting a "condescending attitude" in their opposition to coexistence with Tee-Jay.[55] In addition, he claimed that special treatment accorded the Governor's School was hurting the "self-esteem" of Tee-Jay's students and faculty. West suggested that Tee-Jay sever its ties with the Governor's School.

When the Governor's School board rejected the relocation alternative, Lucille Brown was asked to draft guidelines "for the continued co-existence of the Governor's School for Government and International Studies and Thomas Jefferson High."[56] Richmond City Council, which had issued the request, noted that "ultimate authority" for the facility would rest with Richmond Public Schools. Enrollment numbers for both schools would be adjusted, with city students receiving priority. School board vice-chairman Joseph Carter indicated that, if these arrangements were unacceptable to the Governor's School, it should look for other quarters.

Early in March of 1994 the Richmond school board approved a set of conditions governing the continued coexistence of Tee-Jay and the Governor's School.[57] The action was taken only after the newly appointed state superintendent of public instruction, Dr. William C. Bosher, Jr., had threatened to withhold funding for the Governor's School unless guidelines were forthcoming. The board capped Governor's School enrollment at 600 students for the 1994–95 school year. The following year, enrollment would be limited to no more than 552 students, with a maximum of 138 students admitted per year thereafter. Tee-Jay's total enrollment was set at 800, with annual admission set at 200. Tee-jay and the Governor's School would continue to have separate principals, but the Tee-Jay principal was accorded final authority with regard to building management.

So ends this history of Thomas Jefferson High School. The school's saga, of course, will continue to unfold. Even as final editing on this manuscript was being completed, it was announced that a group of Henrico County parents were holding a meeting of anyone interested in relocating the Governor's School from Tee-Jay to a site in Henrico County![58] In the world of urban education, there is no such thing as certainty. Still, the significance of Tee-Jay's struggle to survive should not be underestimated. The commitment of the city council and the school board to maintain a comprehensive high school in the West End, despite intense pressure from Governor's School supporters, including some of the Richmond area's most influential people, is meaningful because it symbolizes the fact that the dream of integration is not completely dead in the capital of the Confederacy. The determination of black and white students, parents, teachers, and local politicians mattered. Even the *Richmond Times-Dispatch* and one-time supporters of school closure like Roy West were impressed by the tenacity of Tee-Jay's advocates. If the high school can continue to increase its white enrollment without neglecting the educational needs of black students and if faculty and students are able to renew Tee-Jay's reputation for academic excellence, perhaps the skeptics who question the viability of urban comprehensive high schools will be forced to reconsider their position.

PART 3

Interpreting the Tee-Jay Experience

Having recounted the events that helped to shape Tee-Jay and create its special culture and character, we need now to reflect on the significance of the Tee-Jay experience. Preceding chapters tried to capture what it meant to be a member of the Tee-Jay community during important periods in the school's history. The following chapters address what Tee-Jay might mean to others, including policymakers, reformers, and students of educational history. The intention is not to "stretch" Tee-Jay's influence too far beyond the boundaries of a single organization, but simply to assess what can be learned from the school's history with regard to three central organizational challenges—adaptation, continuity, and survival.

The challenge to adapt was represented most dramatically by desegregation. How Tee-Jay responded to desegregation over three decades and what the responses may mean for those committed to diversity and an integrated society are subjects of chapter 7. The following chapter deals with the challenge of continuity, symbolized by Tee-Jay's long-term commitment to academic excellence and its struggle to preserve it during an era of demographic change and fiscal retrenchment. Like so many of its sister high schools in urban areas around the country, Tee-Jay's most pressing problem ultimately became its very survival. Chapter 9 discusses this issue and its relationship to competing pressures for continuity and adaptation.

CHAPTER 7

The Changing Face of School Desegregation

To many blacks living in Richmond in the days before desegregation, Tee-Jay symbolized the inequities of a divided school system.
The textbooks that Tee-Jay discarded became "new" texts for local
black students. The curricular and extracurricular opportunities
available to Tee-Jay students contrasted sharply with the limited
choices facing their peers at Armstrong and Walker. While teachers
at Tee-Jay took graduate work for granted, their counterparts
across town considered themselves fortunate to have obtained an
undergraduate degree. If ever a justification for the *Brown* decision
could be embodied in one school, that school was Tee-Jay.

During the sixties, Tee-Jay's image shifted only slightly. The
school enrolled a small number of black students, and for the most
part they performed well. While they were not subjected to the
cruel harassment that black students frequently received elsewhere, few special efforts were made to welcome these ground-
breakers or accommodate their unique needs. Tee-Jay, along with
Richmond Public Schools, initially embraced a "go slow"
approach to desegregation. Following court-ordered busing in
1970, Tee-Jay came to symbolize, for some, the tragedy of social
experimentation and the loss of a premier center of academic
excellence. For many blacks, however, the full desegregation of
Tee-Jay meant victory in a sixteen-year struggle to realize the
intent of the *Brown* decision. More than a few observers, both
black and white, also saw in Tee-Jay a heartening symbol of reasonable and orderly desegregation.

As the seventies wound down, Tee-Jay's once well-defined
image began to blur into a general picture of urban high schools
across the nation—schools beset by declining enrollment, white
flight, and inadequate resources. Tee-Jay never lost all of its white
students, commitment to excellence, or pride, however. The
school's ability to retain a modest percentage of whites—impres-

sive in comparison with other Richmond high schools—and to maintain relatively high academic standards gradually began to inspire praise instead of pity. By the late eighties, some influential Richmonders felt that Tee-Jay had become the embodiment of hope for their city—a place where racial integration and academic rigor were still possible. Whether its re-emergence as a constructive symbol was a consequence of efforts to prevent Tee-Jay from being closed, or a cause for fighting closure in the first place, is not easily determined.

Consensus regarding Tee-Jay's symbolic value is illusive. Supporters of the Governor's School feel that Tee-Jay constitutes an anachronistic obstacle in their quest for an elite regional high school. With the revival of the neighborhood schools policy by the Richmond school board, others see in Tee-Jay the possibility of a return to a predominantly white high school for the West End. Still others insist that Tee-Jay represents the last hope for integrated comprehensive high school education in the city of Richmond.

These differences in what Tee-Jay has symbolized for Richmonders suggest that the terrain of school desegregation can be ever-shifting. While a detailed map is beyond the scope of the present chapter, several major topographical features will be noted along with some guidance for those traversing the territory.

RESPONDING TO DESEGREGATION

It is misleading, in some ways, to discuss one school's response to an important policy like desegregation. School districts, not individual schools, represent the legal agents charged with developing and implementing educational policies. All schools within a school district typically are expected to implement new policies in a similar manner. Many studies of desegregation understandably have concentrated on school districts as the primary units of inquiry and analysis.[1]

In recent years, however, interest in school-based responses to new policies has grown. Studies of innovations conducted by the Rand Corporation, for example, found that "local factors," more than official intentions and guidelines, determined the nature of policy implementation.[2] Reviewing the Rand studies in light of recent developments, Milbrey McLaughlin concluded that change "continues to be a problem of the smallest unit."[3] In other words, trying to understand how a policy like school desegregation is implemented requires a focus on individual schools and the people in them. Studies of school districts too easily conceal substantial variations across schools.

A central concern of this book has been to describe and understand how an exemplary Southern high school responded to desegregation. The story that emerged was one of shifting responses dictated, to some extent, by changing opinions regarding the nature of the challenge posed by desegregation. During the early years of desegregation, when relatively small numbers of blacks were enrolled at Tee-Jay, teachers and administrators considered the key challenge to be the preservation of academic excellence. "Business as usual" appeared to be the preferred response. Blacks who attended Tee-Jay were expected to adapt to the prevailing culture and organization. No special effort was made to accommodate their unique needs or facilitate racial integration.

The advent of court-ordered busing in 1970 led to a different response. Whereas Tee-Jay's first cohorts of black students consisted mainly of academically able students from middle-class backgrounds, the new students contained large percentages of low achievers, many from relatively poor homes. Teachers and administrators were forced to abandon their business-as-usual approach, though they still clung to their commitment to academic excellence, high expectations, the ideal of the well-rounded student, and other features of Tee-Jay's special culture. The challenges that desegregation now was perceived to pose included remediating academic deficiencies and maintaining an orderly learning environment. The responses—programs like Project Read, in-service training for teachers, new courses such as "Black History," tutorial assistance, learning centers in language arts and mathematics, an informal policy requiring the "best" teachers to teach "basic" courses, and special clubs devoted to interracial understanding—demonstrated Tee-Jay's capacity for adaptation when necessary. As substantial as were these initiatives, none was regarded as a threat to Tee-Jay's basic mission. "Change within tradition" was a Tee-Jay hallmark, and desegregation at this point did not cause a major deviation from this course.

As the seventies progressed, the challenges of desegregation again underwent redefinition. Attracting and retaining white and bright students supplanted remediation and discipline as focal concerns. The percentage of white students attending Tee-Jay dwindled as larger numbers of families moved to the suburbs or private schools. By the early nineties, the Richmond area boasted "nearly fifty" private schools with tuitions ranging from $1,300 to $7,000 per year.[4] Competition for bright students intensified within Richmond Public Schools, as several alternative high schools were created. To respond to these latest challenges, Tee-Jay fought to preserve low-enrollment honors and AP courses in the face of severe budget constraints. Supporters believed that the key to attracting bright students was preserving as much of the "old" Tee-Jay as possible. Turning back the clock completely might be impossible, but maintaining basic elements of school culture such as high expectations, recognition of academic achievement, faculty leadership, an orderly learning environment, and diverse opportunities for student involvement came to be regarded as vital.

What is remarkable, in retrospect, about Tee-Jay's evolving responses to desegregation was the consistent refusal to become "just another city high school." Teachers knew their clientele was changing, and eventually they acknowledged that some accommodation must be made, but they saw little reason why demographic shifts should occasion the abandonment of qualities that had caused Tee-Jay to achieve an admired reputation in the first place and to become an example to black parents of what the fight for equal educational opportunity was all about. In a very real sense, then, Tee-Jay's response to desegregation was to change *and* to remain the same. The significance of this response for students of organizational morphology will be addressed in the concluding chapter.

Having briefly reviewed how Tee-Jay responded to desegregation, we can now explore what those responses might mean in light of the current resegregation of many of the nation's urban schools. Three observations are prompted by the Tee-Jay experience: (1) support for desegregation varies, (2) desegregation may give rise to local markets for students, and (3) the future of integration may not rest exclusively with the urban comprehensive high school.

UNEVEN SUPPORT FOR DESEGREGATION

That many individuals in Richmond, as elsewhere, resisted desegregation in the past, and continue to oppose it, surely is no surprise. Many of these people left the city rather than send their children to desegregated schools. The outmigration for Richmond between 1970 and 1980 exceeded 43,400, more than a 13 percent decline in population.[5] This rate of population loss was comparable to that of some of the largest and most depressed cities in the United States.[6] Others remained in Richmond, but opted to send their children to private and parochial schools.

The history of Tee-Jay also reveals something less obvious—that those who appeared to endorse desegregation did not always share similar views regarding its ultimate importance or how to achieve it. Mary Anne Raywid has written that the "schools are no longer in accord with their political environments—that is, with the desires of the parents and the communities they presumably serve and with the political system whose procedural principles public institutions are obligated to reflect."[7] Such a statement, not uncommon in contemporary critiques of public education, implies that communities and politicians agree about what is important and how to achieve it. The Tee-Jay story indicates, at least for Richmond, that such agreement regarding desegregation never existed. Neither black nor white supporters of desegregation were of one mind concerning a host of matters, including open enrollment, magnet programs, neighborhood schools, selective alternative schools, and the future of Tee-Jay. John Moeser regards such lack of agreement as a central problem facing today's cities:

> Currently, one of the major obstacles encountered in cities . . . is that, instead of a sense of overall community, there is a plurality of communities, one for the race, one for the class, one for the elderly, one for transients, and so on. Also, as urban societies become more complex, urban institutions become more differentiated. Loyalties are directed to particular institutions or groups, seldom to the larger community.[8]

There is nothing new, of course, about such differences of opinion. Prior to desegregation, for example, Virginius Dabney noted that black Richmonders disagreed about a number of matters, including whether black schools should be led by black or white principals.[9] Not all whites supported segregation prior to 1954 either, though vocal public opposition was rare.

Tee-Jay arguably represents one of Richmond's few opportunities for truly integrated comprehensive high school education.

The unwillingness of white supporters of Tee-Jay to send their children to other Richmond high schools was demonstrated clearly in the fall of 1991 when Tee-Jay freshmen were reassigned. Those who have insisted that Tee-Jay remain open have included many black as well as white parents. These individuals—often well-to-do black professionals living in or near the West End—felt that Tee-Jay, alone of Richmond's comprehensive high schools, offered an academic culture, a full range of college preparatory coursework, contact with more than a token number of white students, and a reasonably secure and orderly setting.

Other Richmond parents—both black and white—have remained committed to the goal of integration, but they have preferred to send their children to selective programs or schools, such as the magnet programs, Open High, and Community High. They did not object to blacks and whites studying together as long as assurances existed that students were highly motivated, mindful of authority, and bright. Such assurances, of course, were impossible to give for a comprehensive public high school like Tee-Jay. Blacks and whites also sought admission to the regional Governor's School. A Department of Education official indicated that, in 1993, 21 percent of the Governor School's enrollment was black. Virtually all of the vocal advocates for the Governor's School have been white, however.

A third group, including many people without school-age children, have registered no formal opposition to desegregation per se, but have supported initiatives, such as the closing of Tee-Jay, that might serve, nonetheless, to undermine this cause. These individuals often have flown the banner of cost-cutting and efficiency. One-time mayor and school principal Roy West, a black, was until recently one of the most vocal of this group. He favored shutting down several high schools, including Tee-Jay and Kennedy, to help balance the school system's budget.[10] In the eighties, while principal of Albert Hill Middle School, West said that he did not believe "white flight hurt the school system or that schools should be especially concerned about trying to woo whites back."[1] Whether views such as West's constituted a form of black pragmatism or a genuine preference for "going it alone" is unclear. As mayor, he told reporters, "I never bought the argument that black kids need to sit next to white kids to get an education."[12] Recognizing that the segregation of the nation's black students now exceeds 1970 levels, some policy analysts outside of Richmond have echoed West's sentiments.[13] Since ending racial isolation no longer seems likely, they oppose continued use of scarce resources to promote integration, preferring instead to target funds for minority students left in largely segregated settings.[14]

This position is opposed by black moderates like Claude Steele, who maintains, "Segregation, whatever its purpose, draws out group differences and makes people feel more vulnerable when they inevitably cross group lines to compete in the larger society."[15] Steele feels that the success of any social policy, like desegregation, ultimately depends on the "tactics of implementation." Presumably, there are right and wrong ways to implement policy. In Richmond, no general agreement has existed concerning the best approach to preserving desegregation or achieving real integration.

The recent history of Tee-Jay raises some questions about the extent to which a predominantly black school system and a city government still heavily influenced by a white power structure will go to promote school integration. Has Tee-Jay survived repeated closure threats in spite of Richmond Public Schools and the city council or because of them? Was cost containment a more pressing concern than preserving one of the few high schools with a significant white enrollment? Why have so many people—young and old, black and white, alumni and nonalumni—continued to fight to keep Tee-Jay open?

Tee-Jay's story suggests that there are no simple answers to these questions. The diversity of opinions regarding desegregation is as manifest at Richmond Public Schools and City Hall as it is in the community at large. In a real sense, Tee-Jay has survived *both* because of and in spite of these institutions. Few people oppose cost-cutting, unless they are personally affected. Many people support desegregation. When the two become linked, as in the case of Tee-Jay, and it seems likely that the achievement of one desired goal may interfere with the achievement of another desired goal, reactions can be expected to vary. It would be inspiring to claim that all those who support the continuation of Tee-Jay have done so out of a sincere commitment to school integration, but to do so would be naive. Some supporters have been motivated by convenience—Tee-Jay happens to be close to where they live. Others doubtless would send their children to a private or parochial school or move to the suburbs if they could afford to do so. Lacking sufficient funds, they see Tee-Jay as their "safest" alternative.

Then there are those, like Russell Flammia, who believe Gordon Hill's "dream" is still important. As long as Tee-Jay remains open, these idealists believe there is still hope that black and white students from varying backgrounds and with different aspirations can study together and learn to understand one another. The Richmond school board, in its recent decision to support the continued existence of Tee-Jay, has done its part to keep the dream alive.

Pulitzer-Prize–winning columnist William Raspberry posed the following haunting question in a recent editorial: "Must integration be the overriding priority for those who care about the education of young African Americans?"[16] When, in other words, can scarce energy be concentrated on the quality of learning instead of issues of equal access and opportunity?

The future of school integration, of course, depends on more than the continued existence of one high school. Many scholars doubt whether urban school districts alone can reverse the trend toward resegregation. Gary Orfield and Carole Ashkinaze's study of desegregation in Atlanta led them to conclude that a "metropolitan approach" was necessary.[17] Pressure, they wrote, must be brought to bear on suburbs to desegregate housing and work more collaboratively with urban school systems. After investigating St. Louis's efforts to implement a "metropolitan-type" desegregation plan, Daniel Monti was skeptical, however.[18] He believed no progress would be made unless courts dissolved boards of education that were unable or unwilling to implement school integration.

MARKETS FOR STUDENTS

The focus of desegregation policy initially was to increase black students' access to white schools. In Richmond, as in other cities, court-ordered busing became the policy instrument of choice for achieving this goal. When whites abandoned the city school system, a new focus for desegregation policy began to emerge—the retention of white students. The result was the creation of internal "markets" for students and the official endorsement of seemingly contradictory education policies.

Public school systems long have had to contend with external markets for students. Private and parochial schools traditionally competed for students from advantaged backgrounds. The competition intensified and began to include students from more modest backgrounds following the advent of desegregation. With the onset of court-ordered busing in 1970, however, internal markets have appeared. In other words, competition for students has begun to take place between schools within the same school system. At first, the competition at the high school level in Richmond was limited to several innovative alternative schools—Open High and Community High—that boasted selective admissions policies and challenging college preparatory curricula. The early nineties brought direct competition between comprehensive high schools as magnet programs were created.

An argument can be made that a primary impetus for the creation of Richmond Public Schools' internal market was the retention of white students. Fears existed that the dwindling number of white students in the system would disappear entirely if they were not allowed to choose their schools. These students were not averse to attending school with blacks, but they resisted having to travel to inner-city locations they regarded as unsafe. Many preferred schools where relatively large numbers of black students were interested in challenging academic courses and preparation for college. Bright black students clearly have become a key to the recruitment and retention of white students and vice versa.

Why a school system like Richmond's would be willing to cater so much to white students, despite a preponderance of black students, probably has as much to do with economics as a commitment to integration. With much of Richmond's tax base still controlled by whites, and Richmond Public Schools dependent on the city council for a major portion of its operating revenue, many school officials have felt they had little alternative but to appease those whites who continued to support the public schools.

In their efforts to attract and retain whites, these officials sometimes have endorsed education policies that appeared, on the surface, to operate at cross-purposes. Such conduct might be referred to as "policy balancing." One of the most obvious examples of policy balancing occurred in the late eighties and early nineties when Richmond Public Schools supported both open enrollment *and* neighborhood schools. What makes this particular decision even more interesting is that each policy originally had been intended for purposes somewhat different from those for which it had come to be justified.

"Neighborhood schools" initially was the rallying cry of white parents opposed to busing. Many of those parents also opposed desegregation. Open enrollment derived from similar origins. First encountered in Richmond in the form of "freedom of choice," this policy was intended to slow the progress of school integration by refraining from assigning students to schools for the purpose of racial mixing. School officials believed that most parents, if given a choice of educational programs, would opt to send their children to schools close to home. Since neighborhoods in Richmond remained segregated for the most part, the result would be continued school segregation. Freedom of choice eventually was struck down by the courts, paving the way for court-ordered busing. In 1978, Richmond superintendent Richard Hunter, faced with the large-scale defection of white and middle-class black parents, revived freedom of choice in a limited form. Parents were allowed greater choice for a small number of elementary schools. The schools affected by this policy showed a slight increase in white enrollment.[19]

When neighborhood schools and open enrollment resurfaced in the mid-to-late eighties, circumstances had changed. Richmond had continued to lose population, and the financial condition of the school system had deteriorated. With a small white school population, busing no longer made much sense. Many black parents openly questioned the value of having black children ride school buses in order to attend predominantly black schools. A new commitment to neighborhood schools could mean curtailing transportation costs, appeasing black parents who were disenchanted with busing, and, possibly, encouraging whites to remain in or return to the school system. Tee-Jay stood to benefit from the neighborhood schools policy more than many Richmond schools, since it was still regarded as a viable option by some West End parents and it needed to boost enrollments to forestall threats of closure.

Oddly enough, Tee-Jay would also benefit from a policy of open enrollment. The school long had attracted the interest of parents elsewhere in the city. The creation of a magnet program at Tee-Jay proved that, given the opportunity, students from other parts of Richmond would choose to attend Tee-Jay. Unfortunately, the school district, under pressure from supporters of the Governor's School, restricted Tee-Jay's capacity to compete for middle school students other than those from its two feeder schools, Binford and Hill.

Despite the fact that both open enrollment and neighborhood schools seemed to benefit Tee-Jay, the two policies represented strange bedfellows. While they might have seemed compatible in the sixties and early seventies, by the late eighties they appeared to cancel each other out. Why reintroduce a policy assigning students to schools on the basis of their neighborhood if another policy allowed them to attend the school of their choice? A cynical observer could claim that school officials and board members simply had no idea of what they were doing. Robert L. Crowson and William Lowe Boyd, in fact, argue that "as financial conditions worsen . . . confusion and 'anarchy' seem to prevail in city decision making."[20] While such a contention is possible, a more likely explanation is that Richmond politics demanded policy balancing of the kind just described. Gordon Hill, a newcomer to Richmond, told this writer in the fall of 1991, "Richmond can't get beyond black and white. There are no greys here." To survive in circumstances characterized by a lack of consensus regarding the best approach to desegregation, Richmond Public Schools had little choice but to initiate seemingly incompatible policies in order to placate various constituencies.[21] The policy of neighborhood schools promised to effect some savings while winning support from blacks and whites who opposed busing. The policy of open enrollment, despite its origins, might now ease the sting of returning to a policy—neighborhood schools—that some associated with discrimination and resistance to desegregation. Open enrollment would allow parents to send their children to any city school. Contemporary school officials, like their predecessors, apparently banked on the fact that most parents would not take advantage of the open enrollment option. Long-time civil rights lawyer David Tatel, however, fears that well-intentioned policies like open enrollment eventually will destroy years of efforts to promote integration.[22]

The recent history of Tee-Jay and Richmond Public Schools underscores the fact that the meanings associated with certain policies can change as circumstances change. Circumstances in the late eighties and early nineties dictated the reintroduction of two policies originally regarded as key elements in the fight to impede desegregation efforts. Interestingly, when open enrollment and neighborhood schools resurfaced as official district policies, the former also served to facilitate, while the latter inhibited, the development of internal markets for students. Only time will reveal which policy has the greater effect. One thing seems clear, however. Where markets develop, so too does the potential for winners and losers. Richmond Public Schools currently enroll relatively few white students and college-bound black students. If, for whatever reasons, these students congregate in the same schools, they likely will benefit. How the remaining students in the school system will fare is less clear.

THE VIABILITY OF THE
COMPREHENSIVE HIGH SCHOOL

The development of internal markets within urban school systems like Richmond threatens the viability of the comprehensive high school. Schools designed to serve special populations and address special interests currently appear to be more attractive to many consumers than conventional high schools charged with the responsibility of accommodating everyone.

The comprehensive high school seemingly was well suited to traditional approaches to desegregation, or what has been described as the "command and control model."[23] Based on the assumption that most citizens were unwilling to cooperate, this model relied on restricted choice and coercion. Students were assigned to particular schools, thereby allowing targeted ratios of blacks and whites to be achieved.

The command and control model could not prevent whites and middle-class blacks from moving to the suburbs, however. Furthermore, the *Milliken* decision by the Supreme Court rejected the idea that suburban school systems could be compelled to participate in metropolitan desegregation plans, unless proof existed that they had practiced intentional segregation.[24] School systems like Richmond's consequently have begun to accept the fact that internal markets and parental choice may be their only option for maintaining some semblance of desegregation.

Comprehensive high schools like Tee-Jay may be hampered when school systems become markets because they are seen as trying to be all things to all students. Required by law to accept all students, they enroll some who are not particularly interested in receiving an education. Parents of highly motivated students often prefer more selective schools—such as Open High, Community High, and the Governor's School—that screen out the unmotivated. These alternative schools also are smaller, making it easier for teachers to attend to students' needs and maintain an orderly learning environment. Community High School and the Governor's School currently boast higher percentages of white students than any local comprehensive high school, including Tee-Jay.

An argument could be made, of course, that Tee-Jay would attract a greater percentage of white and college-bound black students if these alternative schools did not exist. The creation of Tee-Jay's magnet program in government and international studies demonstrated that bright students from across the city would attend a specialized program, if artificial enrollment barriers were not created. Transforming comprehensive high schools into magnet schools may prevent urban landmarks like Tee-Jay from being closed, but it is unlikely to save the comprehensive high school or the ideals for which it has stood.

Perhaps these ideals have been more honored in the breach than the observance. To the extent that most comprehensive high schools have been tracked, they have not really lived up to the dream of providing all students, no matter what background, race, ethnicity, or aspirations, with a truly common core of learning. Researchers have found that the quality of the learning experience in low tracks generally is inferior to that found in high tracks.[25] A special report by the Carnegie Foundation for the Advancement of Teaching concluded that urban school systems must acknowledge that "equity and excellence cannot be divided."[26] Despite the current popularity of magnet schools, they may not necessarily ensure the marriage of equity and excellence either. In February 1994 results of a federally funded study of magnet schools were leaked to *Education Week*. The study "cast doubt on the efficacy of magnet schools for desegregating school districts" and questioned the wisdom of federal funding to promote magnet schools in districts with little realistic chance of achieving racial balance.[27] Two months later a study presented at the American Educational Research Association convention in New Orleans indicated that magnet schools appear to have little impact on student achievement.[28] Using data from the National Education Longitudinal Study, the researchers found that no growth in achievement could be detected over the course of students' high school years in magnet programs. Because neither of these studies was available at the time this manuscript was being prepared for publication, their findings must be regarded with caution.

We have reviewed how Tee-Jay and Richmond Public Schools responded to desegregation and the push for educational equity for black students, and we have reflected on what these responses might mean for those committed to school integration. Integration will be of diminished value, it is clear, if the price to be paid for its achievement is inferior education. What can be learned from the history of Tee-Jay that might help those who care about increasing educational quality as well as equity? This question serves as the focus for the next chapter.

CHAPTER 8

The Struggle to Preserve Excellence

The first four decades of Tee-Jay's existence were marked by the development and refinement of a culture of excellence. What was special, if not unique, about this culture was the fact that academic achievement was highly valued, but not to the exclusion of other aspects of adolescent life. Tee-Jay's teachers and administrators were committed to the cultivation of well-rounded students. In the pursuit of this goal, the school amassed an impressive record of individual and collective success, in academics, sports, the arts, publications, and community service. Tee-Jay's legacy of excellence also encompassed a number of "firsts," including (but not limited to) the following:

- First Richmond high school to
  - offer student government
  - provide an honor system
  - offer physical education
  - use a "portable talking movie machine"
  - graduate students in academic gowns
  - have a booster's club
  - send students on school-sponsored trips outside the United States
  - schedule an annual College Day

- First high school in Virginia to
  - provide an astronomy observatory

- Among the first high schools in Virginia and the region to
  - offer a full complement of mathematics courses
  - offer computer courses
  - offer various AP courses

WHAT MAKES A HIGH SCHOOL EXCEPTIONAL?

Opinions vary regarding what makes a high school exceptional. Sara Lightfoot argues, for example, that "good" high schools are those that are conscious of their imperfections and willing to search for ways to improve.[1] All high schools can become better, she assumes, but those that stand out publicly acknowledge this fact, while lesser schools try to conceal or ignore it. Some reformers, like Ernest Boyer, prefer to conceive of school quality in terms of specific criteria. In his highly influential report on secondary education in the United States, Boyer argues that effective high schools possess a "clear and vital mission" and straightforward goals aimed at achieving the mission.[2] Theodore Sizer holds that the best schools are "thoughtful places"—settings where inquiry is respected and nurtured.[3] He condemns those who would equate quality education with indoctrinating young people in their own particular brand of truth.

Aspects of each of these views apply to Tee-Jay during its glory days, but it is this author's opinion that what made the school truly exceptional was its dual commitment to academic excellence *and* well-rounded students. Few who were familiar with Tee-Jay at this time would contest the school's dedication to academic achievement. Great value was placed on earning a seat in advanced courses, receiving good grades, and scoring well on standardized tests. At the same time, importance also was attached to good conduct, integrity, involvement in extracurricular activities, and participation in student government. The Tee-Jay faculty for the most part resisted the temptation, particularly in the late fifties when national attention was focused squarely on academic excellence, to downplay the school's role in shaping character and promoting a balanced view of adolescent development.

Few calls for reform in American secondary education have emphasized the value of a balanced high school education. The phrase "well-rounded student," or its equivalent, is virtually never encountered in the reform literature. From time to time proposals have called on high schools to encourage community service or character development, but the primary target of most blue ribbon reports, at least those during the last quarter century, have been to increase academic achievement, typically measured by standardized test scores, and improve vocational training in order to enhance the nation's economic prospects. An exception has been *High School: A Report on Secondary Education in America*, a collection of recommendations by the National High School Panel. In the prologue to the report, Ernest Boyer, who chaired the panel, wrote:

> Clearly, education and the security of the nation are interlocked. National interests must be served. But where in all of this [the reports linking educational excellence and economic recovery] are students? Where is the recognition that education is to enrich the living individuals?[4]

Many policymakers and other reformers apparently have failed to find a pressing national interest in the preparation of well-rounded students.

That Tee-Jay was able to pursue such a balanced mission for a substantial portion of its history without diluting its academic programs or sacrificing student achievement was due to a variety of factors, including an abundance of bright students and strong community support. Michael Rutter and his colleagues, in their extensive study of secondary education in London, noted the link between school effectiveness and the presence of a nucleus of academically able students.[5] Without such a core group, an academic culture—or what they termed a positive school ethos—is unlikely to develop. Other researchers have acknowledged the contribution to school success of an active and supportive community.[6] Despite their importance, however, able students and supportive community members do not necessarily ensure that a high school will become truly exceptional. H. G. Bissinger, for instance, has written about a high school in Odessa, Texas, that enrolled many able students and enjoyed considerable community support, but that was known more for its gridiron success than its academic accomplishments.[7] According to his year-long account, the culture of Permian High School placed greater value on winning the Texas state football championship and securing football scholarships than the balanced development and intellectual growth of its students. Tee-Jay students, parents, and faculty generally valued athletic prowess and took pride in their teams' victories, but few regarded sports as the school's major priority. What differentiated Tee-Jay from Permian, and many other high schools with which the author is familiar, was the nature of its organizational culture and, to a lesser extent, its structure.

When a school opens, there is nothing but a building and furniture. Students, teachers, administrators, and community members help to shape the school and its culture. In time, if a strong culture develops, the school begins to shape those who work and study there. It begins to symbolize certain qualities that students and teachers feel the need to emulate. These qualities are not always desirable, as is evidenced by some urban high schools where a premium is placed on being "cool" or tough and where academic success is scorned. The culture that formed at Tee-Jay, however, embraced qualities with which the middle class traditionally has identified.

Rossman, Corbett, and Firestone have maintained that the culture of an organization consists of two primary understandings: the way things are and the way things should be.[8] The first encompasses the interpretations that give meaning to events, behaviors, words, and actions. The second includes the norms and expectations that define what is appropriate and desirable. Strong cultures exist when substantial numbers of people in an organization share similar interpretations, norms, and expectations. By this criterion, Tee-Jay's culture was strong.

Teachers expected all students to work hard, tackle challenging material, strive to improve, conduct themselves honorably and courteously, and participate in school life outside as well as within class. "Eggheads" who did little else but study enjoyed no greater esteem than "jocks" who failed to take their coursework seriously. Conscientiousness was the norm, not just in honors and Advanced Placement courses, but in most courses and activities. A passing grade was rarely "automatic." Students who refused to apply themselves or conduct themselves responsibly, of course, could be found at Tee-Jay throughout its school's history, but they neither blended into the mainstream nor were perceived by the majority of their peers and teachers to "fit."

Competition and recognition played important supporting roles in Tee-Jay's culture. Opportunities were available for students to compete at various levels—within class, between classes and grade-levels, on an intramural and homeroom basis, and interscholastically. In keeping with the school's commitment to well-rounded students, competition encompassed all phases of school life, from academics to citizenship, athletics to the arts, fund-raising to community service. Most students could identify at least one area of competition in which they were capable of performing reasonably well. Students were exhorted to compete, not just for themselves, but for the honor of their class, homeroom, team, or school. Those who coveted recognition solely for selfish reasons tended to be held in low regard.

While much about Tee-Jay's culture was laudatory, particularly when viewed against the backdrop of contemporary urban high schools, some aspects of the culture could be considered problematic. Little sympathy, for example, was shown for students who were, or tried to be, "different" and students who, for whatever reasons, declined to try hard and compete. Teachers were much less likely to covet and receive recognition for helping improve the work of "slow learners" than for contributing to the success of the "best and the brightest." The academic expectations held by many teachers overvalued factual knowledge and mastery of required content and undervalued creativity and original thought. There is little reason to believe, however, that these aspects of Tee-Jay's traditional culture were unusual for similar schools at the time.

Tee-Jay's culture was supported by an organizational structure that left little to chance. Virtually all aspects of student life were subject to carefully developed rules, regulations, plans, guidelines, and policies. While outsiders might have regarded the plethora of constraints on behavior as an indication that students could not be trusted to behave appropriately, such an interpretation would have been misleading. Students, in fact, were responsible for developing and enforcing many school rules and regulations through the Student Participation Association and the Honor System. Rules and regulations were accepted by most members of Tee-Jay's community as essential elements of a large and complex organization. Implicit in the school's culture was the belief that everyone benefited from explicit guidelines and expectations. Spontaneity and leaving things to chance were not widely regarded as virtues. School should provide opportunities for fun, to be sure, but fun, like everything else at Tee-Jay, should be well-organized and orderly. Teacher leadership was valued at Tee-Jay. The school was structured so that academic business could be accomplished primarily through the departments, each of which was led by a chairperson. Chairs typically wielded considerable influence and often served as living symbols of the school's culture and traditions. The school's principals enjoyed widespread respect, perhaps in part because they were not regarded as threats to teacher leadership. Today high school principals who have been exhorted to function as institutional leaders often complain that they are unable to do so because of various factors, including an array of pressing noninstructional duties and the sheer curricular complexity of the modern high school. At Tee-Jay, the role of instructional leader almost always was played by department chairs.

Contemporary educational reformers would find much to applaud about Tee-Jay's organizational culture and structure during the glory days. Consider teacher empowerment, for example. Giving teachers a greater role in school decision making currently is considered to be a fundamental element of most "restructuring" schemes. Gerald Grant, a keen observer of high schools and excellent organizational historian, lists as his two "essential" reforms for American education (1) letting schools shape their own destiny and (2) putting teachers in charge of their own practice.[9] Decades before teacher empowerment became a buzzword, the Tee-Jay faculty enjoyed significant influence over their own practice and the destiny of their school. Through their academic departments, they determined course offerings, shaped curriculum content, coordinated expectations, determined assessment and promotion criteria, deliberated student assignments, and planned instructional improvement. Department chairs were *primus inter pares*, helping select new teachers and evaluate their performance, identify department needs, and administer department budgets. The Faculty Senate, along with the chairs, played a central role in school planning and policy development.

The value placed at Tee-Jay on running the school as a rule-governed organization also would receive considerable support among contemporary reformers. After widespread complaints during the sixties and early seventies that schools were obsessed with control and order, opinion seems to have shifted in light of the public's alarm over mounting student misconduct, drug and alcohol use, disrespect for authority, and campus violence.[10] Currently, Goal 6 of the national education agenda calls for every school by the year 2000 to be free of drugs and violence and to offer students a "disciplined environment conducive to learning." Key elements of the action plan for achieving Goal 6 involve "school organization and climate, classroom organization and management, and specific discipline policies and practices."[11] Authors of the action plan share with those who shaped Tee-Jay a belief in the importance of clear guidelines for student behavior and consequences for failure to observe them. Tee-Jay's practice of devolving some responsibility for rule development and enforcement on the student body itself also would appeal to many of today's policymakers. Research at Johns Hopkins has indicated that student involvement in school decisions related to discipline, along with other matters, is positively related to attitudes opposing violence and other inappropriate behavior.[12]

Recent calls for the reform of American high schools have focused on academic achievement, vocational education, and increasingly, discipline and order. Relatively little has been said about student government and extracurricular activities—two areas of vital importance to Tee-Jay's traditional culture and the school's commitment to producing well-rounded students. Reading much of the current reform literature, in fact, fosters the impression that high schools have erred by assuming too many non-academic responsibilities, thereby dissipating precious energy and resources and creating confusion about their real mission. Sara Lightfoot suggests that attending to such "cultural" concerns as school climate, day-to-day living conditions, the need for order, and student relationships can distract teachers, administrators, and students from matters of "academic substance."[13]

On occasion in the past, some teachers and parents complained that Tee-Jay was guilty of tempting students with an overabundance of activities, but no serious initiative was mounted prior to 1970 to eliminate the Student Participation Association or drastically reduce the rich array of extracurricular offerings. The closest Tee-Jay came to an official effort to curtail student participation in nonacademic activities was the creation of the Point System. The primary justification for the Point System, however, was actually (1) to enhance the quality of student involvement and (2) to expand opportunities for participation by discouraging a small group of overzealous students from dominating most student activities.

Importance has been attached in this book to the special culture that developed at Tee-Jay. Contemporary reformers, too, have noted the central role school culture can play in efforts to improve school effectiveness.[14] By recognizing and reinforcing what is important, school culture presumably helps students and teachers focus their efforts, thereby increasing the likelihood of achieving the school's mission. When, however, the mission itself is broad, such as Tee-Jay's commitment to produce well-rounded students, efforts to focus become more difficult. Balance supplants focus as the central value.

Perhaps no other aspect of school culture has received more attention from reformers in recent years than student expectations. Many high schools have been accused of expecting too little of students. The "back to basics" movement of the seventies has been indicted for refocusing the efforts of teachers and students on relatively modest learning outcomes. Conventional wisdom now holds that high expectations may not guarantee excellence, but low expectations assure that excellence will not be achieved. Tee-Jay's traditional culture was universally regarded to embody high expectations for all students, not just those in advanced classes. High expectations, however, were not limited only to coursework, as they sometimes appear to be in the reform literature.[15] Students at Tee-Jay were held to high standards in all phases of school life—deportment, character, student activities, athletics, publications, and the arts.

High expectations at Tee-Jay were reinforced through various forms of competition and recognition. Interestingly, contemporary reformers have embraced the value of student recognition far more readily than student competition. Competition, in fact, frequently is viewed as destructive of school culture, pitting one student against another and ensuring the presence of winners and losers. Reformers may wish to reconsider the value of competition in light of the Tee-Jay experience. In doing so, they should bear in mind two important conditions which characterized competition at Tee-Jay. First, students were not expected to compete only for themselves. More frequently than not, they competed as part of a within-class group, class, homeroom, or grade-level or for the entire school. Second, opportunities to compete were numerous and nonacademic as well as academic. Consequently, most students were assured of being competitive in some area. If they were not a top science or mathematics student, they might be able to raise more funds for charity, sell more subscriptions to the *Jeffersonian*, or maintain a better record of citizenship than their peers.

The factors that helped make Tee-Jay an exceptional high school during its first four decades have not diminished in their importance for public education. There is no reason to believe that teacher leadership, clear and high expectations for student performance, and a strong organizational culture are not as relevant for contemporary high schools as they were for Tee-Jay during its glory days. In fact, reformers frequently have cited these elements as essential to school effectiveness. A case also can be made that several aspects of Tee-Jay that have been overlooked in the current reform literature—such as the mission to produce well-rounded students, the central role of student government and extracurricular activities, and the value placed on student competition—also are worth the consideration of those desiring to improve the nation's high schools.

MAINTAINING EXCELLENCE

Achieving excellence is one thing; sustaining it quite another. This section addresses the extent to which the factors that helped make Tee-Jay exceptional have survived the turmoil and uncertainty of the seventies, eighties, and early nineties.

In *The World We Created at Hamilton High*, Gerald Grant traces the history of a high school in a northeastern industrial city. Similar in many ways to Tee-Jay, Hamilton High began in 1953 as an academically oriented school for the city's growing upper middle class. By 1960, when Hamilton underwent its first accreditation visit, the school was regarded as the premier high school in the area. Over 85 percent of its graduates went on to some form of postsecondary education. Two blacks were among the 350 graduates in 1960.

Hamilton High, like Tee-Jay, experienced the civil rights ferment and desegregation initiatives of the sixties and early seventies. Unlike Tee-Jay, however, Hamilton underwent a series of changes in school ethos that Grant termed "radical."[16] As a result, the "close-knit world adolescents encountered there [at Hamilton High] in 1965 was frayed almost beyond recognition five years later."[17] Adult authority eroded, and students assumed considerable responsibility not only for their own welfare, but the school's.

While the changes wrought by desegregation and related developments at Tee-Jay were substantial, to be sure, they did not constitute a radical break with the past. It is not inevitable, in other words, that desegregation and attendant demographic changes must occasion the total destruction of traditional school culture. Such a finding is important in light of the belief by some observers that organizational continuity always is the victim of desegregation efforts. The racial composition of a school can change dramatically, in fact, without the abandonment of traditional norms and values.

Perhaps Tee-Jay's age was a key to continuity. The origins of its special culture predated Hamilton High by more than two decades. The fact that Richmond also was a very old and conservative city populated by well-established middle-class blacks and whites also could have played a role. Whatever the reasons, Tee-Jay's history has not been characterized by the same dislocations as schools like Hamilton High.

One sign of continuity at Tee-Jay has been a consistent and visible commitment to academic achievement. Even when a majority of graduates no longer went to college, Tee-Jay's faculty and supporters still identified with intellectual rigor, good grades, hard work, and high expectations. Academic success continued to be recognized in public rituals like the National Honor Society induction ceremony as well as on an individual basis. Teachers and administrators went to great lengths to preserve AP courses and academic electives—obvious symbols of the school's unwillingness to abandon its heritage. The price to be paid for saving some of these courses often was higher enrollments in regular courses. In addition, the school day at Tee-Jay was kept seven periods long to accommodate the large number of courses. Tee-Jay students could boast that they enjoyed a greater choice of academic offerings than most of their peers.

Students also continued to select from a variety of extracurricular offerings in areas such as athletics, the arts, and community service. A few activities, such as student publications, fell victim to rising costs or declining interest. Teachers and students for the most part, however, continued to believe that high school entailed more than academic achievement. In several areas, notably community service, evidence even existed that latter-day students at Tee-Jay surpassed their predecessors in the extent and quality of local involvement.

Another indication of continuity at Tee-Jay was the maintenance of an orderly learning environment. With the possible exception of the first year of court-ordered busing, Tee-Jay never experienced the widespread unruly and disrespectful behavior frequently associated with urban high schools. Rules were posted and enforced. Absences were monitored. Classrooms and corridors were not permitted to become unsafe or cluttered with litter.

Unlike Hamilton High, adults did not abrogate authority in the face of a changing student body.

Teacher leadership also remained a characteristic of Tee-Jay. While the size of departments, along with the faculty, shrank as student enrollments declined, departments continued to serve as the locus for much decision making. The principal's office at Tee-Jay remained a sanctuary from the type of autocratic administration that distrusts teachers and questions the wisdom of shared decision making.

Besides these indicators of organizational and cultural continuity, Tee-Jay retained a core of able students and active community support throughout most of the post-1970 period. While the school's current record of achievement may not match that of the glory days, contemporary students actually have performed relatively well as a group, until very recently, in comparison with their local public high school peers, and individual students have continued to chalk up outstanding accomplishments. Considering the competition for able students from private schools and public alternatives, Tee-Jay's continuing ability to attract and retain a nucleus of talented young people has been noteworthy. That community support has remained active and enthusiastic is revealed by the willingness of many parents and alumni to mobilize against any threat to close Tee-Jay.

Having pointed out some examples of continuity, it is only fair to indicate instances where Tee-Jay has changed. The school's much admired Student Participation Association and Honor System are no longer around. Some AP and honors courses have had to be dropped. Change sometimes has meant gradual slippage more than total disappearance. Opportunities for students to compete, for example, have diminished on all but an interscholastic basis. While still perceived as high in relation to other urban high schools, expectations for Tee-Jay students clearly have been eased to accommodate larger numbers of "at-risk" students.

While Hamilton High experienced radical cultural change during the seventies and eighties, Tee-Jay underwent a process that might be more aptly termed "cultural adjustment." Many of the school's traditional values and emphases still can be discerned by the attentive observer, but they no longer stand out quite as vividly as in the past. Most of the faculty has continued to identify with Tee-Jay's traditions and reputation, but few who actually were associated with the school during the glory days remain. The singular commitment to preparing well-rounded, academically able students for college and subsequent positions of leadership has been moderated. For many Tee-Jay students in the eighties and early nineties, passing state proficiency tests and remaining in high school until graduation seem to be sufficiently challenging goals. More than a decade of uncertainty regarding Tee-Jay's future has injected a dose of fatalism into a culture once unabashedly optimistic. What had started as a struggle to preserve excellence in the early days of court-ordered busing has become a struggle for school survival, syphoning off energies that are sorely needed to serve Tee-Jay's growing numbers of needy students.

That Tee-Jay has been able to escape the wholesale deterioration of many "flagship" urban high schools and preserve some semblance of its traditional culture, organization, and record of success is a tribute to its students, teachers, administrators, and community supporters. A high school to whose defense students and parents have been willing, year after year, to rally hardly constitutes a bankrupt or irrelevant enterprise. Obviously they, along with teachers and administrators, believed Tee-Jay is worth fighting for. Special credit must go to a cadre of teachers—people like Edna Davis, Russell Flammia, Ruth Gibson, Kathleen Hancock, and Jim Holdren—who served as caretakers of school tradition, reminding colleagues and students of Tee-Jay's proud past. These individuals, along with particularly capable administrators and influential community members, furnished the leadership and inspiration necessary to sustain the school's protracted struggle for survival.

Supporters may wonder what might have been if Tee-Jay had been allowed to adjust to desegregation without the added pressures of budget crises, closure threats, competition from public alternative schools, school board reversals, and political intrigue. An argument, of course, can be made that the challenges actually are functional, providing important opportunities for students, parents and teachers to reaffirm the mission of their school and to develop a sense of common cause. Whatever the case, schools do not have the luxury of existing in a vacuum. They cannot be insulated from the problems of their communities. Despite their function as vessels of hope for cities like Richmond, urban high schools remain anchored firmly to reality. What can be learned from Tee-Jay's experience that might benefit other schools threatened with extinction is the subject of the concluding chapter.

CHAPTER 9

Keys to Organizational Survival: Continuity and Change

Observers of American education are not in agreement regarding the stability of schools over time. Some, like J. Victor Baldridge and Terrence E. Deal, assume that change is "natural and fundamental" for *all* organizations, including schools.[1] They maintain that schools constantly adjust in order to accommodate a variety of social, economic, demographic, and political changes. Robert Slavin, while acknowledging the pervasiveness of experimentation in schools, finds little evidence that the process has led to sustained improvement. He contends that the motion of educational change has been pendular rather than linear.[2] Noting faddism in the area of instruction, Slavin criticizes educators for neglecting to test with care new approaches to teaching before implementing them. William Lowe Boyd takes a similarly guarded position on change. He characterizes curriculum change in schools as "disjointed incrementalism," a "modest and mundane strategy" calling for "marginal" changes within the "broad outlines of the existing situation."[3] Arthur G. Powell, Eleanor Farrar, and David K. Cohen, on the other hand, contend that the American high school curriculum has undergone revolutionary changes, characterized by shifting emphases, courses of studies, and requirements.[4]

Some observers question whether schools change much at all. Larry Cuban, for example, argues that instruction in secondary schools has remained basically the same for a century.[5] Seymour Sarason believes that educators have consistently tried to innovate, but failed.[6] Claiming that educators do not understand the change process very well, he concludes that the more schools change, the more they remain the same. Daniel Monti reaches much the same conclusion in his assessment of desegregation in St. Louis. His judgment that desegregation was "a ritual that created only an illusion of change" is moderated, however, by the belief that "ritualized conflict" forces people to confront important issues that otherwise might never be debated openly.[7]

While consensus is lacking concerning the extent to which schools actually change, few dispute the desirability, if not outright necessity, of change. Failure to adapt to changing conditions typically is associated with organizational decline. Successful schools, along with other organizations, are portrayed as those that anticipate and accommodate change.

The Tee-Jay story suggests that wholesale endorsements of organizational change may require qualification. Continuity, under certain circumstances, actually may be as crucial to school success as change. Even when change is necessitated, Rosabeth Moss Kanter makes a point with which generations of Tee-Jay teachers and administrators would resonate—"creating change requires stability."[8] Her comprehensive review of research on innovation reveals the fact that successful change often is a function of "organizational structures and cultures that allow continuity."[9] When the need for change arose at Tee-Jay—as it did in the aftermath of busing—school personnel tended to undertake change within the boundaries of tradition. They initiated organizational changes to respond to shifting conditions while continuing to reinforce traditional school values.

Students of organizations tend to concentrate on explaining change rather than continuity. This bias can foster the erroneous impression that little conscious thought goes into preserving organizational culture and structure in the face of changing conditions. The argument goes that, If schools tend to remain largely as they have always been, inertia presumably deserves the credit. It is this author's belief, however, that organizational continuity should not be taken for granted. When examples of continuity are found, as in the case of Tee-Jay, they are just as worthy of analysis, explanation, and interpretation as are instances of change.

The purpose of this chapter is to reflect on the role of continuity and change in the recent history of Tee-Jay and consider what it may mean for the study of organizational morphology. To accomplish these purposes, it will be necessary to show how events at Tee-Jay since 1970 can be interpreted in more than one way.

A CHOICE OF INTERPRETATIONS

History is not just subject to interpretation. To a great extent, history *is* interpretation. Philip Selznick has noted that interpretation is the quest for an understanding of how a phenomenon fits into a "pattern of perception or motivation, history or culture."[10] An important focus of organizational histories is interpreting the meaning of responses to challenges, both from within and outside the organization. The recent history of Tee-Jay—including the school's responses to desegregation, white flight, retrenchment, and closure threats—can be interpreted in at least two ways.

One interpretation regards the Tee-Jay story since 1970 as a tale of slow decline, cultural erosion, and vanishing glory. Such an interpretation has been popular with some retired faculty members and older alumni, as well as Richmonders skeptical of the wisdom of court-ordered desegregation.

A colleague and I once interpreted the history of San Jose High School in a similar fashion. In an article entitled "The Slow Death of a Public High School," we recounted the impact of demographic changes, Proposition 13 (a tax-limitation measure), and several years of serious budget-cutting on the one-time flagship high school of San Jose, California.[11] We felt our motives were respectable. We hoped to draw public attention to the plight of urban high schools and rally support for supplementary funding to offset the destructive effects of California's landmark property tax-limitation measure. We documented in detail how budget cuts had reduced the school's capacity to meet the needs of its diverse student body. We criticized the district's policy of cutting funding for all high schools—both inner city and suburban—by the same percentage. Our argument held that comparable cuts do not affect suburban and urban high schools in comparable ways. The latter are hit much harder by lost resources because their students tend to be further behind.

We were surprised and dismayed when the San Jose High faculty—whose cause we had hoped to champion—roundly criticized our interpretation. They regarded their school's recent history as a saga of survival—a chronicle of valiant efforts by dedicated professionals to serve the interests of an ever-more-needy student body and minimize the impact of Proposition 13. Rather than seeing the decline of a once exemplary high school, they saw themselves rising to the challenge and making the necessary adjustments to larger classes and fewer colleagues. They felt that, by and large, these efforts were succeeding, though some questioned how much longer they could continue to put forth the extra energy.

A similar interpretation to the one preferred by the San Jose High School faculty could also be applied to the recent history of Tee-Jay. For the sake of balance and fairness, then, both interpretations will be discussed in this chapter. One interpretation will not be treated as better or more accurate. Where history is concerned, meaning varies with the beholder. What is important is to understand the assumptions upon which the different interpretations are based and the practical implications that derive from each.

THE SLOW DEATH OF TEE-JAY

Interpreting Tee-Jay's recent history as a persistent process of decline may result from a comparison of the high school during and after its glory days. A dispiriting record of dropping test scores, decreasing numbers of college-bound students, and increasing attention to basic skills and remedial coursework emerges from such a comparison. Enrollments in honors and AP courses fall to levels where consideration must be given to eliminating them. Teachers complain that more time must be spent monitoring student tardiness and absenteeism. Fears of racial incidents are prevalent. Unwilling to witness the loss of preeminence or concentrate on the needs of large numbers of underachieving inner-city youth, some Tee-Jay teachers retire. Those who replace them, along with veterans who decide to hang on, watch the percentage of white students drop steadily until fewer than two in ten are white. Special education students are transferred to Tee-Jay. Retaining academically able students becomes increasingly challenging as the district launches several selective alternative schools. Tee-Jay's much admired culture of academic excellence begins to erode. Standards must be adjusted in light of student deficits. Vital elements of traditional school life, such as the Student Participation Association, Honor System, and publications, fade away. Athletic teams struggle to remain competitive against larger high schools. Competition, once an important element of school culture, is downplayed to prevent discouragement and frustration. Continuing threats of closure syphon off student and teacher energy and cause some parents to search for alternatives, thereby reducing already low enrollments. The overall image is one of a spiralling down process where each new source of bad news serves to accelerate the pace of decline.

It is sobering to think of Tee-Jay's decline in light of all the school once had going for it. And what of the fate of urban high schools with a less glorious heritage and fewer resources upon which to draw? If a high school like Tee-Jay cannot do more to forestall the impact of demographic changes and budget problems, the magnitude of the crisis in urban education is indeed staggering.

Still, a small number of urban high schools are succeeding. Researchers have studied some of these schools to determine how they are defying the odds.[12] Sometimes the key to their success lies less with what they have than what they lack. For instance, they often lack a local context characterized by confusion and outside interference. In addition, they have been able to carve out a local niche for themselves, thereby providing a reasonable degree of security. What of Tee-Jay's context?

Confusion and outside interference certainly have been factors in the school's recent history. Much of the problem can be traced to lack of local leadership—both political and educational. The courts, for example, were compelled to intervene in the operation of Richmond Public Schools because local leaders refused to "do the right thing" and make a sincere effort to promote integration. As a consequence, Tee-Jay, along with other Richmond schools, was given only a few weeks to prepare for student busing and faculty transfers.

In the aftermath of 1970, district officials became absorbed in the politics of placation, trying to retain the support of diverse and sometimes antagonistic constituencies. They neglected some of the conditions associated with quality schooling, including clear mission and expectations and carefully coordinated programs and policies. The creation of Open High School and Community High School as refuges for bright, college-bound students was one example of the district's blurred vision. For Tee-Jay and other Richmond comprehensive high schools to be expected to maintain first-rate college preparatory programs in the face of internal competition from small, well-supported, and selective alternative schools was unreasonable. It was hard enough keeping students from fleeing to private schools. The creation of Open High School and Community High School had the effect of shrinking Tee-Jay's local niche, thereby increasing the comprehensive high school's vulnerability.

In *Savage Inequalities*, Jonathan Kozol describes the tendency of some city school systems to create special schools in a desperate effort to retain local support. He quotes a Washington, D.C., urban planner whose assessment of her city's policy regarding special schools might fit Richmond as well:

> In order not to have an all-poor system with still less political and fiscal backing than they have today, they [school district officials] will accept the lesser injustice of two kinds of schools within one system.[13]

Another example of the politics of placation was the simultaneous endorsement by Richmond Public Schools of both open enrollment and neighborhood schools. While the latter policy aimed to correct the dislocations of busing and bring stability to enrollment patterns, the former policy permitted parents access to any school in the district.[14] Any school but Tee-Jay, that is. To appease supporters of the Governor's School, only Tee-Jay's magnet program, of all those in Richmond high schools, was limited to recruiting students from its two feeder middle schools.

Between 1969 and 1993, Richmond Public Schools employed seven different superintendents, including one individual on two separate occasions. Turnover of school board members was also extensive. A 1991 document entitled *Citizens' Report: A Strategic Plan for Richmond's Future* and published by Richmond Tomorrow included in its list of weaknesses in the city's education system the following: (1) negative perceptions of public school system and long-term politicization and (2) lack of continuity in leadership.[15] The absence of stable district leadership has resulted in a steady stream of reorganization efforts, experiments, and action plans. By almost any yardstick, Richmond Public Schools has been a school system grasping at straws—desperate to do whatever is necessary to secure support and resources. Educational concerns consistently have been forced to the wings as political and economic issues occupied center stage. It would appear that Tee-Jay has not been alone in its struggle to survive. The school system itself is in jeopardy.

By the late winter of 1993, morale among teachers had deteriorated so much that the Richmond Education Association took the unprecedented action of voting "no confidence" in the school board. Teachers vowed to work to "secure an elected school board that is responsible to their employees and constituents."[16] Perhaps the real problem with district leaders was a tendency to be too responsive to too many constituencies. In their efforts to please everyone, no one was satisfied. The school board seemed incapable of taking a firm stand on issues of educational importance.

Interpreting the recent history of Tee-Jay as a tale of decline and lost glory leads to several implications for those concerned about the future of urban high schools. No longer do schools like Tee-Jay enjoy the security that comes from a captive enrollment. Not only has competition from private and parochial schools intensified, but open enrollment policies and within-district competition from selective alternative schools and magnet programs have expanded the options for students who remain in public schools. If comprehensive high schools like Tee-Jay are unable to define their niche in the local school system, they likely will continue to struggle.

It is possible, of course, that no niche exists for today's urban comprehensive high school. With corporations like General Motors and IBM being forced to downsize and subcontract with other organizations in order to remain competitive, the era of large and complex organizations, including high schools, could be ending. Economies of scale traditionally associated with such organizations are offset today by consumer demands for greater responsiveness, specialization, and personalized attention. Comprehensive high schools possibly can survive in affluent suburbs where they are, in effect, specialized college preparatory schools and where competition is slight. In large cities with diverse populations and numerous educational options, however, many students and parents perceive that small magnet programs, schools within schools, and alternative high schools offer more caring and focused environments for learning. The era when one high school could be all things to all students may be passing, at least in the nation's cities.

THE SURVIVAL OF TEE-JAY

Comparing today's Tee-Jay with the vintage version may induce a sense of loss, but comparing it with other contemporary urban comprehensive high schools produces a more favorable impression. Admiration is due a school that has fought to retain its culture and commitments in the face of daunting challenges that have closed down or rendered ineffective similar schools. Despite numerous threats to its existence, Tee-Jay has continued to survive. People have cared enough to fight to save the school. In an age when citizen involvement is mourned as a vestige of a bygone time, the willingness of supporters to rally around Tee-Jay should not be taken lightly.

When Tee-Jay is compared to many contemporary urban comprehensive high schools, it is understandable why students, parents, teachers, and others have fought to keep Tee-Jay open. At a time when many schools seem to have accepted the reality of de facto segregation, Tee-Jay actually reversed the loss of white students and began to lure them back with its new magnet program. Only district interference with Tee-Jay's recruiting efforts prevented the ratio of white to black students from approaching that of Community High School.

While other urban schools have felt compelled to focus exclusively on basic skills and vocational education, Tee-Jay has retained its academic curriculum, including special electives and Advanced Placement courses, and insisted on holding out the possibility of college to any student willing to work hard toward that end. A respectable percentage of students graduate and go on to some form of postsecondary education. Tee-Jay's dropout rate of 5 percent is quite low for an urban high school. The school's brightest students continue to hold their own in comparison to students from other schools.

At a time when high schools across the country are installing metal detectors and electronic surveillance equipment, Tee-Jay manages to provide a safe and orderly environment in which to study without the aid of modern technology. Students find their role models among teachers and coaches, not drug dealers and gang leaders. Considerable credit must go to the caring and commitment of the school's faculty and administration. In fact, Tee-Jay's continuing ability to attract dedicated educators is another reason for regarding it as exceptional. Staffing the nation's urban high schools with capable teachers and administrators has become a cause of considerable concern to school officials and policy makers. Despite decades of challenges, vestiges of Tee-Jay's much admired culture, including high expectations and the valuing of extracurricular activities, still can be found. As in the past, students and teachers are proud to be associated with Tee-Jay.

Why has Tee-Jay fared better than many urban high schools? For one thing, the school has had the good fortune to be located in a safe, attractive, and stable neighborhood. Parents generally have felt comfortable sending their children to Tee-Jay. The fact that whites have not abandoned the city's West End has contributed to the school's ability to attract and retain white students and teachers. Black professionals who have moved into the neighborhood in recent years have swelled the ranks of Tee-Jay's supporters and increased the pool of bright students from which the school can draw.

That Tee-Jay's supporters have been politically savvy is another reason for the school's ability to survive. These people recognized the value of organization, planning, and media attention. Because many were connected to Richmond's power structure, they also knew how to "work the system," get decisions reconsidered, and gain access to top officials. Political skills such as these, coupled with the willingness of Tee-Jay's students to speak up for their school, made it difficult for the school district to follow through on closure threats.

Perhaps engaging students in defending their school pays other dividends as well. Those who have monitored the efforts of Tee-Jay students to save their school are impressed with their responsible behavior and sound arguments. If all students periodically were called upon to fight for their school's future, they just might develop a greater sense of ownership and take their studies more seriously.

Of all the keys to Tee-Jay's survival, though, the most important probably has been its ability to adapt to changing circumstances while simultaneously remaining familiar. Certain challenges, like busing, compel schools to change in order to meet the needs of new students. If schools change too radically, however, they risk losing their traditional symbolic value and, hence, much of their support. Tee-Jay, in the days following court-ordered busing, faced just such a situation. Had too many changes in curriculum, instruction, organization, and culture been made to accommodate incoming students, many of whom came from poor families and possessed modest records of academic achievement, Tee-Jay would have jeopardized its ability to hold bright students, both black and white, who expected to receive a solid college preparatory program. While Tee-Jay eventually lost a large number of white students, its unwillingness to abandon completely a commitment to academic excellence allowed the school to retain more than a token number of whites. This commitment also convinced many college-oriented black students not to abandon the school for other options.

Conventional wisdom holds that the failure of organizations to change invariably leads to decline and dissolution. Such a position ignores the fact that too much change also can lead to disaster. If there is one lesson to be learned from the foregoing "optimistic" interpretation of Tee-Jay's recent history, it is that, under certain circumstances, continuity and change must coexist in order to facilitate organizational survival. Efforts to preserve a strong culture of academic excellence should not be viewed automatically as a rearguard action intended solely to benefit those who traditionally have benefited from rigorous schooling. Thomas Green has argued persuasively that educational equity is more likely to result from the pursuit of excellence than vice versa.[17] The challenge for organizations like Tee-Jay is to embrace change without destroying that which led to greatness in the first place.

The timeliness of this lesson should not be overlooked. The early nineties have witnessed a groundswell of demand for changes in American schools. Terms like "restructuring" and "reinventing" abound. Amidst the general call for reform, it is easy to forget that every school and every community is, to some extent, unique. Determining how best to alter the structure of a school may depend on an understanding of the history and traditions of the school and the community in which it is located. Larry Greiner, a student of organizations, concludes that "the future of an organization may be less determined by outside forces than it is by the organizations."[18] That Tee-Jay has survived repeated external challenges to its existence cannot be understood apart from its unique background.

The Tee-Jay experience offers an additional lesson for students of contemporary change. Organizational success is more than a matter of developing the "right" structure. Restructuring roles, decision making, incentives, expectations, and accountability systems may be necessary to help many schools keep pace with social and economic trends, but these adjustments are no substitute for committed teachers and administrators, supportive parents, and motivated students. In this time of endemic change, it is important to bear in mind that restructuring, while necessary, may be insufficient alone to transform troubled schools.

ORGANIZATIONAL HISTORY:
A SOURCE OF INCREASED
UNDERSTANDING OF SCHOOLS

The great French historian Fernand Braudel noted that there is not one history, but many kinds of history.[1] Library shelves contain histories of societies, nations, religious groups, social movements, ideas, wars, institutions, and organizations. While most of these works share a common commitment to describing human endeavor over time and exploring, to whatever extent possible, primary resources, they vary considerably in scope, perspective, methods of analysis, and implications. This essay explores one particular type of history—organizational history—and how it can be used to understand the development of schools. The opening section describes the nature and focus of organizational history. Discussions of the importance of this methodology and how it can be undertaken follow. Several examples of organizational histories of schools, including the preceding study of Thomas Jefferson High School, are used to illustrate key aspects of the process.

WHAT IS ORGANIZATIONAL HISTORY?

The unit of inquiry and analysis for organizational history is the organization. While people in the organization, their motives and beliefs, and the sociopolitical context in which the organization exists are important, these subjects are studied primarily for the light they shed on the organization as an entity, not vice versa. The organization occupies the foreground; its context and membership the background. Organizations are collections of people ostensibly pursuing a set of common purposes within a relatively formal structure of rules, roles, and relationships. The particular type of organization that serves as the focus for this essay is the ubiquitous precollegiate school.

Organizational history represents a merging of the goals, perspectives, and methods of historical research and the language, concepts, and frameworks of sociology-based organization theory for the purpose of understanding the evolution of particular organizations over time. A 1954 report of the Social Science Research Council's Committee on Historiography noted that the function of theory in history is to "suggest problems, to provide categories for organizing data, to supply hypotheses by which various interpretations of the data may be tested, and to lay down criteria of proof."[2] The report goes on to observe that the main function of theory is to provide the investigator with questions, not answers.

In its reliance on organization theory, the field of organizational history follows in the tradition of the New History.[3] For example, organizational history stresses close links with social science and a broad view of the subject matter appropriate for historical study. Prior to the twentieth century, most historians would not have found the study of individual organizations such as schools worthy of their efforts. Where organizational history deviates from the tenets of the New History is in its concern for the unique and the particular as well as broad generalizations and regularities.

Dray maintains that historical understanding is a function of two scholarly endeavors—description and explanation.[4] Of these, description necessarily comes first. This position has been advanced most convincingly by Husserl and other phenomenologists, as well as by advocates of the New Sociology.[5] All agree that it is pointless to attempt to explain phenomena until the phenomena have been described as precisely as possible.

History, however, is not just description and explanation. It also involves interpretation and the search for meaning. As Rickman noted in his introduction to Dilthey's *Pattern and Meaning in History*, historical understanding entails uncovering "the meaning of an action, or sequence of actions" in order to provide observers with "criteria for selecting what is relevant and deciding what is important."[6] Sometimes this process is referred to by historians as "interpretation." Ritter defines interpretation as

The ensemble of procedures by which the historian—according to personal perspective, temperament, social conditioning, and conscious choice—imposes a pattern of meaning or significance on his subject; the process of selection, arrangement, accentuation, and synthesis of historical facts that establishes the personal stamp of an individual historian on an account of the past.[7]

Let us now review briefly the three elements of historical research as they might relate to the study of schools as organizations.

Undertaking an organizational history of a school requires describing the school at various stages in its development. Here, however, we encounter for the first time what Dray terms "the problem of selection."[8] What is to be described? Obviously it is impossible to describe everything about an organization. At this point the value of organization theory becomes apparent. Organization theory offers a variety of concepts related to organizational structure and culture. These concepts specify different dimensions of organizations that are considered by theorists to be important in differentiating among organizations and explaining what they accomplish and how. A control theorist, for example, may choose to describe mechanisms established to ensure that members of the organization attend to the organization's goals. Such mechanisms often include supervision, evaluation, rewards, and sanctions. Other theorists may prefer to describe decision-making processes (authority structure), designated roles and relationships between roles, policies and rules governing the behavior of organization members, or informal organizational factors.

Whatever the structural or cultural dimensions of the organization that are chosen to guide descriptive research, the focus of attention is the collection of data over time. Unlike many case studies and examinations of innovations in organizations, organizational history demands descriptive information covering the "life" of the organization (or, at least, a substantial portion of the organization's existence). Beginning with the circumstances surrounding the organization's creation and a description of the initial characteristics of the organization, the organizational historian proceeds to describe changes in the organization and the temporal contexts in which the changes have occurred. At the same time that changes are chronicled and contextualized, the organizational historian also notes aspects of the organization that remain relatively unchanged.

The problem of selection also must be faced when explanation is the focus of attention. What aspect or aspects of the organization's history should be explained? Some historians, notably Dilthey, have argued that what is most important historically are patterns of action or regularities rather than unique events. He contended that that which recurs tends to reflect what people regard as meaningful. Such a view may lead the organizational historian to identify and attempt to explain those dimensions of an organization that remain relatively stable or unchanged over time.

Other historians are drawn more to change than stability. They seek to explain disjunctions, breaks with the past, unexpected developments, and the like, finding in these atypical events keys to understanding social problems and collective aspirations. Explaining organizational changes may lead historians to try to account for shifts in goals and mission, the emergence of new roles and relationships, efforts to restructure decision making or elements of the organization's technical core, alterations in policies and procedures, and changes in cultural values and norms.

It is this writer's opinion that stability and change *both* merit explanation where organizations are concerned. In other words, it is insufficient to *assume* that organizations exist in a natural state of either homeostasis or constant change. Organizational stability and organizational change both have "causes," and it is the duty of the organizational historian to understand as much as possible about these causes.

Chronicles of stability and change often reveal stories of the struggle to survive. No organization, however essential or revered, is assured of continued existence. Schein observes that the survival of all organizations is a function of how well they address two central needs—internal integration and external adaptation.[9] Organizations, like people, are driven by needs. They must see that their members continue to work together toward common goals while simultaneously ensuring that these goals reflect the interests of the external environment.

The issue of organizational survival therefore provides another focus for historical explanation and, hence, another choice for the historian. How should the "story" of survival be told? Is it best presented as a triumph or a tragedy, a case of missed opportunity, a tale of irony, an epic, or a satire?[10] Facts and explanations can be arranged in various ways according to a number of possible "plots," depending on what the historian finds significant about an organization's history.

At each stage of an organization's development, from its inception through assorted changes, various real and perceived threats to its existence may be encountered. On occasion, particular threats are so potent that the organization ceases to exist. No organizational history would be complete without some effort to account for the organization's responses to threats. Just as organizational stability and change should not be assumed, historians must never take for granted the existence of an organization. Sometimes it is at the very time when an organization appears most secure to the casual observer that its vulnerability is greatest. As the adage goes, nothing breeds failure more than success.

Forty years ago many students of public education seemed to assume that public schools were a relatively fixed part of every community. The era of school consolidation had passed; school enrollments were growing. Issues of school survival could not have been further from their thoughts. Several decades of declining birth rates, desegregation, white flight, taxpayer revolts, private and parochial school expansion, homeschooling, and the popularization of school choice have demonstrated, however, that no public school is totally "safe." Understanding why one school is closed while another remains open may require the historian to track the activities of special interest groups, local political "deals," and school-based initiatives. Threats can be thought of as "choice points." On occasions when organizations are threatened, they usually are faced with a range of alternatives, from resistance to capitulation, adjustment to radical reform. How an organization chooses to respond to threats constitutes an important part of its story.

Reflecting on the meaning of an organization's history is the third task for the organizational historian.[11] What is the significance, for example, of the fact that a school remains relatively stable during a period of rapid social change? What meaning can be attached to periodic efforts to restrict or expand the curriculum choices available to students? Should an attempt to decentralize decision making during a period of expansion be interpreted differently from a similar attempt during a time of retrenchment? Ultimately the meanings associated with historical events, rather than the events themselves, justify the historian's efforts. Historians therefore must be careful to specify when they are attempting to understand (1) the contemporary meanings of historical events and (2) the meanings of those events at the time of their occurrence.

In summary, then, *organizational history is a form of systematic inquiry intended to describe, explain, and find meaning in the creation and evolution of particular organizations.* Why such endeavors are worth doing is the subject of the next section.

WHY IS ORGANIZATIONAL HISTORY IMPORTANT?

The value of understanding the history of particular organizations derives from various factors. First, organizations are important because most people spend a good portion of their lives in them. The more that is known about organizations, the easier it becomes to create and maintain hospitable and productive organizational environments. Second, organizations do not exist in a vacuum. The changes they experience can provide insight into what certain segments of society regard as meaningful at particular points in time. Third, there is currently a great deal of concern about the viability of many organizations. Efforts to "restructure" or otherwise alter contemporary organizations so that they may better serve human needs can be informed by an understanding of what these organizations are and how they got to be this way. Finally, understanding the history of particular organizations eventually may help us understand the evolution of organizations in general. Let us briefly look at each of these reasons.

In Western society, virtually everyone spends a considerable portion of their childhood and adolescence in educational organizations. They also may become members of churches and youth organizations. With maturity comes employment, possible military service, and membership in community organizations and voluntary groups. Because most people spend much of their existence in organizations and because organizational structure and culture influence human action, those who seek to understand human behavior can benefit from understanding organizations and how they become what they are.

How is it, for example, that two elementary schools serving similar groups of students in contiguous neighborhoods of the same city differ dramatically in terms of look, "feel," and success? Conventional efforts by social scientists to answer this question often involve comparisons of current school characteristics. School A has a dynamic principal, a committed faculty, and involved parents. School B does not. While important, such observed differences are only the beginning of the story, not the end. The organizational historian asks, "How has it evolved that one neighborhood tolerates an ineffective school while an adjacent neighborhood boasts an exemplary one?" Has School B always been a marginal operation, or was there a time when its leadership, faculty, and parental involvement were comparable to School A's? Has School A always been a model, or did it once resemble School B? Only by investigating these and related questions is it possible to appreciate how some organizations serve the needs of their clients while other organizations simply compound their clients' misery.

Organizational history not only provides insight into the lives of those in and affected by organizations, but it offers a window on the world in which organizations are located. Schein observes that organizations which consistently fail to accommodate the needs, norms, and values of their communities rarely survive.[12] Organizational change often results from external pressure. As a consequence, understanding the ways in which organizations change over time can reveal important information about the contexts in which they exist.

Consider a suburban high school that eliminates most of its vocational programs. Such a change may reflect a shift in the socioeconomic composition of the community. As the percentage of middle- and upper-middle-class patrons increases, the importance of college preparatory courses rises. Enrollment in vocational programs drops. Even though some students still do not go on to college, the community has come to regard preparation for college as the central purpose of high school. They grow unwilling to provide financial support for relatively expensive vocational programs serving small numbers of students.

A third reason it is important to study organizational history concerns organizational change. It is one thing to understand *why* an organization changes. *How* it changes is quite another matter. Studies of the history of organizations provide details concerning the processes by which organizations adjust and transform themselves. How an organization goes about change in turn reveals key assumptions about human behavior, local values, and what those in charge understand about the change process. What alternatives, for example, were considered prior to making changes in the organization? Were some options never entertained? Once implemented, were changes evaluated? If so, by what criteria were the changes judged? Such information can be invaluable to those involved in organizational development.

Of particular interest is the pattern of organizational change over time within particular organizations. Does organizational change tend to be symmetrical or asymmetrical? Consider, for example, changes occasioned by increasing and decreasing resources. Do organizations contract in the reverse order in which they expand? What elements of an organization's structure are most and least likely to change? Relatively little is known about the "life cycle" of particular innovations or the relationships over time among organizational changes within the same organization.

Present efforts to "restructure" schools offer rich opportunities for the study of organizational history. Since this movement is not the first to address the need for reform in school structure, the chance exists to compare restructuring at different points in time within the same schools. Historically, particular schools and school systems have experimented with increasing and decreasing teacher and parent involvement in decision making, tightening and loosening rules and regulations, and expanding and reducing academic requirements, to mention but a few types of organizational change. Those who have studied these and other educational changes note that no two schools are likely to implement an innovation in the same way.[13] Understanding the history of a particular school can help local change agents tailor the change process and increase the possibility of successful change. While not foolproof, the best predictor of how an organization will respond to change probably is a knowledge of how the organization previously responded to change.

By amassing information on how and why particular organizations develop as they do, organizational historians contribute to a general understanding of organizations, thereby making it possible for organization theorists to test and extend their theories.

An example may be helpful. The importance of organizational focus or mission has been noted by various students of organizations. What remains unclear, though, is whether the critical role of mission is constant over time or episodic. At certain times (when external conditions are unstable, for instance), it may be appropriate for organizational mission to be relatively vague. W. T. Grant, the retailing giant, went bankrupt when it insisted on maintaining its traditional mission during a period of demographic shifts. Efforts to focus organizational energies prematurely—while external conditions are still in flux—may not be prudent. To confirm such a contention, an understanding of the histories of particular organizations is needed.

Arriving at generalizations about organizations as a result of in-depth histories of particular organizations is not prevailing practice, however. Typically, organization theorists rely on multiple case studies, surveys of organizations, and cross-sectional analyses. These methods are useful, but they do not provide the richness of detail or the temporal perspective of organizational history. Studies of the history of individual organizations enhance the theorist's appreciation for the variability across organizations. Theory that ignores such variability may fail to capture the complexity to which reality is heir.

Having noted various reasons why organizational history can be a worthwhile endeavor, we need also to point out some possible limitations of the approach. By focusing on a single organization, the historian may foster the illusion of autonomy—of a vessel periodically buffeted by winds, but essentially steering its own course. Critics can counter, however, that organizations—particularly schools—are part of greater systems and that the only history worth undertaking is the history of these systems.

A second limitation is related to the assumption that the past is relevant to understanding the present. If, as some observers contend, the contemporary relevance of an organization's history cannot be assumed, then focusing on the past could obscure, rather than illuminate, explanations of the present nature of an organization.[14]

UNDERTAKING ORGANIZATIONAL HISTORY

To engage in the process of organizational history requires a variety of operations. Seven activities in particular seem to be important: selecting an organization, identifying a time period, determining subjects for description, collecting descriptive information, selecting critical events, explaining critical events, and determining the meaning of descriptive and explanatory information. Each of these steps will be discussed by drawing on examples from several recent organizational histories of schools. A note of caution is in order. Discussing the seven steps separately creates the impression of a linear, cookbook-like approach. In reality, though, conducting an organizational history is likely to be a much "messier" and integrated process.

Selecting a School

In selecting a school, certain considerations should be taken into account. For example, it makes little sense to conduct a history of a relatively new school. Case study methodology may be more appropriate. Only with the passage of time comes the variety of internal and external challenges and subsequent organizational responses that shape the school's "character" and make its story worth telling. Another consideration involves the availability of primary and secondary resources. If few documents related to the history of a school are available and if informants are scarce, the value of undertaking an organizational history must be questioned.

What types of schools have been chosen for organizational histories to date? First of all, it should be noted that most organizational histories have involved corporations, private schools, colleges, and universities. Relatively few published histories of public elementary and secondary schools exist. Several histories of school districts have been written, including most recently histories of the Richmond (Virginia) Public Schools from 1954 to 1989 and the Seattle Public Schools from 1901 to 1930.[15] The problem with district histories, though, is that they rarely examine individual schools in any detail. As a result, organizational variation within the school system can be overlooked. Pratt's history of Richmond Public Schools, for instance, seems to suggest that all schools in the district adjusted to desegregation in similar ways. The preceding historical investigation of Thomas Jefferson High School indicates that organizational responses to desegregation probably varied considerably among Richmond's high schools.

Over the past few decades, relatively few books about schools have met all of the criteria of an organizational history. *McDonogh 15* and *Race War in High School*, for example, are highly personal accounts of a New Orleans elementary school and a Brooklyn high school.[16] Neither focuses on school organization per se, though both deal with the topic in the process of relating personal anecdotes about a principal's triumphs over adversity, in the case of the former book, and a teacher's tortured journey through desegregation, in the case of the latter. *Inside High School* and *Adolescent*

Life and Ethos: An Ethnography of a U.S. High School are highly informative ethnographic accounts of life in a high school, but the first is based on six months' and the second on one year's field-work.[17] The authors draw on historical data periodically to enhance their descriptions and analyses of student life, but their efforts hardly can be classified as systematic organizational histories. Neither describes organizational structure in detail nor tries to capture changes in structure over time. *Friday Night Lights* provides fascinating insights into the evolution of Permian High School in Odessa, Texas, but the primary purpose of the narrative is to chronicle one year in the life of Permian's football program.[18] School organization receives some treatment, but only when it enhances, or interferes with, the culture of competitive athletics that dominates the community.

The two recent books which, in this author's judgment, best represent the preceding conception of organizational history are *The World We Created at Hamilton High* and *The Making of an American High School*.[19] In the former, Grant offers a "sociologically informed history" of a high school in a northeastern city from 1953 to 1987. Labaree looks at Philadelphia's Central High School from 1838 to 1939. Referring to his work as a "case study," the author undertakes what is essentially a school history informed by sociological, political, and economic frameworks.

In selecting a school, the organizational historian may be interested primarily in locating one that is presumed to be typical. While Hamilton High had been an elite, all-white urban high school, Grant did not treat it as if it were unlike other urban high schools experiencing desegregation. Labaree, on the other hand, makes a point of Central High's special status. Central was the first public high school in Philadelphia, and one of the first in the country. Its unique curriculum initially prepared boys to enter the business world and pursue careers as proprietors of commercial enterprises. His approach to the story of Central is that of one who has identified an exemplar.

A third choice may be a school which represents an alternative to typical schools. Alternative schools may or may not be exemplars, but they are never typical, at least in comparison to conventional public schools. This is because they purposefully strive to be what conventional public schools are not. A few histories of alternative schools were written in the sixties and early seventies.[20] Since alternative schools tended to be short-lived phenomena, however, these histories rarely covered more than a few years. Understandably, the focus of attention was the creation of the alternative school, not its subsequent development. Such brief lifespans do not permit the kind of in-depth analysis and understanding of organizational development that are possible with more established schools.

Thomas Jefferson High School was selected for the preceding study for several reasons. Like Hamilton High, Tee-Jay had been an exemplary academic high school prior to desegregation. Token desegregation and court-ordered busing did not convince school officials to alter the school's mission, though some efforts were made to accommodate a more diverse student body. For three decades Tee-Jay struggled to maintain an academic culture and retain white students against formidable odds, including numerous efforts by the Richmond school board to close it. Why a predominantly black school system would seek to shut down one of its few comprehensive high schools with more than a tiny number of white students was one of the interesting questions that prompted Tee-Jay's selection for study. Another reason concerned the survival strategies employed by Tee-Jay supporters to forestall closure. Since little was known about what schools do to prevent their own demise, the choice of Tee-Jay promised to shed light on an important aspect of organizational morphology.

Selecting a Time Period

Conducting an organizational history requires the identification of a time period for study. Case studies of organizations and organizational histories are similar in many respects, but they differ in terms of the length of time to be covered in detail. While historical information serves as background material for the case study, it is the central concern of organizational history. For this reason, as much care must be devoted to investigating prior periods in the history of an organization as the present or culminating period.

Organizational history need not encompass the entire span of an organization's history. Labaree's history of Central High School, for instance, covered a century, stopping just before World War II. Of greater importance is the fact that the author began with the opening of the school in 1838. Given the significance of circumstances surrounding the birth of an organization, it would be difficult to undertake a history without covering the organization's early years. Determining a point at which to stop is relatively easy when an organization ceases to exist or reaches a natural watershed. In the case of Central High, 1939 marked the school's move to a new building and the return of its status as Philadelphia's only selective high school for boys. The latter event marked a victory for Central's long-time supporters and a logical stopping place. Labaree elected not to carry on his project until 1983, when Central faced a court order to admit girls, but this date also could have served as an end-point.

Selecting a stopping place can be more difficult when dramatic events continue to unfold. When I began my history of Thomas Jefferson High School in Richmond, Virginia, the school had just survived its second closure threat in four years. The occasion seemed a perfect place to conclude the history. Within a few months, however, district officials again were hinting that the future of the school was in jeopardy. Ending the history when I originally had planned would have excluded an important example of policy reversal and fostered the erroneous impression of organizational stability at the close of the story.

Focusing the Descriptive Investigation

Identifying a focus or foci for the descriptive part of the organizational history represents another decision point. Asserting that organizational data about a school will be collected is insufficient. What constitutes "organizational data" can vary from one researcher to another. In addition, theorists disagree about which elements of organizations are most worthy of study. Some shun the more formal dimensions of organizational structure in favor of informal organization. Others focus on the classical elements of structure—goals, control mechanisms, organization charts, decision-making processes, policies, rules, roles, and the like. The past decade has witnessed heightened interest in organizational culture, encompassing such elements as norms, values, unofficial roles, and rituals. Any of these features of an organization is subject to change. Describing changes in a school's formal structure, informal organization, or culture can lead to insights regarding the school's needs and challenges and increased understanding of how it has developed over time. Even when change does not occur, there is a story to be told. For example, the fact that a school's rules governing student behavior remain the same despite dramatic shifts in student conduct may be a "non-event," but one clearly worthy of description and, ultimately, explanation and interpretation.

In *The World We Created at Hamilton High*, Gerald Grant concentrates on how the school's mission was defined before, during, and after a period of school desegregation. The story of Hamilton High is one of initial rejection and subsequent acceptance of student diversity. To enhance readers' understanding of this shift, the author describes the gradual evolution of the school's culture and authority structure. Hamilton High started out as an all-white high school, the pride of the prominent in the community. Desegregation occasioned the breakdown of the school's "old order," plunging Hamilton High into an eight-year period when students essentially did what they wanted and educators largely abdicated their authority. From 1980 until 1985, the faculty and administration reasserted their authority in a variety of formal and informal ways. The resulting stability was accompanied by widespread support for student diversity, support that had been lacking during the preceding period of anarchy. Grant provides a valuable account of how Hamilton High's organizational structure and culture adjusted to changing demographics, at first unsuccessfully and eventually successfully.

School mission and authority structure also serve as foci in David Labaree's *The Making of an American High School*. In addition, however, the author describes stability and change in Central High's curriculum, discipline policies, and pedagogy. For instance, Labaree writes of the early days of the school:

> From the opening day in 1838, Central High School took on a form that closely expressed the mixed purposes embedded in its founding ideology. It presented students with a curriculum that was both common, permitting little choice (and later, no choice at all), and practical, oriented toward the preparation of students for business. The early system of discipline was explicitly designed to mold character rather than simply keep order, and conduct was incorporated into academic grades. Also, the school's pedagogy was extraordinarily meritocratic. Students could gain admission only through a highly competitive entrance examination.[21]

As Labaree proceeds to relate the story of Central High, he continually refers to these aspects of the school's organization.

Changes in rules and policies governing the behavior of students and teachers are chronicled. Descriptions are provided of new courses, tracks, and graduation requirements. Shifts in leadership and governance procedures receive considerable attention. Some of these changes in school organization are treated by the author as particularly important. These are the changes that eventually become the focus of explanation and interpretation.

In studying the history of Tee-Jay, the decision was made to concentrate on the school's mission, formal structure, and culture. How these aspects of school organization originally developed in the thirties, forties, and fifties and then were affected by the withering array of challenges faced by the school from the time of initial desegregation through recent threats by the Governor's School constitute the basis for much of this book's historical narrative. Trying to explain why some aspects of these organizational elements changed while others remained basically the same is an important part of the latter half of the book.

Collecting Data

Primary sources are the historian's grail. Dating from the time period under consideration, these materials provide direct access to the perceptions of participants. They allow the historian "to take on, mentally, the circumstances, views, and feelings of those being studied so as to interpret their actions appropriately."[22] Labaree, for example, draws heavily on the minutes of faculty meetings to describe changes in mission and governance at Central High. Grant consults student and community newspapers and yearbooks in his efforts to reconstruct the evolution of Hamilton High.

Primary sources must not be treated as if they are free of interpretation and bias, however. Recorders of minutes and journalists, for example, may allow personal impressions and judgments to comingle with their "objective" accounts of events. For this reason, organizational historians must seek, whenever possible, multiple sources of primary data. This process sometimes is referred to as "triangulation." Data pertaining to the same subject that are derived from different sources permit corroboration.[23] Trustworthiness increases when several sources share similar views or point to the same set of "facts."

Secondary sources provide additional information for the organizational historian. These sources of data include efforts subsequent to the events under consideration to describe, explain, and "make sense" of the events. The works of historians and social scientists are a chief source of secondary material.

Data derived from retrospective interviews with individuals who actually participated in the events under consideration combine elements of primary and secondary material. While these persons have the benefit of firsthand knowledge, their memories are imperfect and their recollections are subject to modification in light of subsequent events. For instance, teachers who were greatly concerned over student conduct during the sixties may look back wistfully on that period as a time of relative innocence in light of subsequent violence on campuses. Organizational historians need to keep one eye on the past as they scan descriptive material obtained in the present, making sure to balance recollections with primary resources whenever possible.

It goes without saying that the quality of historical explanation and interpretation can be no greater than the quality of the descriptive data upon which the historian draws. An illustration is provided by Maris Vinovskis's reexamination of Michael B. Katz's study of Beverly High School. In *The Irony of Early School Reform*, Katz recounted the March 14, 1860, vote at the Beverly (Massachusetts) town meeting to abolish the town's two-year-old high school.[24] The availability of voting records and descriptive data on voters allowed Katz to determine the types of people who had voted to close the school and to keep it open. His analysis of these data led Katz to conclude that public secondary education should not necessarily be viewed as "the fulfillment of working-class aspirations," as other historians had suggested.[25] Katz discovered that those who voted to keep Beverly High open were not the workers of the town, but its social and financial leaders.

In his reexamination of Katz's work, Vinovskis questioned the data upon which Katz's findings were based.[26] First, he pointed out that Katz had failed to investigate educational discussions in Beverly prior to 1860. Had he done so, he would have realized that, although Beverly High began in 1858, it had been proposed in the early 1840s. Katz pinned much of his argument about Beverly High's origins to socioeconomic conditions in the late 1850s, a time of "economic dislocation." Vinovskis pointed out that the early 1840s, when discussions regarding a high school started, was a favorable economic period.

Vinovskis went on to scrutinize Katz's analysis of voting behavior, criticizing him in the process for failure to corroborate his statistical data sufficiently with other primary sources:

> Thus, one can often learn as much about an historical event from the reading of the town meeting records or the local newspaper as from analyzing the pattern of voting. Combining both of these analytic strategies permits us to reconstruct the past more accurately than if we had to choose between them.[27]

Vinovskis concluded that Katz overstated the opposition of the working class to the new high school and understated the support of the local clergy for the fledgling organization.[28] In so doing, he fostered the impression that Beverly High School was intended as a mechanism of social control by the town's most well-to-do citizens. Vinovskis's judgment was that Beverly's workers were not opposed to the idea of secondary schooling, only to the tax burden it represented during tight times.

In studying the history of Tee-Jay, I used a variety of sources. Primary sources included memoirs, school board minutes, annual reports published by the Richmond Public Schools, school newspapers and yearbooks, official documents and public relations materials, and local newspapers. Interviews were conducted with current, as well as retired, teachers and administrators, central office officials, parents, and students, including graduates and those currently enrolled at Tee-Jay. Written impressions of Tee-Jay were solicited from a large number of retired teachers.

The process that generally was followed for each phase of Tee-Jay's history was to identify several key informants and, based on their interviews, to construct a tentative record of central events and themes. Additional sources then were tapped in an effort to support or disconfirm these records of events and themes. When determining whether or not an account was accurate proved difficult, a note was made in the text. These notes became more frequent as debate intensified over Tee-Jay's future. Vexing problems were encountered, for example, in trying to identify the origin of particular recommendations regarding school closure and tracing the course of school board deliberations, the most important of which often took place in executive session. Partisan views predominated when respondents concentrated on the most recent events in Tee-Jay's history. Editorials supporting Tee-Jay's closure in Richmond's two major newspapers suggested that these sources might not be relied upon for unbiased accounts of circumstances related to the school's future. The prevalence of rumor, accusation, and conflicting enrollment figures and target dates for closure were treated, in the end, as indicators of the highly complex and political nature of public education in Richmond. Believing they often had been misrepresented and occasionally mistreated by the press and others seeking data, Richmond school officials were reluctant to share information, even though it might have helped to clarify some areas of confusion concerning Tee-Jay's recent history.

While data collection problems such as these might seem to warrant reconsideration of the selection of an organization on which to focus, they also imply that the organization is, or has been, associated with important issues—issues worthy of study. In one sense, then, the prevalence of obstacles actually can serve to justify the organizational historian's choice of a subject.

Critical Events

Another step in organizational history entails reviewing descriptive information to identify *critical events* in the organization's development. These critical events can serve as a focus for explanatory and interpretive efforts. For Katz, a critical event in *The Irony of Early School Reform* was the 1860 town vote on the future of Beverly High School. His study, while less an organizational history than an account of social and economic dynamics in an industrial town, provides valuable insights into how an early high school struggled to survive. The Beverly town meeting offered an opportunity for the historian to examine such issues as social stratification and identify local perceptions of the nascent high school's mission.

The identification of critical events is very important because it is unwarranted to treat all past events as if they were of equal significance. Besides, it is impossible, in practical terms, to collect and analyze data on all events in an organization's history. Historians may try to select events they feel are representative of an organization's experience or that have been instrumental in shaping the organization. In recounting Tee-Jay's first three decades, during which its unique culture was formed, an effort was made to focus on representative events. Selected events, chosen because they constituted challenges to this culture and eventually to the school itself, served as the basis for the second half of Tee-Jay's history.

Writing on the trend toward merging sociological and historical methods, Griffin observes that certain events are "imbued with sociological import because it is *in* and *through* their unfolding that we see the collision of social structure and social action."[29] To social structure could be added organizational culture and structure. Critical events in the histories of organizations provide opportunities for in-depth study of the interactions between structural dimensions of organizations and social forces within and outside the organization. Sometimes these interactions cause organizational change, while at other times they result in the illusion of change or resistance to change. In either case, the historian is faced with circumstances necessitating understanding and explanation.

In *The World We Created at Hamilton High*, Grant initially chooses to concentrate on events related to the desegregation of the high school. He devotes only a brief introductory chapter to the school's first twelve years—from 1953 to 1965—and its development into an "elite school." The history of Tee-Jay suggests that how a school has responded to challenges in its "maturity" cannot be appreciated fully without a thorough understanding of how it developed during its formative years.

The period from 1968 to 1971 receives special emphasis by Grant because racial tension and even violence flared at Hamilton, despite the fact that black enrollment was less than 20 percent. During this time, the school's conventional control structure began to erode, students started to organize, and the principal resigned. Discipline soon absorbed much of the faculty's and administration's time, leaving less time to address the increasingly diverse needs of Hamilton's students.

The event on which Grant next focuses is the advent of mainstreaming for handicapped students in the mid-seventies. While the increased number of special needs students in regular classes added to Hamilton's diversity and placed additional demands on teachers, tension did not result as it had when black students enrolled. Educators and students were becoming accustomed to heterogeneity.

The appointment of a new principal in 1982 marked a third significant event, one that symbolized the reestablishment of adult authority at Hamilton High. Interestingly, Grant treats the hiring of the new principal as an outgrowth of, rather than an impetus for, improving conditions. The change in leadership indicated that the school was mature enough to face succession without destabilization.

While Grant focuses on changes in Hamilton's student body and leadership, Labaree concentrates on events linked to political and economic developments in Philadelphia. For example, the decision by the school board in the 1880s to open a series of public high schools broke Central High School's 50-year monopoly on secondary education. Simultaneously the middle class of Philadelphia "began to pin their hopes for status attainment on the professions—which required college attendance and thus made Central's practical and terminal curriculum look much less attractive."[30] As a result of these challenges Central entered upon a sustained period of organizational change, culminating in a stratified (tracked) curriculum and a new authority structure (with reduced faculty prerogatives).

Critical events serve not only as a framework for description, but as a target for the organizational historian's explanatory efforts. Description without explanation is like food consumption in the absence of taste and smell. Sustaining, perhaps, but definitely not satisfying. Edward Carr, in fact, has characterized history as a "study of causes."[31] Explanation provides an opportunity for the historian to exercise skills of interpretation, analysis, evaluation, synthesis, and imagination. Critical events may be thought of as choice points in an organization's history. They typically represent occasions when consequential decisions are likely to be made. Even the choice to refrain from acting is a decision. For the organizational historian, the causes not only of critical events, but of the particular decisions they prompt merit explanation.

The critical events that initially challenged the culture of academic excellence at Tee-Jay were related to local desegregation efforts. Later, financial problems arose to threaten the school's very existence. A variety of organizational responses were made in the face of these circumstances. At first, the responses entailed the creation of special programs and the reallocation of school resources. When the possibility of school closure surfaced, more drastic measures were occasioned. Tee-Jay was incorporated into a multi-high-school "complex" for seven years. Later, a magnet program was added to boost enrollment. Eventually, Tee-Jay was compelled to share its site with a Governor's School. Explaining the decisions that were made to protect its "core" organization and culture while adjusting to these changes represented an important dimension of the Tee-Jay story.

A central question in the history of Tee-Jay, as in most organizational history, is *What causes an organization to survive?* As noted earlier, the ongoing existence of an organization should not be assumed. Survival is an empirical issue. Under some circumstances, organizations must change or adapt to survive. Under other circumstances, organizations must resist change to survive. Tee-Jay was called on to do both—sometimes simultaneously! Accounting for continuity and change are primary tasks for the organizational historian.

Labaree, as mentioned before, explains change and stability in terms of factors exogenous to Central High. To assist him in his efforts, Labaree employs Lindblom's twin constructs—politics and markets. Politics encompasses democratic, inclusionary forces. Markets represent competitive, exclusionary forces. The history of Central High unfolds as a continuing struggle between political and market forces. When the school board approved the establishment of other high schools for Philadelphia, Central High found itself in the unprecedented position of having to compete for students. At the same time, the school's traditional mission of preparing the sons of the middle class for small proprietorships was fast becoming outdated. In the 1880s, professional careers requiring college attendance had become the aspiration of the middle class. Had Central High failed to adjust its mission in light of this market shift, the venerable school never might have survived the onset of competition from other public high schools. Instead, sweeping changes in mission, curriculum, and authority structure allowed Central High to remain an important part of the education scene in Philadelphia. Interestingly, despite these changes, Central High managed "to preserve much of its distinctiveness and autonomy" and avoid becoming just another comprehensive public high school.[32]

Carr has noted that there is rarely a single way to explain historical events.[33] Historians sometimes compile lists of possible causes. As they reduce these lists or arrange them in hierarchies of causes, they engage in what Carr has referred to as "interpretation." How historians interpret the causes of events may be influenced by what they know about the events, how they came to this knowledge, their personal values and beliefs, and the times in which they live. Historians often become known by their causal preferences. Labaree, for example, would be expected to explain organizational events in terms of political and market forces. Had Grant studied Central High as he did Hamilton High, he probably would have opted to focus on the influences of local culture.[34] While both Labaree and Grant acknowledge that schools are shaped by their contexts, they choose to focus on different contextual factors. Other historians might stress different causes, such as leadership, psychological needs, group dynamics, and ideology. That historians concentrate on dissimilar causes is less a sign of the weakness of the discipline than an indication of the richness and complexity of historical subject matter.

Among the causal factors that proved to be instrumental in the development of Tee-Jay were the aspirations of Richmond's growing white middle class, the politics of desegregation, the redistribution of educational resources, and the evolution of markets within Richmond Public Schools. Making sense of Tee-Jay's history without reference to these contextual factors would be futile. Had Tee-Jay's faculty, administration, and supporters failed to understand their importance, it is unlikely the school would have survived as long as it has.

Finding Meaning

For many historians, the most rewarding aspect of their craft involves speculating on the meaning of their efforts. Dilthey observed that meaning could be approached from three distinct perspectives: the meaning of events for the original actors, for those directly affected by the events, and for those living in the contemporary period.[35] Far from a static dimension, meaning is subject to change as additional data become available and as current developments compel historians to reinterpret past history.

In reflecting on the meaning of Hamilton High's history, Grant sounds a note of encouragement for those committed to school integration and pluralism. Though the school experienced a period of racial tension, it eventually became a place where black, white, and later Asian students could work and play together. For Grant, the history of Hamilton High signifies the possibility that urban schools have a bright future. White flight, racial isolation, and academic decline need not be their destiny. As the author concludes, "Moving about its halls, I could not help be moved by what the school represented in the way of extending educational opportunities to students of every social class and color and every level of ability and disability."[36]

Had a revisionist historian like Michael B. Katz written about Hamilton High, different meanings might have been attached to its history. For Katz, public high schools were created as sorting and selecting mechanisms designed to reproduce society as it has been, rather than agencies of vision committed to fostering a new society. In his history of the high school's development in nine-teenth-century Massachusetts, for example, Katz concluded that,

> the extension and reform of education in the mid-nineteenth century were not a potpourri of democracy, nationalism, and humanitarianism. They were the attempt of a coalition of the social leaders, status-anxious parents, and status-hungry educa-tors to impose educational innovation, each for their own rea-sons, upon a reluctant community.[37]

Katz published these lines, of course, two decades before Grant's history of Hamilton High appeared. In the late 1960s it was not uncommon to question the motives behind the creation and operation of social institutions. While similar questions con-tinue to be raised, the intervening period has witnessed a variety of developments, many of which could not have been anticipated by Katz. If Dilthey was right, these developments might well have prompted the attachment of different meanings to the history of the high school. Twenty years of de facto segregation and urban deterioration cannot help but influence the meaning of the Hamil-ton High experience. The fact that at least one city high school avoided the discouraging pattern of so many of its sister organiza-tions is a finding of no small consequence and an important rea-son for undertaking school histories.

Had it not been for the intensely political nature of educa-tional decision making in Richmond, the meaning of Tee-Jay's experience might have been as full of promise as that of Grant's Hamilton High. Here, after all, was an urban high school with a well established and widely respected academic culture; an out-standing track record of success after, as well as prior to, desegregation; and the ability to retain a respectable percentage of white students when many of its peer schools had become virtually all black. These advantages, however, proved insufficient to ensure Tee-Jay's future. Years of financial retrenchment and the development of within-district competition for white and bright students forced Tee-Jay to contend with chronic uncertainty. The stability so vital to ongoing school improvement and staff and student recruitment has been absent for over a decade. That Tee-Jay has survived is more a testament to the tenacity and political savvy of its supporters than any carefully crafted long-range plan in which Richmond Public Schools and the city council acknowledged the school's central role in a campaign to reaffirm the value of academic excellence *and* racial integration.

The Promise of Organizational History

Dilthey reminded historians of his era that the proper focus of history should be the actions and thoughts of individuals. He also noted, however, that individuals cannot be understood in isolation.[38] They are situated in terms of time, society, and circumstance. People today spend a large portion of their lives in organizations, and how they think and behave is a function, to some extent, of the structures and cultures of these organizations. By studying the history of organizations, light can be shed on the development of organizational structure and culture and their role in mediating the influence of society on human action and thought.

Organizational histories of schools are less common than accounts of many other types of organizations. Historians typically have preferred to address the history of schools in the aggregate, a tendency that can conceal important variations and exaggerate commonalities across schools. It is hoped that more organizational histories of schools will be undertaken in the future, thereby creating a rich body of knowledge that can be drawn on by organization theorists and educational historians alike. Generalizations are important outcomes of research, but their validity depends, ultimately, on the quality of the knowledge of individual cases upon which they are based. The first step toward sound theories of school organization is, therefore, to understand as much as possible about how particular schools form, develop, and confront the challenges of survival.

NOTES

INTRODUCTION

1. *Richmond Times-Dispatch*, 26 March 1989, p. D-1.
2. *Richmond News Leader*, 19 April 1989, p. 12.
3. Getting accurate racial breakdowns of students in Richmond schools proved more difficult than expected for certain periods. Some of the figures which appear in the book are derived from visual counts of students pictured in school annuals. These should be regarded as approximate.
4. *Washington Post*, 14 December 1993, p. 1.
5. Jonathan Kozol, *Savage Inequalities* (New York: Crown Publishers, 1991), p. 4.
6. Gary Orfield and Carole Ashkinaze, *The Closing Door* (Chicago: University of Chicago Press, 1991).
7. Edgar H. Schein, *Organizational Culture and Leadership* (San Francisco: Jossey-Bass, 1985), p. 6.

CHAPTER 1

1. The inscription comes from a letter written in 1810 by Thomas Jefferson and sent to future president John Tyler. The full quotation is as follows:

I have two great measures at heart, without which no republic can maintain itself in strength. (1) That of general education, to enable every man to judge for himself what will secure or endanger his freedom. (2) To divided every county into hundreds, of such size that all children of each will be within reach of a central school in it.

2. Virginius Dabney, *Richmond: The Story of a City* (Charlottesville: University of Virgina Press, 1990), p. 133.
3. Ibid.
4. Ibid., p. 110.
5. Ibid., p. 200.

6. Christopher Silver, *Twentieth Century Richmond: Planning, Politics, and Race* (Knoxville: University of Tennessee Press, 1984), p. 31.

7. Ibid, p. 32.

8. Ibid., p. 31.

9. Ibid., pp. 3–14.

10. Ibid., p. 18.

11. Details of the convention are provided by Allen W. Moger in *Virginia: Bourbonism to Byrd, 1870–1925* (Charlottesville: University of Virginia Press, 1968), pp. 6–9.

12. The development of Richmond's public school system is described in Margaret Meagher, *History of Education in Richmond* (Richmond: City School Board, 1939) and Rebekah Roberts Sharp, "A History of the Richmond Public School System 1869–1958" (Master's thesis, University of Richmond, 1958).

13. Details regarding *Stuart v. School Dist. No. 1 of the Village of Kalamazoo* can be found in Kern Alexander, *School Law* (St. Paul: West Publishing Co., 1980), pp. 36–40. The case determined that Michigan law allowed taxes to be levied on the general public to expand free public schooling beyond the elementary level to high school.

14. Dabney, *Richmond: The Story of a City*, p. 230.

15. *Fourth Annual Report of the Superintendent of the Public Schools of Richmond, Virginia, 1872–1873* (Richmond, Union Steam Press, 1874), p. 291.

16. A detailed description of Richmond's growth is contained in Christopher Silver's *Twentieth Century Richmond*.

17. The initial decision to raze the Chief Justice's residence in order to build the new school was reversed in the face of vociferous public opposition.

18. A brief description of the history of John Marshall High School can be found in *John Marshall High School: A Richmond Legend* (Richmond: Dietz Press, 1985).

19. Silver, *Twentieth Century Richmond*, p. 121.

20. Ibid., p. 122.

21. Ibid., p. 296.

22. Ibid.

23. Ibid., p. 294.

24. Ibid.

25. Marion N. Moody, "A History of Thomas Jefferson High School" (Master's thesis, University of Richmond, 1958), p. 7.

26. Notes on the planning of Thomas Jefferson High School were provided by Shirley Callihan, Clerk of the Richmond Public Schools Board of Education.

27. Silver, *Twentieth Century Richmond*, p. 118.

28. Ibid., pp. 106–9.

29. Ibid., p. 108.

30. Minutes of the Richmond School Board, 31 May 1929.

31. *Sixty-first Annual Report of the Superintendent of the Public Schools of the City of Richmond, Virginia, 1929–1930*, p. 9.

32. Ibid., p. 11.

33. *Richmond Times-Dispatch*, 12 September 1930, p. 1.

34. The superintendent's annual report for 1930–31 indicated that the eventual first-term enrollment for Tee-Jay was 909 students. The figure rose to 1,086 students for the second term.

35. Aspects of Shawen's life were gathered from his privately published memoirs, "Recollections of a Principal" (1963). I am indebted to his daughter, Mrs. W. Lawrence Weaver, for sharing a copy of her father's work.

36. Moody, "A History of Thomas Jefferson High School," p. 64.

37. This practice was eventually stopped in 1937. The reasons given by school officials included the crowded conditions in the high schools and the disruptive influence of some overage students.

38. *Jeffersonian*, 13 February 1931, p. 2.

39. Ibid., p. 1.

40. Ibid., 3 June 1931, p. 1.

41. Ibid.

42. Ibid., 13 March 1931, p. 2.

CHAPTER 2

1. Edgar H. Schein, *Organizational Culture and Leadership*, p. 9. A more straightforward definition of organizational culture is offered by Robert E. Quinn in "Mastering Competing Values: An Integrated Approach to Management," in David A. Kolb, Irwin M. Rubin, and Joyce S. Osland (eds.), *The Organizational Behavior Reader*, 5th ed. (Englewood Cliffs, N. J.: Prentice Hall, 1991), p. 35: "culture is the set of values and assumptions that underlie the statement, 'this is how we do things around here.'"

2. Robert Hampel, *The Last Little Citadel: American High Schools Since 1940* (Boston: Houghton Mifflin, 1986), p. 15.

3. Ibid., p. 17.

4. *Sixty-ninth Annual Report of the Superintendent of the Public Schools of the City of Richmond, Virginia, 1937–1938*, pp. 43–44.

5. *Sixty-sixth Annual Report of the Superintendent of the Public Schools of the City of Richmond, Virginia, 1934–1935*, p. 12.

6. *Sixty-fifth Annual Report of the Superintendent of the Public Schools of the City of Richmond, Virginia, 1933–1934*, p. 13.

7. A study in 1935 by Richmond Assistant Superintendent F. H. Norris reported that "out of some 7,428 students entering high school in September over a ten-year period, 3,333 were graduated while 4,095 dropped out" (*Sixty-sixth Annual Report of the Superintendent of the Public Schools of the City of Richmond, Virginia, 1934–1935*, p. 25).

8. *Jeffersonian*, 4 March 1938, p. 1.

9. Ibid., 24 September 1938, p. 1.

10. *Sixty-fourth Annual Report of the Superintendent of the Public Schools of the City of Richmond, Virginia, 1932–1933*, p. 16.

11. Ibid.

12. *Richmond Times-Dispatch*, 30 August 1934, p. 5.

13. Information on the work of the Committee of Ten is drawn from Edward A. Krug, *The Shaping of the American High School* (New York: Harper and Row, 1964), pp. 18–92.

14. Ibid., p. 65.

15. *Sixty-seventh Annual Report of the Superintendent of the Public Schools of the City of Richmond, Virginia, 1935–1936*, p.25.

16. Ibid.

17. *Sixty-ninth Annual Report of the Superintendent of the Public Schools of the City of Richmond, Virginia, 1937–1938*, p. 44.

18. Marion N. Moody, "A History of Thomas Jefferson High School," pp. 29–30.

19. *Seventy-first Annual Report of the Superintendent of the Public Schools of the City of Richmond, Virginia, 1939–1940*, p. 13.

20. Moody, "A History of Thomas Jefferson High School," p. 30.

21. This explanation was advanced by Marion Moody in "A History of Thomas Jefferson High School," p. 63.

22. *Jeffersonian*, 15 October 1943, p. 1.

23. The typical student at the time attended four courses a day, not counting Cadet Corps or physical education. Academic credit was not awarded for these two programs.

24. *Jeffersonian*, 20 October 1944, p. 1.

25. *Seventy-third Annual Report of the Superintendent of the Public Schools of the City of Richmond, Virginia, 1941–1942*, p. 33.

26. Ibid., p.43.

27. *Jeffersonian*, 1 March 1932, p. 1.

28. A useful discussion of the issues concerning ability grouping can be found in Francis F. Archambault, Jr., "Instructional Setting and Other Design Features of Compensatory Education Programs," in Robert E. Slavin, Nancy L. Karweit, and Nancy A. Madden, *Effective Programs for Students at Risk* (Boston: Allyn and Bacon, 1989), pp. 241–49.

29. *Sixty-sixth Annual Report of the Superintendent of the Public Schools of the City of Richmond, Virginia, 1934–1935*, p. 24.

30. *Sixty-ninth Annual Report of the Superintendent of the Public Schools of the City of Richmond, Virginia, 1937–1938*, pp. 38–39.

31. Ibid., p. 38.

32. Moody, "A History of Thomas Jefferson High School," p. 44.

33. *Jeffersonian*, 30 October 1931, p. 4.

34. Ernest Shawen, "Recollections of a Principal" (privately published, 1963), p. 13.

35. Ibid., p. 12.

36. Ibid., p. 13.

37. Ibid., pp. 13–14.

38. *Jeffersonian*, 9 April 1937, p. 1.

39. Ibid., 22 January 1937, p. 1.

40. Ibid., 13 March 1931, p. 4.

41. Ibid., 3 June 1931, p. 1.

42. Ibid., 14 April 1932, p. 1.

43. Ibid., 12 May 1932, p. 1.

44. Ibid., 4 December 1942, p. 3.

45. Interview with Roland Galvin, 11 August 1992.

46. *Jeffersonian*, 16 October 1936, p. 2.

47. *Sixty-sixth Annual Report of the Superintendent of the Public Schools of the City of Richmond, Virginia, 1934–1935*, p. 24.

48. *Jeffersonian*, 28 November 1932, p. 2.

49. I am indebted to Mary Maddox for sharing her experience with the fiftieth reunion of her first homeroom. Her students, who remained together in school until 1942, came back to Richmond from all over the United States in 1992.

50. The number of homerooms at Tee-Jay during the 1930s ranged up to about sixty.

51. *Jeffersonian*, 27 November 1931, p. 1.

52. Ibid., 18 January 1932, p. 2.

53. Ibid., 31 March 1932, p. 1.

54. One current educational researcher who finds merit in competition is Robert E. Slavin of Johns Hopkins University. Slavin has incorporated within-class competition into some "cooperative learning" activities. He finds that the desire to help one's team serves as a powerful incentive for many students to learn. Furthermore, competition among class groups stimulates within-group cooperation.

55. *Sixty-ninth Annual Report of the Superintendent of the Public Schools of the City of Richmond, Virginia, 1937–1938*, p. 44.

56. *Richmond Times-Dispatch*, 11 June 1932, p. 3.

57. *Sixty-sixth Annual Report of the Superintendent of the Public Schools of the City of Richmond, Virginia, 1934–1935*, p. 23.

58. *Sixty-ninth Annual Report of the Superintendent of the Public Schools of the City of Richmond, Virginia, 1937–1938*, p. 47.

59. *Seventieth Annual Report of the Superintendent of the Public Schools of the City of Richmond, Virginia, 1938–1939*, p. 61.

60. *Seventy-second Annual Report of the Superintendent of the Public Schools of the City of Richmond, Virginia, 1940–1941*, p. 30.

61. *Jeffersonian*, 4 December 1942, p. 1.

62. Ibid., 2 October 1942, p. 2.

63. Shawen, "Recollections of a Principal," p. 29.

64. *Jeffersonian*, 2 October 1942, p. 1.

65. Ibid., 16 October 1942, p. 2.

66. Ibid.

67. *Seventy-fourth Annual Report of the Superintendent of the Public Schools of the City of Richmond, Virginia, 1942–1943*, p. 15.

68. *Jeffersonian*, 30 October 1942, p. 2.

69. Ibid., 22 September 1944, p. 2.

70. *Seventy-fifth Annual Report of the Superintendent of the Public Schools of the City of Richmond, Virginia, 1943–1944*, pp. 13–15.

71. *Jeffersonian*, 18 March 1938, p. 1.

72. *Seventy-fifth Annual Report of the Superintendent of the Public Schools of the City of Richmond, Virginia, 1943–1944*, pp. 14–15.

CHAPTER 3

1. *Jeffersonian*, 20 February, 1953, p. 1.

2. Robert A. Pratt, *The Color of Their Skin: Education and Race in Richmond, Virginia, 1954–1989* (Charlottesville: University Press of Virginia, 1992).

3. Marion Moody, "A History of Thomas Jefferson High School," p. 42.

4. *Jeffersonian*, 1 April 1960, p. 1.

5. Ibid., 20 February 1959, p. 1.

6. Thomas Toch, *In the Name of Excellence* (New York: Oxford University Press, 1991), p. 3.

7. Douglas L. Wilson, "Thomas Jefferson and the Character Issue" *The Atlantic Monthly*, November 1992, p. 62.

8. "The Pursuit of Excellence," *Time*, 7 July 1958, pp. 55–56.

9. "Wasteland, U.S.A.," *Time*, 17 February 1958, p. 72.

10. *Jeffersonian*, 10 April 1959, p. 2.

11. M. Elizabeth Beaman, who taught foreign language at Tee-Jay from 1938 until 1973, reported that a group of fifty Spanish students inaugurated foreign travel by Richmond high schoolers when they traveled in 1954 to Mexico by bus. Subsequently, groups visited Cuba, Italy, and Mexico again.

12. Moody, "A History of Thomas Jefferson High School," p. 59.

13. Ernest L. Boyer, *High School* (New York: Harper and Row, 1983). For an example of more typical mission statements for the contemporary American high school, see Ray Marshall and Marc Tucker, *Thinking for a Living* (New York: Basic Books, 1992).

14. In his classic study of the "suburban temper" of the fifties, William H. Whyte noted the value placed on well-roundedness in the schools for Organization Man's children. Well-roundedness was important because it increased the likelihood of adaptability, and adaptability was considered a cardinal virtue by Organization Man. See William H. Whyte, Jr., *The Organization Man* (New York: Simon and Schuster, 1956), p. 393.

15. *Richmond Times-Dispatch*, 9 May 1978, p. B-2.

16. *Jeffersonian*, 25 September 1952, p. 1. The mathematics courses offered at Tee-Jay included General Math 1-2-3-4, Practical Math 1-2, Algebra 1-2-3-4, Geometry 1-2-3, Senior Arithmetic, Advanced Arithmetic, Trigonometry, and Trigonometry-Algebra 5-6.

17. Moody, "A History of Thomas Jefferson High School," pp. 68–69.

18. College Day originated as a result of colleges sending representatives to Tee-Jay to recruit individual students. In 1956 it was decided to set aside an entire day for the purpose of disseminating information on college. As a result of the initiative of the Tee-Jay Guidance Department, College Days spread all over the Commonwealth. See the *Jeffersonian*, 24 October 1957, p. 1.

19. *Jeffersonian*, 20 October 1961, p. 1.

20. Ibid., 15 December 1961, p. 3.

21. Moody, "A History of Thomas Jefferson High School," p. 69.

22. *Jeffersonian*, 26 September 1958, p. 1.

23. Ibid.

24. Ibid., 8 May 1959, p. 2.

25. Ibid., 6 March 1953, p. 6.

26. Moody, "A History of Thomas Jefferson High School," pp. 75–78.

27. Shirley Callihan, "A Mini-History of the Richmond Public Schools: 1869–1992" (Richmond: Richmond Public Schools, 1992), p. 374.

28. *Annual Report of the Richmond Public Schools: Fiscal Year 1962–1963*, p. 7.

29. William H. Whyte, Jr., *The Organization Man*, pp. 3–14. It should be noted that Whyte was critical of over-reliance on group identification, fearing it spelled the demise of individualism and creativity.

30. "The Interpreter," p. 19.

31. Ibid., pp. 19–20.

32. *Jeffersonian*, 6 November 1952, p. 1.

33. To illustrate the size of these groups, the membership figures for 1957–58 appear in parentheses.

34. *Jeffersonian*, 24 October 1958, p. 2.

35. Ibid., 30 March, 1962, p. 2.

36. Ibid., 23 October 1959, p. 2.

37. *Richmond Times-Dispatch*, 13 January 1962, p. 5.

38. Ibid.

39. Moody, "A History of Thomas Jefferson High School," pp. 83–84.

40. Callihan, "A Mini-History of the Richmond Public Schools: 1869–1992," p. 365.

41. *Jeffersonian*, 22 November 1957, p. 6.

42. Ibid.

43. Ibid., 13 March 1958, p. 6.

44. Ibid., 9 March 1962, p. 1.

45. Ibid., 22 September 1961, p. 1.

46. "The Interpreter," p. 22.

47. The complete story of the integration of Richmond Public Schools has been told very ably by Robert A. Pratt in the *The Color of Their Skin*.

48. *Jeffersonian*, 11 October 1957, p. 2.

49. Pratt, *The Color of Their Skin*, p. 7.

50. Ibid.

51. Whites in Prince Edward County continued to defy integration efforts until May 25, 1964, when the United States Supreme Court ordered county officials to reopen their public schools.

52. Pratt, *The Color of Their Skin*, p. 7.

53. Ibid., p. 13.

54. Ibid., p. 31.

55. *Richmond Times-Dispatch*, 2 September 1962, p. A-16.

56. Maurice Duke wrote of Richmond's tradition of uniqueness in "Cabell and Glasgow's Richmond: The Intellectual Background of the City," *Mississippi Quarterly* 27 (Fall 1974): 375–91.

CHAPTER 4

1. *Jeffersonian*, 6 November 1964, p. 1.

2. The author was a sophomore at Tee-Jay in the fall of 1962 and was unaware of any planned or spontaneous actions intended to ridicule or frighten the school's first black student.

3. *Richmond Times-Dispatch*, 7 September 1963, p. 1.

4. A discrepancy seems to exist in reports of the actual number of black students enrolled in white schools. While Robert Pratt reported the

figure of 312 (*The Color of Their Skin*, p. 36), the *Richmond Times-Dispatch* (7 September 1963) indicated on page 1 that 369 black students were enrolled.

5. Not all Tee-Jay students were pictured in the yearbook. The official enrollment figure for 1969–70 was 1,701. It is difficult to find official statistics on the numbers of black students at each Richmond high school during the pre-busing years.

6. Pratt, *The Color of Their Skin*, p. 93. Black enrollment exceeded white enrollment for the first time in Richmond in the fall of 1958 (James A. Sartain and Rutledge M. Dennis, "Richmond, Virginia: Massive Resistance without Violence," in Charles V. Willie and Susan L. Greenblatt (eds.), *Community Politics and Educational Change* [New York: Longman, 1981], p. 219).

7. Pratt, *The Color of Their Skin*, pp. 36–55.

8. Ibid., p. 37.

9. Ibid.

10. Ibid., p. 38.

11. Ibid., p. 42.

12. Ibid., p. 43.

13. Ibid., p. 44.

14. Ibid., p. 46.

15. Ibid.

16. Ibid., p. 48.

17. Virginius Dabney, *Richmond: The Story of a City*, p. 82.

18. James L. Doherty, *Race and Education in Richmond* (privately printed by the author, 1972), p. 82.

19. *Jeffersonian*, 15 February 1963, p. 1.

20. *Richmond Times-Dispatch*, 5 September 1963, p. 2.

21. Ibid.

22. Several remedial reading classes were offered toward the end of the sixties.

23. *Jeffersonian*, 22 January 1965, p. 1.

24. Ibid., 20 December 1963, p. 6.

25. Ibid., 14 February 1964, p. 2.

26. Ibid., 12 February 1965, p. 2.

27. Ibid., 21 May 1965, p. 2.

28. Ibid., 9 February 1968, p. 2.

29. At the end of the 1962–63 school year, for example, Tee-Jay lost fifteen teachers, or about one-fifth of its faculty. Some teachers retired, while others moved away or switched to private schools. That this large turnover of teachers—the greatest number in a given year prior to 1970—should have occurred at the end of Tee-Jay's first year of desegregation seems too unusual to be due to coincidence alone.

30. Terrence Deal and Allen Kennedy, *Corporate Culture* (Reading, Mass.: Addison-Wesley, 1982), pp. 88–90.

31. Tee-Jay's total of 28 semifinalists was second only to Freeman's 35 and ahead of Collegiate's 14, Hermitage's 3, Huguenot's 22, John Marshall's 11, and Wythe's 22. See James L. Doherty, *Race and Education and Richmond*, p. 83.

32. *Jeffersonian*, 7 December 1962, p. 1.

33. Ibid., 27 September 1963, p. 1.

34. Ibid., 26 April 1963, p. 1.

35. Ibid., 7 December 1962, p. 6.

36. Ibid., 7 May 1965, p. 1.

37. Ibid., 26 April 1963, p. 2.

38. Ibid., 7 May 1965, p. 2.

39. Ibid., p. 1.

40. Ibid.

41. *The Monticello: 1967–1968*, p. 27.

42. Ibid.

43. *High Schools in the South* (Nashville: Center for Southern Education Studies, George Peabody College for Teachers, 1966), p. 70.

44. *Annual Report of the Superintendent of Public Instruction of the Commonwealth of Virginia: 1968–1969* (Richmond: State Board of Education, 1969), p. 54.

45. *Richmond Times-Dispatch*, 1 June 1969, p. B-7.

46. For a comprehensive review of research concerning disadvantaged students, see Robert E. Slavin, Nancy L. Karweit, and Nancy A. Madden, *Effective Programs for Students at Risk*.

47. *Richmond News Leader*, 13 March 1971, p. 17.

48. Ibid., p. 13.

49. Ibid.

50. Ibid., p. 17.

51. Ibid.

52. *The Monticello: 1970–1971*, p. 14.

53. *Richmond News Leader*, 3 March 1971, p. 17.

54. Ibid.

55. Ibid.

56. Ibid.

57. *The Monticello: 1970–1971*, Finis.

58. *Mini-Jeffersonian*, 25 February 1972, p. 3.

59. *Jeffersonian*, 12 November 1971, p. 6.

60. Ibid., p. 1.

61. Ibid., 8 October 1971, p. 1.

62. *Richmond News Leader*, 12 June 1976, p. 1.

63. Ibid.

64. Ibid.

65. In 1972–73, Tee-Jay enrolled nineteen special education students. For the next two years, enrollments were twelve and eighteen, respectively.

66. *Richmond Times-Dispatch*, 19 March 1992, p. C-5.

67. Data were not available concerning how "lower economic background" is operationally defined or on the actual income levels of parents of Community High students.

68. *Richmond Times-Dispatch*, 19 March 1992, p. C-5.

69. *Richmond News Leader*, 25 February 1971.

70. *Jeffersonian*, 7 October 1977, p. 5.

71. Ibid., 15 December 1970, p. 2.

72. Ibid.

73. Ibid. The Cadet Corps was discontinued in the spring of 1971.

74. Ibid.

75. Ibid., 12 November 1971, p. 2.

76. James L. Doherty, *Race and Education in Richmond*, p. 3.

77. According to the *Annual Report of the Superintendent of Public Instruction of the Commonwealth of Virginia: School Year 1973–1974*, Virginia had 480 public and 69 nonpublic secondary schools (pp. 44–45).

78. *The Monticello: 1976–1977*, p. 6.

CHAPTER 5

1. *Richmond Times-Dispatch*, 3 April 1979, p. B-1.

2. *Richmond News Leader*, 21 October 1977, p. 13. Similar proficiency tests were scheduled for all Virginia school divisions by 1981.

3. Ibid.

4. Ibid., p. 1-A.

5. Ibid., 30 November 1977, p. 19.

6. Ibid., 8 February 1978, p. 1.

7. Ibid., 12 April 1979, p. 9. The school board actually voted to accept Plan G in November of 1978, but months of lobbying for other options followed. Hunter finally reiterated the board's support for Plan G in April of 1979.

8. *Jeffersonian*, April 1979, p. 1.

9. Ibid.

10. Allen McCreary, "Richmond Public Schools: A Decade of Change," *Richmond News Leader*, 29 August 1980, p. 1.

11. Ibid., p. 5.

12. *Richmond Times-Dispatch*, 26 August 1979, p. C-8.

13. Ibid., 4 September 1979, p. B-1.

14. In the first "complex" graduations, 500 JHW, 375 Armstrong-Kennedy, and 305 Marshall-Walker students received diplomas.

15. *Richmond Times-Dispatch*, 4 April 1979, p. B-3.

16. *Odyssey 1984*, p. 3.

17. Jefferson-Huguenot-Wythe self-study 1984–85, Visiting Committee Report, November 1985.

18. Richmond Newspapers, Inc., et al. v. Vernelle M. Lipscomb, 234 Va. 277 (1987), p. 277.

19. *Washington Post*, 31 January 1993, p. A-10.

20. Jefferson-Huguenot-Wythe High School Self-Study 1984–85, p. 50.

21. Ibid., pp. 50–51.

22. Ibid., p. 2.

23. Ibid., p. 3.

24. *Richmond News Leader*, 29 August 1986, p. 4.

25. Ibid.

26. Robert Pratt, *The Color of Their Skin*, pp. 89–90.

27. It is worth noting that when George Allen succeeded L. Douglas Wilder as governor in 1994, he opted to enroll his child in a Henrico County elementary school.

28. Jefferson-Huguenot-Wythe High School Self-Study 1984–85, pp. 4–5.

29. *Odyssey 1984*, p. 57.

30. *The Monticello 1988*, p. 6.

31. Pratt, *The Color of Their Skin*, p. 15.

32. *Richmond Times-Dispatch*, 13 March 1989, p. B-1.

33. *Richmond News Leader*, 24 March 1989, p. 8.

34. Ibid., 19 April 1989, p. 12.

35. "Recommendations Before the City of Richmond School Board Involving Changes in Building Utilization," Richmond Public Schools, 22 March 1989.

36. Ibid.

37. Ibid.

38. *SOS Newsletter*, updated.

39. One of the school district's arguments for closing Tee-Jay concerned the estimated $1,161,800 required for building repair and maintenance. SOS contended that such costs actually were greater for Armstrong than for Tee-Jay.

40. *Richmond News Leader*, 22 March 1989, p. 30.

41. Ibid.

42. *Richmond News Leader*, 23 March 1989, p. 4.

43. "Alternatives to Recommended Changes in Building Utilization," Richmond Youth Council, National Association for the Advance-

ment of Colored People, presented to the Richmond School Board, 22 March 1989.

44. Ibid.

45. *Richmond News Leader*, 23 March 1989, p. 1.

46. Minutes of a Special Meeting of the School Board of the City of Richmond, 22 March 1989.

47. Minutes of the Regular Meeting of the School Board of the City of Richmond, 18 April 1989.

48. Lawrence Douglas Wilder, "Excerpts from Remarks Made for Thomas Jefferson High School Commencement Exercises 4:00 P.M. June 15, 1989, The Mosque, Richmond, Virginia."

49. *Richmond Times-Dispatch*, 28 March 1989, p. B-1.

50. Ibid.

51. Evans Clinchy, "Magnet Schools Matter," *Education Week* (8 December 1993), p. 28.

52. Mary Haywood Metz, *Different by Design: The Context and Character of Three Magnet Schools* (New York: Routledge, 1992), p. 1.

53. Harvey Kantor and Barbara Brenzel, "Urban Education and the 'Truly Disadvantaged': The Historical Roots of the Contemporary Crisis, 1945–1990," in Michael B. Katz (ed.), *The "Underclass" Debate: Views from History* (Princeton: Princeton University Press, 1993), p. 385.

54. Minutes of the Regular Meeting of the School Board of the City of Richmond, 3 January 1990.

55. Ibid.

56. Much of the groundwork for corporate support of the Tee-Jay magnet program had been laid by Morgan Edwards and the team that prepared the original federal magnet program grant. Edwards later would register dismay that this earlier planning was largely ignored by Albert Jones in his efforts to create a Tee-Jay magnet.

57. "Magnet Schools in Richmond," brochure published by Richmond Public Schools, January 1990.

58. Frances Helms, "Magnet Schools Attract 'Choice' Students," *The City Magazine* (April/May 1991), p. 39.

59. Biographical statement prepared by Cassandra Fletcher on February 7, 1992.

CHAPTER 6

1. *Style Weekly*, 27 November 1990.

2. *Richmond Times-Dispatch*, 25 January 1991, p. B-1.

3. Rosabeth Moss Kanter, "When a Thousand Flowers Bloom: Structural, Collective, and Social Conditions for Innovation in Organization," in Barry M. Staw and L. L. Cummings (eds.), *Research in Organization Behavior*, vol. 10 (Greenwich, Conn.: JAI Press, 1988).

4. *Richmond Times-Dispatch*, 9 June 1991, pp. B-1, B-2.

5. Ibid., p. B-2.

6. Ibid.

7. Minutes of the Regular Meeting of the School Board of the City of Richmond, 19 March 1990.

8. Ibid.

9. *Richmond News Leader*, 11 June 1990, p. 10.

10. Minutes of the Regular Meeting of the School Board of the City of Richmond, 3 April 1990.

11. *Richmond Times-Dispatch*, 10 August 1991, p. B-3.

12. Minutes of the Regular Meeting of the School Board of the City of Richmond, 7 May 1991.

13. Ibid.

14. *Richmond Times-Dispatch*, 1 September 1991, p. C-3.

15. Ibid.

16. Interview conducted with Dr. Steven Ballowe on 20 December 1991. Also see *Richmond Times-Dispatch*, 18 December 1991, p. C-8.

17. *Richmond Times-Dispatch*, 18 December 1991, p. C-8.

18. Interview conducted with Dr. Steven Ballowe on 20 December 1991.

19. *Richmond Times-Dispatch*, 10 August 1991, p. B-3.

20. Ibid.

21. *Richmond News Leader*, 24 September 1991, p. 19.

22. Ibid.

23. *Richmond Times-Dispatch*, 10 December 1991, p. B-4.

24. Ibid.

25. Ibid., 27 December 1991, p. 1.

26. Ibid.

27. Ibid., 10 January 1992, p. B-6.

28. Ibid.

29. Ibid., 9 January 1992, p. B-1.

30. Minutes of the Regular Meeting of the School Board of the City of Richmond, 4 February 1992.

31. Ibid.

32. Minutes of the Special Meeting of the School Board of the City of Richmond, 14 February 1992.

33. Minutes of the Special Meeting of the School Board of the City of Richmond, 25 February 1992.

34. *Richmond Times-Dispatch*, 16 February 1992, p. B-1.

35. Minutes of the Regular Meeting of the School Board of the City of Richmond, 3 March 1992.

36. *Richmond Times-Dispatch*, 17 June 1992, p. B-1.

37. Ibid., 2 August 1992, p. S–67.

38. Ibid., 9 August 1992, p. B-6.

39. Though reported in May of 1992, the OAP data refer to student performance in the 1990–91 school year. Therefore, the eleventh graders who were reported on in the OAP data were not the same group represented in the August 1992 TAP data.

40. *Richmond Times-Dispatch*, 30 August 1992, p. B-10.

41. Ibid.

42. Ibid., 21 October 1992, p. B-1.

43. Ibid.

44. Ibid., 20 March 1993, p. B-3.

45. Ibid.

46. Ibid., 31 March 1993, p. L–1.

47. Ibid., 29 April 1993, p. B-9.

48. Ibid.

49. Ibid., 26 May 1993, p. B-1.

50. Ibid., 2 June 1993, p. B-1.

51. Ibid., 16 June 1993, p. A-1.

52. Ibid., 21 August 1993, p. B-3.

53. Ibid., 20 October 1993, p. B-1.

54. Ibid., 8 December 1993, p. B-6.

55. Ibid., 17 December 1993, p. B-6.

56. Ibid.

57. Ibid., 2 March 1994, p. B-3

CHAPTER 7

1. Besides Robert Pratt's study of desegregation in Richmond, see Daniel J. Monti, *A Semblance of Justice: St. Louis School Desegregation and Order in Urban America* (Columbia: University of Missouri Press, 1985), and Gary Orfield and Carole Ashkinaze's study of Atlanta's desegregation experience, *The Closing Door*.

2. Milbrey W. McLaughlin, "The Rand Change Agent Study Revisited: Macro Perspectives and Micro Realities," *Educational Researcher* 19 (December 1990): 11–16.

3. Ibid.

4. *Richmond Surroundings* (Newcomer Edition 1992), p. 56.

5. John V. Moeser, "What's Ahead for Our City," in Maurice Duke and Daniel P. Jordan (eds.), *A Richmond Reader: 1733–1983* (Chapel Hill: University of North Carolina Press, 1983), p. 231.

6. Ibid.

7. Mary Anne Raywid, "Rethinking School Governance," in R. F. Elmore et al. (eds.), *Restructuring Schools: The Next Generation of Educational Reform* (San Francisco: Jossey-Bass, 1990), p. 152.

8. Moeser, "What's Ahead for Our City," pp. 233–34.

9. Virginius Dabney, *Richmond: The Story of a City*, p. 295.

10. *Richmond News Leader*, 11 June 1990, p. 10.

11. Ibid., 30 August 1986, p. 4.

12. Ibid.

13. *Education Week*, 12 January 1994, p. 5.

14. Ibid.

15. Claude M. Steele, "Race and the Schooling of Black Americans," *The Atlantic Monthly*, April 1992, p. 78. Opposition to de facto segregation is voiced by Gary Orfield and Carole Ashkinaze in *The Closing Door*. They argue that tacit acceptance of segregation by black leaders in Atlanta did not result in greater achievement or better opportunities for blacks.

16. Washington Post, 12 April 1994, p. A-13.

17. Orfield and Ashkinaze, *The Closing Door*, pp. 223–24.

18. Daniel J. Monti, *A Semblance of Justice*, p. 185.

19. J. Harvie Wilkinson, *From Brown to Bakke: The Supreme Court and School Integration, 1954–1978* (New York: Oxford University Press, 1979), pp. 151–54.

20. Robert L. Crowson and William Lowe Boyd, "Urban Schools as Organizations: Political Perspectives," in James G. Cibulka, Rodney J. Reed, and Kenneth K. Wong (eds.), *The Politics of Urban Education in the United States* (Washington, D.C.: Falmer Press, 1992), p. 90.

21. The "politics of placation" also was in evidence in 1992 when a Richmond elementary school was accused of "clustering" its small number of white students at each grade school in the same classes. The principal justified clustering for the "social and emotional" welfare of the white students and referred to School Board policy. Lucille Brown, the superintendent, ordered an end to clustering, but not before the U.S. Department of Education threatened legal action.

22. Mark Walsh, "Counsel for the Cause," *Education Week* (May 11, 1994): 25.

23. Brian L. Fife, *Desegregation in American Schools: Comparative Intervention Strategies* (New York: Praeger, 1992), p. 176.

24. Ibid., p. 178.

25. Michael W. Sedlak, Christopher W. Wheeler, Diana C. Pullin, and Philip A. Cusick, *Selling Students Short* (New York: Teachers College Press, 1986), pp. 37–57.

26. *An Imperiled Generation: Saving Urban Schools* (Princeton: The Carnegie Foundation for the Advancement of Teaching, 1988), p. 4.

27. Peter Schmidt, "Magnets' Efficacy As Desegregation Tool Questioned,' *Education Week* (February 2, 1994): 1.

28. Debra Viadero, "Magnet Schools Appear to Have Little Impact on Student Achievement, Researchers Find," *Education Week* (April 13, 1994): 12.

CHAPTER 8

1. Sara Lawrence Lightfoot, *The Good High School* (New York: Basic Books, 1983), p. 309.
2. Ernest L. Boyer, *High School*, pp. 58–67.
3. Theodore R. Sizer, *Horace's School* (Boston: Houghton Mifflin, 1992), pp. 120–32.
4. Boyer, *High School*, p. 5.
5. Michael Rutter, Barbara Maughan, Peter Mortimore, and Janet Ouston, *Fifteen Thousand Hours: Secondary Schools and Their Effects on Children* (Cambridge: Harvard University Press, 1979).
6. Karen Seashore Louis and Matthew B. Miles, *Improving the Urban High School* (New York: Teachers College Press, 1990), pp. 172–74.
7. H. G. Bissinger, *Friday Night Lights* (Reading, Mass.: Addison-Wesley, 1990).
8. Gretchen B. Rossman, H. Dickson Corbett, and William A. Firestone, *Change and Effectiveness in Schools* (Albany: State University of New York Press, 1988), p. 5.
9. Gerald Grant, *The World We Created at Hamilton High* (Cambridge: Harvard University Press, 1988), pp. 220–21.
10. *Reaching the Goals: Goal 6, Safe, Disciplined, and Drug-free Schools* (Washington, D.C.: U.S. Department of Education, Office of Educational Research and Improvement, 1993).
11. Ibid., p. 5.
12. James M. McPartland and E. L. McDill, "The Unique Role of Schools in the Causes of Youthful Crime," Report no. 216 (Baltimore: Center for the Social Organization of Schools, Johns Hopkins University, 1976).
13. Sara Lawrence Lightfoot, *The Good High School*, p. 356.
14. Rossman, Corbett, and Firestone, *Change and Effectiveness in Schools*.
15. For example, see Ray Marshall and Marc Tucker, *Thinking for a Living*.
16. Grant, *The World We Created at Hamilton High*, p. 117.
17. Ibid.

CHAPTER 9

1. J. Victor Baldridge and Terrence E. Deal (eds.) *The Dynamics of Organizational Change in Education* (Berkeley: McCutchan, 1983), p. 3.

2. Robert E. Slavin, "PET and the Pendulum: Faddism in Education and How to Stop It," *Phi Delta Kappan* 70 (June 1989): 752–58.

3. William Lowe Boyd, "The Politics of Curriculum Change and Stability," in Baldridge and Deal (eds.), *The Dynamics of Organizational Change in Schools*, p. 233.

4. Arthur G. Powell, Eleanor Farrar, and David K. Cohen, *The Shopping Mall High School* (Boston: Houghton Mifflin, 1985), pp. 233–308.

5. Larry Cuban, *How Teachers Taught* (New York: Longman, 1984).

6. Seymour B. Sarason, *The Culture of the School and the Problem of Change*, 2d ed. (Boston: Allyn and Bacon, 1982).

7. Daniel J. Monti, *A Semblance of Justice*, p. 182.

8. Rosabeth Moss Kanter, "When a Thousand Flowers Bloom: Structural, Collective, and Social Conditions for Innovation in Organization," p. 195.

9. Ibid.

10. Philip Selznick, *The Moral Commonwealth* (Berkeley: University of California Press, 1992), p. 76.

11. Daniel L. Duke and Adrienne M. Meckel, "The Slow Death of a Public High School," *Phi Delta Kappan* 61 (June 1980): pp. 674–77.

12. See Patrick B. Forsyth and Marilyn Tallerico (eds.), *City Schools* (Newbury Park, Calif.: Corwin Press, 1993); Sara Lawrence Lightfoot, *The Good High School*; Karen Seashore Louis and Matthew B. Miles, *Improving the Urban High School*; and Gary G. Wehlage, Robert A. Rutter, Gregory A. Smith, Nancy Lesko, and Ricardo R. Fernandez, *Reducing the Risk: Schools as Communities of Support* (London: Falmer Press, 1989).

13. Jonathan Kozol, *Savage Inequalities*, p. 186.

14. Interestingly, support for parental choice by city leaders did not extend to the selection of school board members. On April 28, 1992, the Richmond City Council rejected a measure urging a referendum on elected school boards!

15. Richmond Tomorrow was created in 1988 when the city council appointed a steering committee of ten civic leaders to undertake a long-range strategic planning effort. The 1991 Citizens' Report was based on a series of community forums held in June of 1990 and the recommendations of various citizen task forces.

16. *Richmond Times-Dispatch*, 3 March 1993, p. B-9.

17. Thomas F. Green, "Excellence, Equity, and Equality," in Lee S. Shulman and Gary Sykes (eds.), *Handbook of Teaching and Policy* (New York: Longman, 1983).

18. Larry Greiner, "Evolution and Revolution as Organizations Grow," in Daniel A. Kolb, Irwin M. Rubin, and Joyce S. Osland (eds.), *The Organizational Behavior Reader*, 5th ed., p. 385.

APPENDIX

1. Fernand Braudel, *In History* (Chicago: University of Chicago Press, 1980), p. 64.

2. *The Social Sciences in Historical Study: A Report of the Commmittee on Historiography*, Bulletin 64, (New York: Social Science Research Council, 1954), p. 26.

3. Lawrence Stone, "History and the Social Sciences in the Twentieth Century," in C. F. Delzell (ed.), *The Future of History* (Nashville: Vanderbilt University Press, 1977).

4. William Dray, "The Historian's Problem of Selection," in R. H. Hash (ed.), *Ideas of History*, vol. 2 (New York: E. P. Dutton, 1969), p. 218.

5. G. F. Kneller, *Movements in Thought in Modern Education* (New York: Macmillan, 1984), pp. 56–57.

6. Wilhelm Dilthey, *Pattern and Meaning in History* (New York: Harper and Row, 1962), p. 49.

7. Harry Ritter, *Dictionary of Concepts in History*, (New York: Greenwood Press, 1986), p. 243.

8. Dray, "The Historian's Problem of Selection," pp. 216–27.

9. Edgar H. Schein, *Organizational Culture and Leadership*, p. 6.

10. Ritter, *Dictionary of Concepts in History*, p. 247.

11. The sequencing of organizational history presented in this essay should not be regarded as invariant or necessarily linear. In actual practice, description, explanation, and interpretation may overlap, occur simultaneously, or recur periodically.

12. Schein, *Organizational Culture and Leadership*, p. 6.

13. Gene E. Hall and Shirley M. Hord, *Change in Schools* (Albany: State University of New York Press, 1987).

14. I am indebted to an anonymous reviewer for this cautionary note.

15. Robert A. Pratt, *The Color of Their Skin*; Bryce E. Nelson, *Good Schools: The Seattle Public School System, 1901–1930* (Seattle: University of Washington Press, 1988).

16. Lucianne B. Carmichael, *McDonogh 15* (New York: Avon, 1981); Harold Saltzman, *Race War in High School* (New Rochelle, N. Y.: Arlington House, 1972).

17. Philip A. Cusick, *Inside High School* (New York: Holt, Rinehart and Winston, 1973); Heewon Chang, *Adolescent Life and Ethos: An Ethnography of a U.S. High School* (London: Falmer Press, 1992).

18. H. G. Bissinger, *Friday Night Lights* (Reading, Mass.: Addison-Wesley, 1990).

19. Gerald Grant, *The World We Created at Hamilton High* (Cambridge: Harvard University Press, 1988); David F. Labaree, *The Making of an American High School* (New Haven: Yale University Press, 1988).

20. Steve Bhaerman and Joel Denker, *No Particular Place to Go: The Making of a Free High School* (New York: Simon and Schuster, 1972); John Bremer and Michael von Moschzisker, *The School Without Walls: Philadelphia's Parkway Program* (New York: Holt, Rinehart and Winston, 1971); George Dennison, *The Lives of Children: The Story of the First Street School* (New York: Random House, 1969).

21. Labaree, *The Making of an American High School*, p. 3.

22. Earl Babbie, *The Practice of Social Research*, 4th ed. (Belmont, Calif.: Wadsworth, 1986), p. 294.

23. Ibid.

24. Michael B. Katz, *The Irony of Early School Reform* (Cambridge: Harvard University Press, 1968).

25. Ibid., p. 19.

26. Maris A. Vinovskis, *The Origins of Public High Schools: A Reexamination of the Beverly High School Controversy* (Madison: University of Wisconsin Press, 1985).

27. Ibid., p. 118.

28. Ibid., pp. 112–16.

29. Larry J. Griffin, "Temporality, Events, and Explanation in Historical Sociology," *Sociological Methods and Research* 20 (1992): 413.

30. Labaree, *The Making of an American High School*, p. 6.

31. Edward H. Carr, *What Is History?* (New York: Vintage Books, 1961), p. 113.

32. Labaree, *The Making of an American High School*, p. 7.

33. Carr, *What Is History?*, pp. 113–43.

34. Grant, *The World We Created at Hamilton High*, pp. 117–37.

35. Dilthey, *Pattern and Meaning in History*, p. 50.

36. Grant, *The World We Created at Hamilton High*, pp. 113.

37. Katz, *The Irony of Early School Reform*, p. 218.

38. Dilthey, *Pattern and Meaning in History*, p. 97.

BIBLIOGRAPHY

Alexander, Kern. *School Law*. St. Paul: West Publishing Co., 1980.

Archambault, Francis S., Jr. "Instructional Setting and Other Design Features of Compensatory Education Programs." In Robert E. Slavin, and Nancy A. Madden (eds.), *Effective Programs for Students at Risk*. Boston: Allyn and Bacon, 1989.

Babbie, Earl. *The Practice of Social Research*, 4th ed. Belmont, Calif.: Wadsworth, 1986.

Baldridge, J. Victor, and Deal, Terrence E. (eds.). *The Dynamics of Organizational Change in Education*. Berkeley: McCutchan, 1983.

Bhaerman, Steve, and Denker, Joel. *No Particular Place to Go: The making of a Free High School*. New York: Simon and Schuster.

Bissinger, H. G. *Friday Night Lights*. Reading, Mass.: Addison-Wesley, 1990.

Boyd, William Lowe. "The Politics of Curriculum Change and Stability." In J. Victor Baldridge and Terrence E. Deal (eds.), *The Dynamics of Organizational Change in Education*. Berkeley: McCutchan, 1983.

Boyer, Ernest L. *High School*. New York: Harper and Row, 1983.

Bremer, John, and von Moschzisker, Michael. *The School Without Walls: Philadephia's Parkway Program*. New York: Holt, Rinehart and Winston, 1971.

Callihan, Shirley. "A Mini-History of the Richmond Public Schools: 1869–1992." Richmond Public Schools, 1992.

Carmichael, Lucianne B. *McDonogh 15*. New York: Avon, 1981.

Carr, Edward H. *What Is History?* New York: Vintage Books, 1961.

Chang, Heewon. *Adolescent Life and Ethos: An Ethnography of a U.S. High School*. London: Falmer Press, 1992.

Cibulka, James G.; Reed, Rodney J.; and Wong, Kenneth K. (eds.). *The Politics of Urban Education in the United States*. Washington, D.C.: Falmer Press, 1992.

Clinchy, Evans. "Magnet Schools Matter," *Education Week* (8 December 1993): 28.

Crowson, Robert L., and Boyd, William Lowe. "Urban Schools As Organizations: Political Perspectives." In James G. Cibulka, Rodney J. Reed, and Kenneth K. Wong (eds.), *The Politics of Urban Education in the United States*. Washington, D.C.: Falmer Press, 1992.

Cuban, Larry. *How Teachers Taught*. New York: Longman, 1984.

Cusick, Philip A. *Inside High School*. New York: Holt, Rinehart and Winston, 1973.

Dabney, Virginius. *Richmond: The Story of a City*. Charlottesville: University Press of Virginia, 1990.

Deal, Terrence E., and Kennedy, Allen. *Corporate Culture*. Reading, Mass.: Addison-Wesley, 1982.

Delzell, C. F. (ed.). *The Future of History*. Nashville: Vanderbilt University Press, 1977.

Dennison, George. *The Lives of Children: The Story of the First Street School*. New York: Random House, 1969.

Dilthey, William. *Pattern and Meaning in History*. New York: Harper and Row, 1962.

Doherty, James L. *Race and Education in Richmond*. Privately printed by the author in 1972.

Dray, William. "The Historian's Problem of Selection." In R. H. Hash (ed.), *Ideas of History*, vol. 2. New York: E. P. Dutton, 1969.

Duke, Daniel L., and Meckel, Adrienne M. "The Slow Death of a Public High School." *Phi Delta Kappan* 61 (June 1980): 674–77.

Duke, Maurice. "Cabell and Glasgow's Richmond: The Intellectual Background of the City." *Mississippi Quarterly* 27 (Fall 1974): 375–91.

Duke, Maurice, and Jordan, Daniel P. (eds.), *A Richmond Reader: 1733–1983*. Chapel Hill: University of North Carolina Press, 1983.

Elmore, R. F. (ed.). *Restructuring Schools: The Next Generation of Education Reform*. San Francisco: Jossey-Bass, 1990.

Fernand Braudel, *In History* (Chicago: University of Chicago Press, 1980), p. 64.

Fife, Brian L. *Desegregation in American Schools: Comparative Intervention Strategies*. New York: Praeger, 1992.

Forsyth, Patrick B., and Tallerico, Marilyn (eds.). *City Schools*. Newbury Park, Calif.: Corwin Press, 1993.

Grant, Gerald. *The World We Created at Hamilton High*. Cambridge: Harvard University Press, 1988.

Green, Thomas F. "Excellence, Equity, and Equality." In Lee S. Shulman and Gary Sykes (eds.), *Handbook of Teaching and Policy*. New York: Longman, 1983.

Greiner, Larry. "Evolution and Revolution As Organizations Grow." In David A. Kolb, Irwin M. Rubin, and Joyce S. Island (eds.), *The Organizational Behavior Reader*, 5th ed. Englewood Cliffs, N.J.: Prentice Hall, 1991.

Griffin, Larry J. "Temporality, Events, and Explanation in Historical Sociology." *Sociological Methods and Research* 20 (1992): 413.

Hall, Gene E., and Hord, Shirley M. *Change in Schools*. Albany: State University of New York Press, 1987.

Hampel, Robert. *The Last Little Citadel: American High Schools Since 1940.* Boston: Houghton Mifflin, 1986.

Hash, R. H. (ed.). *Ideas of History.* Vol. 2. New York: E. P. Dutton, 1969.

Helms, Frances. "Magnet Schools Attract 'Choice' Students." *The City Magazine* (April/May 1991), 39.

High Schools in the South. Nashville: Center for Southern Education Studies, George Peabody College for Teachers, 1966.

An Imperiled Generation: Saving Urban Schools. Princeton: The Carnegie Foundation for the Advancement of Teaching, 1988.

John Marshall High School: A Richmond Legend. Richmond: Dietz Press, 1985.

Kanter, Rosabeth Moss. "When a Thousand Flowers Bloom: Structural, Collective, and Social Conditions for Innovation in Organization." In Barry M. Staw and L. L. Cummings (eds.), *Research in Organizational Behavior,* Vol. 10. Greenwich, Conn.: JAI Press, 1988.

Kantor, Harvey, and Brenzel, Barbara. "Urban Education and the 'Truly Disadvantaged': The Historical Roots of the Contemporary Crisis, 1945–1990." In Michael B. Katz (ed.). *The "Underclass" Debate: Views from History.* Princeton: Princeton University Press, 1993.

Katz, Michael B. (ed.). *The "Underclass" Debate: Views from History.* Princeton: Princeton Unviersity Press, 1993.

Katz, Michael B. *The Irony of Early School Reform.* Cambridge: Harvard University Press, 1968.

Kneller, G. F. *Movements in Thought in Modern Education.* New York; Macmillan, 1984.

Kolb, David A.; Rubin, Irwin M.; and Osland, Joyce S. (eds.), *The Organizational Behavior Reader,* 5th ed. Englewood Cliffs, N.J.: Prentice Hall, 1991.s

Kozol, Jonathan. *Savage Inequalities.* New York: Crown Publishers, 1991.

Krug, Edward A. *The Shaping of the American High School.* New York: Harper and Row, 1964.

Labaree, David F. *The Making of an American High School.* New Haven: Yale University Press, 1988.

Lightfoot, Sara Lawrence. *The Good High School.* New York: Basic Books, 1983.

Louis, Karen Seashore, and Miles, Matthew B. *Improving the Urban High School.* New York: Teachers College Press, 1990.

Marshall, Ray, and Tucker, Marc. *Thinking for a Living.* New York: Basic Books, 1992.

McLaughlin, Milbrey W. "The Rand Change Agent Study Revisited: Macro Perspectives and Micro Realities," *Educational Researcher* 19 (December 1990): 11–16.

McPartland, James M., and McDill, E. L. "The Unique Role of Schools in the Causes of Youthful Crime." Report no. 216. Baltimore: Center for the Study of Social Organization of Schools, Johns Hopkins University, 1976.

Meagher, Margaret. *History of Education in Richmond*. Richmond: City School Board, 1939.

Metz, Mary Haywood. *Different by Design: The Context and Character of Three Magnet Schools*. New York: Routledge, 1992.

Moeser, John V. "What's Ahead for Our City." In Maurice Duke and Daniel P. Jordan (eds.), *A Richmond Reader: 1733–1983*. Chapel Hill: University of North Carolina Press, 1983.

Moger, Allen W. *Virginia: Bourbonism to Byrd, 1970–1925*. Charlottesville: University of Virginia Press, 168.

Monti, Daniel J. *A Semblance of Justice: St. Louis School Desegregation and Order in Urban America*. Columbia: University of Missouri Press, 1985).

Moody, Marion N. "A History of Thomas Jefferson High School." Master's thesis, University of Richmond, 1958.

Nelson, Bryce E. *Good Schools: The Seattle Public School System. 1901–1930*. Seattle: University of Washington Press, 1988.

Orfield, Gary, and Ashkinaze, Carole. *The Closing Door*. Chicago: University of Chicago Press, 1991.

Powell, Arthur G.; Farrar, Eleanor; and Cohen, David K. *The Shopping Mall High School*. Boston: Houghton Mifflin, 1985.

Pratt, Robert A. *The Color of Their Skin: Education and Race in Richmond, Virginia, 1954–1989*. Charlottesville: University Press of Virginia, 1992.

"The Pursuit of Excellence." *Time* (7 July 1958), 72.

Quinn, Robert E. "Mastering Competing Values: An Integrated Approach to Management." In David A. Kolb, Irwin M. Rubin, and Joyce S. Osland (eds.), *The Organizational Behavior Reader*, 5th ed. Englewood Cliffs, N.J.: Prentice Hall, 1991.

Raywid, Mary Anne. "Rethinking School Governance." In R. F. Elmore and Associates (eds.), *Restructuring Schools: The Next Generation of Educational Reform*. San Francisco: Jossey-Bass, 1990.

Reaching the Goals: Goal 6, Safe, Disciplined, and Drug-free Schools. Washington, D.C.: United States Department of Education, Office of Educational Research and Improvement, 1993.

Ritter, Harry. *Dictionary of Concepts in History*. New York: Greenwood Press, 1986.

Rossman, Gretchan B.; Corbett, H. Dickson; and Firestone, William A. *Change and Effectiveness in Schools*. Albany: State University of New York Press, 1988.

Rutter, Michael; Maughan, Barbara; Mortimore, Peter; and Ouston, Janet. *Fifteen Thousand Hours: Secondary Schools and Their Effects on Children.* Cambridge: Harvard University Press, 1979.

Saltzman, Harold. *Race War in High School.* New Rochelle, N.Y.: Arlington House, 1972.

Sarason, Seymour B. *The Culture of the School and the Problem of Change,* 2d ed. Boston: Allyn and Bacon, 1982.

Sartain, James A., and Rutledge, M. Dennis. "Richmond, Virginia: Massive Resistance without Violence." In Charles V. Willie and Susan L. Greenblatt (eds.), *Community Politics and Educational Change.* New York: Longman, 1981.

Schein, Edgar H. *Organizational Culture and Leadership.* San Francisco: Jossey-Bass, 1985.

Schmidt, Peter. "'Magnets' Efficacy As Desegreation Tool Questioned," *Education Week* (2 February 1994): 1, 16.

Sedlak, Michael W.; Wheeler, Christopher W.; Pullin, Diana C.; and Cusick, Phillip A. *Selling Students Short.* New York: Teachers College Press, 1986.

Selznick, Philip. *The Moral Commonwealth.* Berkeley: University of California Press, 1992.

Sharp, Rebekah Roberts. "A History of the Richmond Public School System 1869–1958." Master's thesis, University of Richmond, 1958.

Shawen, Ernest. "Recollections of a Principal." Privately published, 1963.

Shulman, Lee S., and Sykes, Gary (eds.), *Handbook of Teaching and Policy.* New York: Longman, 1983.

Silver, Christopher. *Twentieth-Century Richmond: Planning, Politics and Race.* Knoxville: University of Tennessee Press, 1984.

Sizer, Theodore R. *Horace's School.* Boston: Houghton Mifflin, 1992.

Slavin, Robert E. "PET and the Pendulum: Faddism in Education and How to Stop It." *Phi Delta Kappan* 70 (June 1989): 752–58.

Slavin, Robert E.; Karweit, Nancy L.; and Madden, Nancy A. *Effective Programs for Students at Risk.* Boston: Allyn and Bacon, 1989.

Social Science Research Council. *The Social Sciences in Historical Study: A Report of the Committee on Historiography.* Bulletin 64. New York: Social Science Research Council, 1954.

Staw, Barry M., and Cummings, L. L. (eds.). *Research in Organization Behavior.* Vol. 10. Greenwich, Conn.: JAI Press, 1988.

Steele, Claude M. "Race and the Schooling of Black Americans." *The Atlantic Monthly* 269 (April 1992): 78.

Stone, Lawrence. "History and the Social Sciences in the Twentieth Century." In C. F. Delzell (ed.), *The Future of History.* Nashville: Vanderbilt University Press, 1977.

Toch, Thomas. *In the Name of Excellence*. New York: Oxford University Press, 1991.

Viadero, Debra. "Magnet Schools Appear to Have Little Impact on Student Achievement, Researchers Find," *Education Week* (13 April 1994): 12.

Vinovskis, Maris A. *The Origins of Public High Schools: A Reexamination of the Beverly High School Controversy*. Madison: University of Wisconsin Press, 1985.

Walsh, Mark. "Counsel for the Cause," *Education Week* (11 May 1994): 22–25.

"Wasteland U.S.A." *Time* (17 February 1958), 2.

Wehlage, Gary G.; Rutter, Robert A.; Smith, Gregory A.; Lesko, Nancy; and Fernandez, Ricardo R. *Reducing the Risk: Schools As Communities of Support*. London: Falmer Press, 1989.

Whyte, William H., Jr. *The Organization Man*. New York: Simon & Schuster, 1956.

Wilkinson, J. Harvie. *From Brown to Bakke: The Supreme Court and School Integration, 1954–1978*. New York: Oxford University Press, 1979.

Willie, Charles V., and Greenblatt, Susan L. (eds.), *Community Politics and Educational Change*. New York: Longman, 1981.

Wilson, Douglas L. "Thomas Jefferson and the Character Issue," *The Atlantic Monthly* 270 (November 1992): 57–74.

INDEX